An absorbing and timely account of a pioneering voyage on board the *Canna* – the first sailing yacht from Britain and Ireland to visit Leningrad (and other Baltic ports beyond the Iron Curtain) since the Russian Revolution.

In 1987 Roger Foxall and his crew (including members of his family) left Derrynane Harbour in southern Ireland on the first leg of an extraordinary enterprise. Their year of preparation for this goodwill journey through a dozen countries was finally rewarded with permission to test the waters of *glasnost*, after an intriguing round of ambassadorial visits, visa hunts and Cyrillic despatches.

As a sailing voyage the cruise was remarkable enough: in one summer season the *Canna* circumnavigated England and Ireland, twice crossed the North Sea, sailed through Scotland, Sweden and Germany, and made a complete circuit of the Baltic. Its main aim, however, was to sail into Russia, Estonia, Latvia and Poland, and this it handsomely achieved.

From Leningrad onwards, the *Canna* and her crew encountered a dizzying array of characters and quirky officials, fascinating landscapes and enthralling architecture (not to mention patrol boats and submarines, sudden gales and a butter mountain). While revelling in the camaraderie of fellow-yachtsmen, the sharp wit of supposedly 'dour' Russians and the special entrancements of Riga, they gained an unusual insight into the enigmatic relationships between Poland, Russia and her south Baltic republics.

Filled with practical advice and information, this is a book which will inspire yachtsmen while also appealing to sedentary travellers. It is, perhaps above all, proof positive of *glasnost*.

Sailing to Leningrad

ROGER FOXALL

Sailing to Leningrad

A Voyage through the Baltic

SHERIDAN HOUSE

First published in the United States of America 1989 by
Sheridan House Inc.
145 Palisade Street
Dobbs Ferry, NY 10522

ISBN 0 911378 98 7

Copyright © Roger M. Foxall 1989

Typeset by Rowland Phototypesetting Ltd
Bury St Edmunds, Suffolk
Printed and bound in Great Britain by
Hartnolls Ltd, Bodmin, Cornwall

Contents

To our friends along the Baltic coasts,
and to neighbours in Kerry,
for their help and friendship

Preface

'One tool will only do one job,' my mathematics tutor warned sternly, giving me a prize of a simple penknife, when I'd really hoped for an all-purpose gadget, complete with cork-screw and hoof-pick. He was right, of course, and the lesson stuck; but what follows is, for better or worse, neither entirely a salty adventure nor wholly an account of travels among sensible people onshore. But there is simply no help for it, since that's the way it turned out for *Canna*'s crew. My excuse will have to be that all the countries of the Baltic owe their very existence, to a great degree, to the sea they border. An approach from seaward is in many ways the most revealing, and I hope to carry the sailor and landsman alike through what to us has come to seem a single composite voyage, without frustrating the one too much with interruptions from sailing, nor fazing the other with boating technicalities. Soviet ports are already becoming more accessible to foreign yachtsmen; and extra pilotage information will be found in the Appendix.

Acknowledgements

The planning, execution, and aftermath of *Canna*'s voyage have occupied more than two years, so that the sailing itself now seems like a sudden brief apex of physical effort.

In connection with the planning of the cruise, I particularly wish to thank the staff of the Department of Foreign Affairs in Dublin, the Russian Embassy in Ireland, and the Polish Embassy in London. Special thanks are also due to Adrian Lucey and his staff in Waterville for their tireless help with telexes; and many other individuals and organizations who gave advice in the early stages and along the route are mentioned in the text.

In the course of preparing the boat, valuable assistance in kind was provided by Union Chandlers, of Cork, Kilmacsimon boatyard, and Mc William Sailmakers. David John Hare of London secured equipment for filming, and produced the resulting film: *40° East*, and Agfa-Gevaert generously donated film.

Since our return, I have been submerged for more than a year in paper. Various people contributed: my thanks go particularly to Clive C. Martin, for his permission to publish extracts from the *Oriana* log; and to Winkie Nixon of Howth for timely information on crucial points. Subsequently, the editors Richard Johnson and Penelope Isaac have kept me on the straight and narrow. Marie O'Carroll typed some of the text.

I had noted the convention of reserving special thanks for one's wife, if she lasted the course to the end. Only now do I understand why; that Susan was half the instigation of the plan in the first place, and participated in the most exciting sailing, now does little to diminish my debt. She hardly expected to be typing half a million words as a result, nor to be keeping me sane at the same time with liberal helpings of common sense. I would scarcely have got through it without her.

PHOTOGRAPHS are by Shay Fennelly, except where otherwise marked; and two (in the Russian yacht and in Tallinn) were kindly provided from Alan Balfe's collection.

Glossary

BEAM, on the: appearing, relatively, at right-angles to the boat

BEAR AWAY, to: to turn the boat away from the wind

BEAT, to; BEATING: to sail as close as possible towards the direction from which the wind comes

BILGE: space in the hull under the floorboards

BLOCKS: pulleys

BOOM: Heavy spar to which the mainsail foot is secured

CABLE: one-tenth of a nautical mile (q.v.), approx. 608 feet (185 metres)

CLOSE-HAULED: with sails hauled in flat in order to beat

COCKPIT: the steering well

DAN BUOY: a marker buoy with staff and flag; in a yacht, for man overboard

DECCA: proprietary European navigation system utilizing transmitting stations on shore, and receiving device on boat

FREE, to sail: to sail in any way except 'close-hauled', ie, 'free' to steer to port or starboard of one's course without having to tack (q.v.)

GENOA: a particularly large foresail

GOOSEWINGED: sailing with the wind from exactly astern, with sails set to both sides

GUNWALE: the top edges of a boat's hull above the deck line

GYBE, to: when sailing with the wind from astern, to change course so that the boom swings across – highly dangerous if done accidentally

HEAD WIND: wind from the direction of one's destination

HEAVE TO, to: to stop the boat by setting the sails to work against each other

JAM CLEAT: an automatic gripper for a sheet (q.v.)

JIB: foresail

LAT. and LONG.: latitude and longitude, the north/south and east/west co-ordinates of position

LOOM: vague first or last appearance, especially of light from lighthouse

MILE: 'miles' at sea in the text are nautical miles. 1 naut. mile = 6076 feet (1852 metres) = 1.15 statute miles

MOLE: harbour pier or breakwater

PORT: left-hand side, when looking forward

PULPIT/PUSHPIT: safety railings at the bows/stern

REACH, to; REACHING: to sail with the wind across the boat. 'A reach' is a course which achieves this

REEF, to: to temporarily reduce the size of a sail, or sails, to cope with strong winds

RUN, to; RUNNING: to sail with the wind astern

SHEET: the rope controlling the loose corner of a sail

SHROUDS: fixed wires from the sides of the boat to keep the mast in place

SLOOP: yacht with two-sail rig, one before and one aft of mast

SOLE: floor of boat cabin

SPINNAKER: very large and flimsy foresail for running in light winds

SPRING TIDES: tides at or near their maximum range, ie, high 'highs' and low 'lows', causing strong currents

STARBOARD: right-hand side, when looking forward

TACK, a: a 'zig' or 'zag' when beating, ie, a 'port' or 'starboard' tack

TACK, to: to change from 'zig' to 'zag' = 'to go about'

TRANSOM: the rear of a boat's hull above the waterline

VARD: a Norwegian pillar beacon

VHF: Very High Frequency communications radio

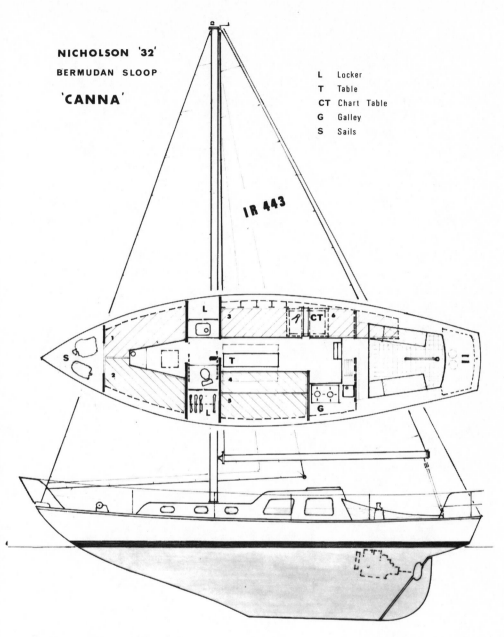

NICHOLSON '32'

BERMUDAN SLOOP

'CANNA'

L	Locker
T	Table
CT	Chart Table
G	Galley
S	Sails

IR 443

32' 0" x 9' 3" x 5' 6"   L O A   Beam   Draught   9·75 x 2·82 x 1·67 m

DISPLACEMENT: 7 tons
BERTHS: 6
ENGINE: Volvo diesel, 23 HP
NAVIGATIONAL EQUIPMENT:
   Marine radio receiver/RDF.
   Echo sounder. Log. VHF.
   Decca Navigator.

MAPS

The Route of <u>Canna</u>

Nordkapp (North Cape)

16° 24° 32° 40° 48°

68°

WHITE SEA

Archangel

64°

N O R W A Y

Gulf of Bothnia

S W E D E N

Karelia

FINLAND

L. Ladoga

60°

Helsinki Haapasaari Leningrad

Ahvenanmaa (Åland Is.)

Oslo

Hanko Narva

Stockholm Tallinn

Hiiumaa ESTONIA

L. Vänern Göta Canal

Norrköping Saaremaa

L. Vättern Mem

Gulf of Riga 56°

Göteborg

Gotland Ventspils Riga

BALTIC SEA LATVIA

aw

RSFSR (RUSSIA)

Kattegat Öland Liepāja

Daugava

Copenhagen LITHUANIA U S S R

DARK Klaipēda Kaunas

Stubbeköbing Bornholm Vilnius

Ustka Kaliningrad Minsk 52°

Stralsund Rügen Kolobrzeg Gdynia Elblag BYELORUSSIA

Rostock Świnoujście Gdansk

amburg Szczecin Wisla

Berlin (Vistula) Brest-Litovsk

Frankfurt Warsaw

Elbe Odra POLAND

EAST GERMANY Wroclaw UKRAINE Kiev

Dnieper

Y Krakow Lvóv 48°

CZECHOSLOVAKIA

MOLDAVIA Odessa

HUNGARY

ROMANIA BLACK SEA

oyage, 1987

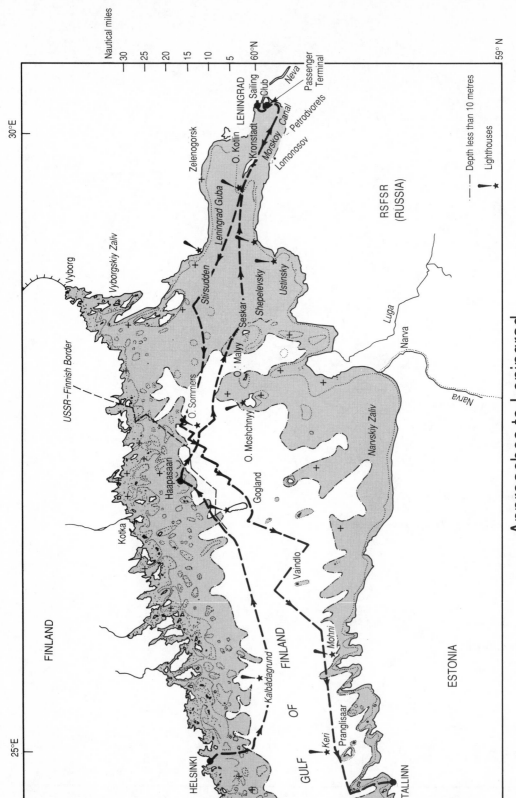

Approaches to Leningrad

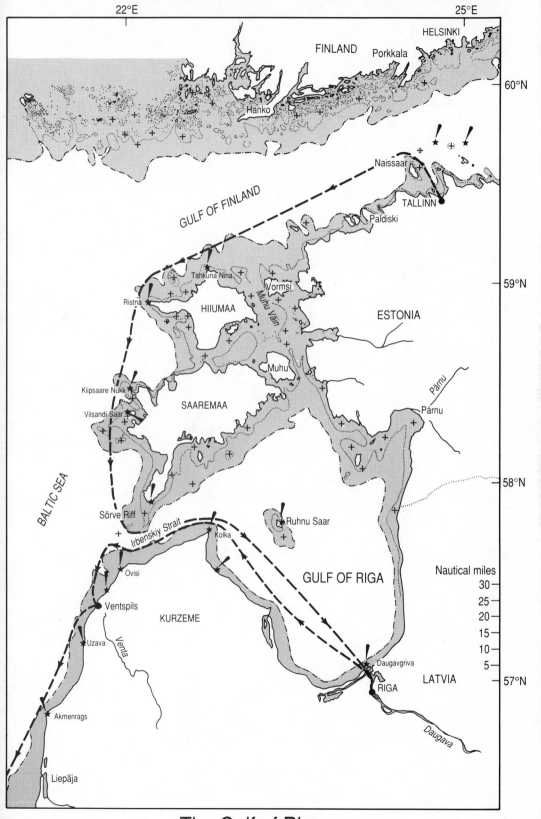

The Gulf of Riga

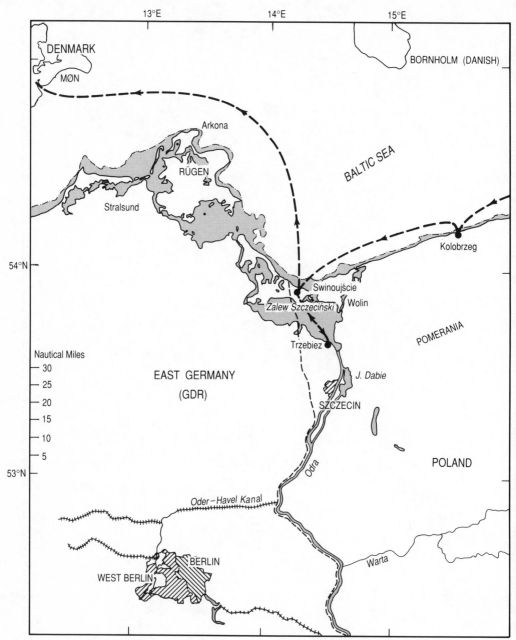

West Poland and the Odra River

Part I
EAST
TO
LENINGRAD

CHAPTER 1

Departure

'Get it in a bit more!' I yelled, hooking my elbow over the upper coaming of the slanting cockpit.

Fenny's face creased with concentration as he took a grip on the sheet controlling the mainsail boom, and heaved on it until it hummed.

'And more again!'

Fenny had it bar-taut now. The boat heeled further, and a splatter of salt water drenched him as he squinted forward.

'That's about right,' I called. 'Now bear away a little.'

Three pairs of eyes peered to the head of the 40-foot mast, gyrating giddily against the clouds. The wind-vane arrow lurched fitfully until it pointed about 30 degrees away from the bows, its tail oscillating over the fixed tab on the port side.

The new crew were getting the feel of the boat; I wanted them to know how she behaved in the next few hours, before evening fell.

It was not an easy task. Out to starboard the mountainous outposts of south-west Ireland thrust seaward, capped by wild, tearing cloud. The offshore wind, bitterly cold for June, chased squalls across the steely water, piling up a steep chop which slammed against the hull. We were heavily reefed down already, with almost half the mainsail rolled around the boom, and only a small triangle of foresail hauled out to balance it. Even so, we were heeling well to port as we surged west, the gunwale disappearing underwater from time to time when rolled an extra few degrees by a sharp crest.

Canna, our 32-foot sloop, was a very traditional workhorse. Although a glassfibre boat, the first of her type had been built nearly 25 years ago, and her design owed much more to the sturdy timber yachts that were her immediate predecessors than to the lightweight speed machines that had since swept the board. For one thing, she had a full-length keel and plenty of ballast in her bottom – nearly three tons of it – which encouraged her to stay upright and 'stand up to her sails', as the sailmakers had put it. I was certainly glad of her stability now; if we were heeling too far it was because we were pushing her hard, maybe too hard, to force her through the seas. Certainly, we didn't need another square inch of canvas. Even Maxwell McKeever's 18-odd stone, wedged against me on the uphill side, was having no apparent effect.

We braced our legs against the opposite lockers, half-standing, half-lying, adjusting our backsides and armholds every time a roll or a jolt threatened to hurtle us against the lower guardrails. At least, I consoled myself, we were moving well; the force of the wind was sucking her onward, plucking her eight- or nine-ton weight out towards the open sea at about five knots. It was no wonder the decks were awash with spray.

Maxwell had seen it all before, both in his own boats and, for a short spell in the previous year, in this one. A doughty farmer from the east of the country, for 40 or 50 of his 64 years he'd not only tilled, and traded cattle, but had also spent some time at sea. He was unconcerned, but for Fenny it was different. Younger than Maxwell but less robust, he was a doctor from Northern Ireland, and although a very keen sailor in his spare time, this was to be his first long offshore voyage. Also, he wasn't quite fit. A fever due to a kidney infection had plagued him for the last two months, but having prescribed for himself to stave off attacks, he had arrived, pale but determined, on the eve of our departure. Now, his knuckles showed white against the mahogany tiller as he fought to keep the boat straight.

I wasn't even beginning to think about initiating our other crew member. Shay Fennelly, the youngest among the four of us, was below in the saloon sorting out cameras. Tousled, solidly-built and soft of voice, he was originally from Dublin but had spent the previous few years fishing and fish-farming on the mid-west coast. There he'd developed a latent passion for photography, which he'd combined with ample experience in many types of working boat; he had, however, never set foot in a sailing yacht, and this was certainly no time to be inculcating the rudiments. Before setting out I had put everyone through a crash course on safety drills, and that would have to do for now. Besides, there would be – should be – plenty of time to make a sailor of him. Shay was due to be on board for three and a half months at least.

Four or five miles astern lay our point of departure, Derrynane Harbour in south Kerry, a tiny cove set among rocky hills now dwindling to an outline of painted cardboard; Bolus Head, a dark truncated promontory, loomed on our starboard bow. Between the two, Ballinskelligs Bay fell back in a wide horseshoe; out of its two-mile-wide mouth the winds gusted to a near gale, foretelling what we should soon be encountering in the open Atlantic.

Fenny's wife Snoo, driving with a friend northwards around the bay's edge, had caught sight of us passing the gap. A blast buffeted the car as she pointed out a white speck far off beyond the headlands.

'But they'll surely not be going far in that small boat?' the friend exclaimed.

'Oh aye,' replied Snoo, in her strong northern accent. 'Fenny's to crew as far as Sweden, but the rest of them are bound for *Russia* and back!'

That was indeed our hope. It was June 1987, and we had just embarked on the first leg of a goodwill cruise to the Baltic Sea, with the intention of visiting every nation and country around its borders, but particularly the communist ones; Russia and the other Soviet Republics, Poland and East Germany. Among the ship's papers, wedged into a case above the twin batteries, were full authorization documents for four or five ports in Poland, and partial ones for four more in the Soviet Union. We hoped to collect the missing visas along the way.

Behind us lay a great deal of effort. As far as we knew, ours would be the first western yacht since the Revolution to secure permission to visit so many ports in the eastern bloc and the necessary research and applications had occupied most of a year. My wife Susan, still grappling with telexes and diplomatic procedures, was due to join the cruise in Sweden with one of our sons.

Ahead lay 2,000 miles of sailing to reach our first Russian port – Leningrad, at the extreme eastern end of the Baltic; but we were scarcely off the starting block, and already the race looked hard.

Today, Sunday 7 June, was our second attempt at departure: we had been ignominiously beaten back the day before by the northerly gale-force winds. By this morning, reporters, photographers and helpers had vanished; but, as we left the harbour, between waving briefly to Susan and a much-diminished group of friends, and sorting out the spaghetti-like tangle of lines in the cockpit, I'd had the sudden lift of wild elation, the tingling thrill that always confirms departures. We were on our way to foreign shores, and the relief of getting clear was enormous. That had been before the weight of the weather struck home; now the full fetch of wind and sea was surging down from the Arctic 1,500 miles away.

When planning our route, we'd reckoned on the usual south-westerlies – in fact, anything between south-east and north-west would do fine – to carry us up the west coasts of Ireland and Scotland and on to Orkney, and across the North Sea. It should be a following wind, an easy run or a reach at least; good sailing, anyway. We'd been looking forward to it. But now! – here we were, already a day late, with an out-and-out aberration, an unbelievable northerly, foul in every sense – cold, strong, gusty, kicking up a nasty sea where no shelter offered and, worst of all, unlikely to change for days.

The Meteorological Office had tendered only a vestige of encouragement – the gale, still from the same point, should ease down to a barely manageable Force 6 or 7. To follow our plan we'd have to beat against it, sailing as close to the wind as we could, zigzagging to and fro like a demented snail. Just now it hardly seemed likely we could do even that.

Canna in cruising trim, with hundredweights of tinned stores amidships, hundreds of feet of chain and three anchors in the bows, and a hefty self-steering gear perched right on the stern, had the momentum of a rocking-chair. If she didn't roll she'd pitch back and forth instead, bucking ponderously over walls of water, swooping down the troughs and up again or, if they were too steep, driving right through them in an explosion of foam; the stem-head and pulpit rails disappeared for seconds on end, and torrents of green water charged aft along the side decks, hitting the cockpit coamings and bursting away in all directions.

In the valleys our horizon shrank to the crests of the waves but, as they lifted us, twin pinnacles lurched into view in the distance dead ahead – the Skellig Rocks.

'Rocks' is an understatement. The Skelligs are gigantic splintered pyramids shooting straight from the sea-bed, 300 feet beneath. Great Skellig, to the west, carries the remains of a monastery on its 700-foot peak and, lower down, two lighthouses. Little Skellig, 400 feet high, is strung with white necklaces of contrasting strata on its sheer rock shoulders, which when disturbed dissolve into clouds of flying birds and melt away: it's one of the biggest gannetries and seabird refuges in Europe. Our course was taking us towards it, and although it was more dangerous than significant, it made a logical waypoint.

Shay by now was agog. An ardent wildlife enthusiast, he couldn't wait to get to close quarters. His wide, bespectacled face appeared in the companionway under a blue stocking hat, as he passed up a thermos of soup. It was already afternoon.

Yet more water arrived on board, swilling around the afterdeck, and sluicing into the cockpit; I made for the saloon to pump the bilge which would be inexorably filling, and to check that nothing other than crew was careering around on the loose. Shay was on his way up, festooned with apparatus.

'Now look!' I called to the deck crew. 'Don't stand on too far towards the Little Skellig. It'll be on the windward side of us, it has a huge wind shadow, and the squalls beneath it can be fierce. We want to stay clear.'

Down below, I pumped, sharply to begin with, to clear air from the suction pipe. It took quite a while.

'Fifty,' I gasped, 'that's about normal.' Sixty. Eighty! – that's a lot – we'd taken a good deal of water already.

'Hey. Look out! The boom! Watch the gybe!' came a rumbling bellow from Maxwell, up top.

The boat lunged, came upright, heeled the other way. I dashed up. The rock face seemed only feet away, a sort of bloodshot grey, full of slabs and splits, sucking white froth through its teeth, streaked with bird-shit above. Thousands of birds wheeled overhead, screaming alarm and abuse. Shay was oblivious, photographing like an automaton. The tail end of the massive aluminium boom swung dangerously close to his ear. The jib was filling from the wrong side, stretched tight against the wire shrouds; the mainsail shivered and slammed as Maxwell eased it out. We weren't sailing forward but sideways – towards the cliff, lurching towards the foam. What I had feared had happened, we'd fallen into the wind shadow; and the blast roaring clear across the top of the island was rolling over like a giant curl of hair, slamming down on the water, flattening out the chop, and shoving us bodily on to the cliff. The mast was now slanting parallel to the rock.

'Can we get in any closer?' called Shay, his eye still glued to a view-finder.

For answer, I dived for the controls and fired the engine.

'Maxwell, the jib. Fenny, stand by the main!'

With the jib sheet freed, *Canna* forced her way seaward, but we weren't free yet: violent flukes of wind were rasping the water around the eastern tail of the rocks into blue-black scars. Slam! They hit us. The mainsheet blocks rattled sharply, then went quiet.

As Fenny struggled to ease the sheet from the jam-cleat, the boat heeled to starboard, the mast-head pointing at the sun, and the rigging twanged and shrieked. With relief, I heard the bow-wave build and burble, and within seconds, we were back in the noisy world of flying spray. The island, cheated, stretched out a last rocky claw – we were clear, certainly, but it had not been the most seamanlike operation ever seen.

Shay's interest seemed faintly stirred as he finished polishing and stowing his lenses with meticulous concentration.

'Those wires must be fairly strong,' he commented, eyeing the three port-side shrouds.

'They're supposed to be able to lift the full weight of the boat,' I said, following his gaze upward.

They didn't seem to be doing much less than that now; the stainless-steel cables were rigid with tension, hauling the windward gunwale way out of the water, while the leeward ones hung slack. I'd been up the mast to refit the rigging only weeks before. The lives of all the crew depended on my having done it right, I thought, as I watched it gleam and strain under the clearing sky. Had I tightened the terminals enough? There was nothing to be done about it now, and it was unwise to peer aloft too long – it had a notoriously sickening effect. 'Vomited lunch, crew pasty' records the journal bleakly.

It was time to take stock of our choices. If conditions had been right, we'd expected not to make port until Stornoway in the Outer Hebrides, but now . . . After our first tack of the voyage, the Kerry coast still barred our way, and an early evening was threatening. The wind and swell were not slackening, and slogging up-wind all night would only weaken the crew further. There was only one option – six or seven miles ahead, the southern approach to Valentia Harbour; but we'd have to be quick. The Channel was tidal, unbuoyed and flanked by sunk hazards.

'Sail her on a bit free,' I called out, 'keep her moving – we'll go on in to Portmagee.'

'She's right as she goes,' returned Maxwell, and there was silent assent from the others to the abandonment of our plans.

Far ahead a fishing launch scurried through a gap in the dark blue cliffs and vanished.

At last we followed her in, rounding up to drop sail in a wide bend of the Channel and motoring the last mile to the small fishing village. Orange lights on the pier already accentuated the dusky tinge in the sky. Houses crouched under the hillsides like mice in a skirting board, their windows winking out.

Tying up to a trawler in the twilight, tension drained away as we went about our chores, quietly setting and coiling the mooring warps, re-stowing the sail, lashing out the halyards, stripping off lifejackets and wet oilies, wiping salt from our eyes.

Shay was soon rooting for the frying-pan, and Fenny and Maxwell headed off to refill tanks: the boat's and their own. I watched them pick their way across the nets and gunwales of two trawlers, rear up tall on the dockside for a moment, and disappear. I hadn't wanted to join in, feeling a curious heavy reluctance to set foot ashore. We shouldn't really be in this port at all; a few days before, I'd made an urgent enquiry about outward customs clearance.

'Of course, you know,' the local official came crackling over the phone. 'We can't clear you out of Derrynane. You'd have to bring the boat around . . . could you come into Portmagee?'

'Not really,' I'd explained. 'It's out of our way and we couldn't spare the time to break our journey. We have a very tight programme and it is a rather unusual cruise,' I pressed. 'We have had a lot of support for the idea.'

Bending the rules, he'd arrived in the expedition office on our official departure date, ploughed through a thicket of papers with good grace, and attached his best wishes for the voyage.

Now, here we were, all cleared, in Portmagee. I could just imagine his surprised black eyebrows lifting over a pint glass, but that wasn't the whole, or even the main point of what was gnawing me. We were just far too close to home. Our efforts had got us nearly nowhere – we were north-west from Derrynane, the general windward direction we needed, but although we'd skipped two minor headlands, we were only 11 miles away. *Only 11 miles!* Leningrad was much more than 2,000 miles away if we had to carry on beating, but we had only 39 days left in which to do it: there was part of an ocean and two seas to cross, canals to crawl through, crew to change and foreign charts to find; we had no room for failures or delays. With a feeling like a lift falling, I realized the mathematics made no sense at all.

Maxwell and Fenny might also recognize that, but neither was sailing all the way to Russia; Shay was new to the game, and the log showed, didn't it, that we'd actually sailed three times as far?

Only I knew the full extent of the superstructure which the cruise was carrying: a full year's work committed, by myself and my wife; my professional career set aside; recommendations and letters of greeting sought and received from some of the most prominent public figures in the country; the bank manager blarneyed and cajoled into acquiescence; the small but crucial sponsorships; the air-flights and arrangements for all the crew due to join us along the way; the advance greetings from foreigners we'd not yet met, anxious for our arrival; the newspaper articles already published detailing our bold endeavour; all the film equipment begged, provided and stowed on board: the ramifications were as endless as the sea was wide. And here was I, responsible for balancing the whole edifice in one hand while with the other putting the boat and four crew through a hoop which in my mind's eye was shrinking by the minute. One of the crew was unfit, and one untried . . .

A smell of steak unconcernedly frying wafted up as I peered out. Being holed up in a land-locked estuarine cut seemed to make the whole thing worse. While we had been immersed in planning, the possibility of failure was a shadowy doubt, something to think one's way out of. Here, I realized, the possibility might come to stare me in the face. Nearly all the parameters were fixed: the tides, the weather, the places, the dates – thinking couldn't change them. The rigid outlines of the chart glared back at me. I could be about to reap the results of the most massive misjudgement of my life. How on earth had I contrived to paint myself into such a small corner?

The idea was conceived of frustration and delivered by lateral thought.

The initial prick of provocation had come from Arthur, a computer programmer and somewhat erratic friend, in the autumn of 1986. Our charter yacht was already hauled up on the slip a few hundred yards from our home, and it was time to be thinking about the next year's programme.

'Would you consider making an Atlantic crossing next summer?' he said.

I wasn't at all averse. Arthur had sailed with us before and shown himself to be a good seaman and companion, and I had already sailed the first leg of the normal south-about route to the Americas as far as the Spanish-Portuguese border. But when Arthur had loped away again toward his droopy tapes and floppy disks, problems began to plop in the lake of intention like fish taking flies. It was mainly a matter of time and distance. The conventional cruising man leaves Europe in the late summer, which we couldn't now do; and unarguable diagrams of hurricane tracks showed it would be almost impossible to squeeze in a full circuit between the Caribbean hurricanes of early summer and the autumn gales of Europe.

Even a very bare round of the Azores, Bermuda, Canada and back would be a 5,000 or 6,000-mile gallop with just about enough time to holler a greeting to the spectators at the far end and charge straight back again. I had too high a regard for American and Canadian scenery and hospitality to want to revisit charabanc style.

'It isn't working out,' I said to Susan.

This specific frustration was laid down on top of much older, sedimentary strata which had just as much to do with Russia as with the Americas – more, probably, because we'd never been there. The convention seems to have arisen that, when introducing the subject of Russia, writers delve back into a grey void in their subconscious and haul into view a full menu of their fears and phobias. I can't remember having had many. Being born near the blitzed city of Coventry in the English Midlands during the War, it's not surprising that the first few crumbs to fall my way had been, as it were, black bread: the dark mutterings of my mother about Winston Churchill's ordeals with Stalin – 'What a time he had with him', she'd say, wagging her head and tutting – and images of ice, ice everywhere, threatening to overturn the convoy ships as they thumped through the northern seas to supply the Russian war effort. But any imbalance of feeling was quickly redressed. I was still wearing short trousers when I saw my first real Russians, and important ones too: Khrushchev and Bulganin leaving a trade fair at the Bingley Hall in Birmingham and being ushered into the street. The crowds stood back in ranks and watched in a dead silence; even now I can feel the seconds tick by until one or two hoarse boos broke out. I read the next day that someone had shaken his fist. A great shame, I had felt, for people who had come so far, and looked so bleak and nervous. It was perfectly plain that they didn't have horns, and I accepted without question that they were the descendants of the real people with real emotions that stalked the pages of Russian literature.

The trouble was that in the twenty and more years since, the human connection seemed to be very heavily blurred, perhaps by the effort needed to make it. The paperback cover of Hedrick Smith's *The Russians*, for instance, which soberly filled in much of the social and factual background of the 1970s, strangely didn't illustrate any of the people at all, but featured a tiny Kremlin glimpsed through an impregnable-looking livid red key-hole in the shape of a star. There always seemed to be a curious discrepancy between the human ingredient and the stereotype, which carried right through news and commerce, and politics; but even at the height of the Cold War it was possible to know that this mismatch was artificially ramified and had little to do with the man in the street – or the field.

Laurens van der Post related an incident from his tour of the Soviet

Union in the 1960s which stuck in the mind: he had been brought to visit a fellow-author's parents who were farmers deep in the country near Kiev. After laying out a meal for their unexpected guest and enquiring a little about life in Britain, the old couple had fallen into an embarrassed silence, obviously wanting to ask something more, but declining with a shake of their heads. Eventually their son had explained – their worry was the risk of their treasured livelihood vanishing into oblivion.

'Why had people to be so wicked as still to want to make war against their country . . . ?' They hadn't been able to believe van der Post's replies and denials, preferring to trust the responses of the sky and the soil, for as long as they would last. For years after, it had conjured an aggravating recurrent image, a sort of Salvador Dali triptych: the silent peasants in Kiev on one side and on the other, out of touch, people in their English villages or elsewhere, shaking their heads over the same central problem but to different rhythms, while above and between, the outsize figures of two fighting cocks crowed and clawed at each other in a frenzy of din and dust, with whole arsenals of weapons secreted in their feathers.

Such frustrations and a generalized curiosity about Russia had not diminished during the years in which we had worked a smallholding by the sea, in a spot about as far removed from Russia as it's possible to get in Europe. In fact, they had become more acute as our self-imposed attachment to the land locked us in almost as firmly as van der Post's Ukrainian peasants; travel as a family had been impossible and a Russian visit merely a pipe-dream. As our two sons struggled toward independence, however, and summer neighbours fuelled reveries by accounts of a recent visit to Leningrad, the dream stirred.

Leningrad! It had always stood as a symbol and focus of our fascination. Built by Peter the Great as a huge new porch to his national house, with a very generous door facing west, who did not have an image of its grand ranks of public buildings glowing golden over the banks of the Neva?

We asked our friends for their impressions of the city.

'Oh, fine,' said Clare. 'The ballet was absolutely splendid. Petrodvorets Palace was lovely, but it was spring and all the statues were covered by wooden boxes.'

You got hauled over the coals by the police if you went jay-walking, they warned. Money exchange was a bother.

'The main thing I noticed,' said David, 'was that rainwater down-pipes on all the buildings were far too big, and as ugly as hell.'

Down-pipes! I mused. Here was a curious disconnection. It was an awfully long way to go to find you didn't like the plumbing. So Leningrad had ugly down-pipes; but what about the people? He hadn't really met them, David had said; he'd been travelling with a group. They looked better off in Moscow.

Our curiosity about the city was pricked. Surprisingly, historians agreed that a few hundred years ago there had been nobody worth talking about in the lowlands of the Neva estuary. Tsar Peter had been an avid seaman, however, and early in his career had prised open the mandibles of his neighbouring opponents and driven in a wedge of territory to get at the tongue of water that would connect him through the Baltic to the North Sea, and open up ship-borne trade to Europe. Leningrad, or rather St Petersburg, had been the maritime capital of the whole country, its wealth and fabled architecture built on the comings and goings of boats. To arrive there now by train or plane, I realized with a jerk, was to approach the city back to front.

The other factor present in the summer of 1986 was a fresh breath of wind in international affairs: the fighting cocks were backing off; there were new, encouraging sounds, and mostly from the Russian house.

During Peter's reign, his door to the west had stood wide open; after his death it had hung creaking on its hinges through the period of the Crimean War, Russian setbacks in Japan and mounting internal problems. At the onset of the Revolution, the draught coming in through it had proved such a menace it had been decisively slammed shut while the new regime got on with fanning the flames of a new home fire on a different hearth. It had stayed that way, it seemed, ever since, with only a little cat-flap remaining to admit rationed portions of tourists.

A sudden lurch of lateral thought set our fingers trailing to the right across the fold in the atlas. If not sail west, then why not east? Scandinavia – we'd never seen it! Finland next, another fascination. Then through the Gulf of Finland, up to the furthest end, to Leningrad. It was surprisingly far east, just beyond the 30° meridian; further east, in fact, than Istanbul. But then, like Istanbul, Venice, or indeed any maritime city, perhaps it should be approached from the sea to appreciate it to the full. For a boat, the common denominator of sea water is a connection between countries, not a barrier.

Peter himself had sailed widely around Europe and it would be very satisfying to arrive at his city in a way he would have immediately understood.

Perhaps it hadn't been done for a very long time, but wasn't it worth a try? We glanced at each other with a wild surmise.

The indented coastline of the South Baltic gave us an obvious route for return. The Baltic Republics, then Poland and East Germany stretched invitingly for more than a thousand miles, leading on towards Denmark and West Germany.

In a few seconds we had described on paper a full clockwise circuit of the Baltic, taking in every country on its shores.

Why not a sort of informal goodwill cruise to visit all of them? The communist countries would be a particular fascination – in all the sailing magazines and books there was never one word about them, unless a comment betraying unrequited curiosity from a skipper passing, say, from West Germany to Sweden, who had no permission to enter their waters. And yet, there had to be some kind of sailing activity going on there: the odd Polish name cropped up from time to time in the annals of long-distance cruising, and both Poland and the Soviet Union had very substantial sail-training ships. Smaller ones, too, Susan reminded me: in the 1984 Tall Ships' gathering in Liverpool, there had been Russian yachts much closer to our own in size, the crews of which had been entertained at local sailing clubs. Perhaps there was a sort of one-way valve here, which needed re-setting to work in both directions? The distance, four and a half thousand miles or so, should be manageable in a summer, but Susan, who began to see an active role for herself in all of this, shuddered slightly.

'Bound to be cold,' she said.

The atlas, again, contradicted – the further one went east in the Baltic, the more deeply one became embedded in a continental climate: Leningrad was a lot warmer in summer than we were used to.

'Besides,' I said, 'the Atlantic is getting dangerous; thick with ships and junketing sailors heading for the sun, zooming around on automatic pilot and not keeping watch – probably safer to go East!'

We nodded in unison, and I made a beeline for the telephone. It was the starting-gun for a hectic hurdle-chase that occupied us body and soul for the next year. Already, it was late October.

CHAPTER 2

Preparations

My first call was to a long-standing friend and colleague, Eric Healy, an ex-merchant captain and sail-training ship skipper. Greatly respected for his commitment to international goodwill through sailing, I felt sure he would support the idea. Perhaps he had even been into the eastern Baltic as a ship's officer?

'No,' he replied. 'And I don't know if it can actually be done. I have a friend who will have a good idea – I'll be meeting her in the next two or three weeks, and I'll telephone you.'

An enquiry was also fired off to the Cruising Association, a long-established voluntary organization of cruising yachtsmen, with premises in London and a library of charts, pilot books and old logs.

In the meantime Arthur, acquiescing in the change of plan, arrived with references.

The Admiralty chart of the Baltic was impressive, an oversize sheet stretching from 54° to 66°N, and from 9° to 30°31′E, nearly 800 nautical miles (1,100 statute miles) each way. The land areas, conforming to a common mental picture, were undefined grey masses; but the sea itself, sprawling out to the margins, was crowded with incident. The Gulfs of Bothnia and Finland stretched north and east like a pair of dislocated jawbones and, among the lines of old-fashioned fathoms soundings, there were islands everywhere. Gotland, 75 miles by 30, looked across toward Estonia, where a pair of Siamese twins with the entrancing names of Hiiumaa and Saaremaa screened the Latvian Gulf of Riga from the west. Into the maw of Bothnia were crammed the Åland Islands, a semi-independent part of Finland about 30 miles square. South of these, along the Swedish coast, and fringing the Finnish coast to the east, lay a vast scatter of rocks and shoals and banks and islets, so chaotic as to look more like the work of a demonic demolitioner or an accident with cosmic condiments than part of God's creation. This cluster of hazards, extending 20 miles and more offshore, would form the left bank of any passage in toward Leningrad, with bright magenta exclamation-marked lighthouses at its outer edges. Towards the eastern end of the Gulf of Finland were islands we'd never heard of: Gogland, standing centrally north-south, like a sentinel in a doorway; Ostrov Moschnyy, Ostrov Malyy, Seskar; finally one I did know, Kronstadt, right in the eastern tip of the tongue, the last staging post near Leningrad. This was the naval fortress which had featured so crucially in the early days of the Revolution, and had threatened to throw the whole of the Leninist programme off balance: a sensitive, emotive place indeed. Could a single, six-man yacht get permission to pass by? And assuming we should get so far, where in fact could we land?

The Admiralty Pilots for the Baltic, three big hard-bound volumes, were no less impressive than the charts. The bulk of the text was a painstaking description, bay by bay, mile by mile, of coastal features, the only relief in the inexorable listing of rocks, beacons, anchorages and port facilities being sketches of navigational marks. Thumbnail views of 'Vilsandi Saar Light-house', or 'Panga Nukh Headland' seemed to carry romantic nuances far beyond the plain lines of the drawings and prose.

From the first chapters we took the list of ports open to foreign merchant shipping as a reasonable point of departure, or rather approach, as we guessed that we could land only at those equipped with customs posts. In Russia proper, the Russian Soviet Federative Socialist Republic, there weren't too many of them; only Vyborg and Gavan Vysotsk in the north-east corner of the Gulf, and Leningrad itself. In Estonia, opposite Helsinki, there was Tallinn, the capital of the Republic and the venue for the 1980 sailing Olympics. Next was Latvia, where the ports open to foreign merchant shipping were Riga, the capital, and Pärnu, both deep-set in an enclosed Gulf, and Ventspils on the main west-facing Baltic coast. Finally, on the clockwise route, was Klaipėda in Lithuania – eight possible ports of entry spaced between about one hundred and two hundred miles apart.

'We should try for at least one port in every Republic,' I mused.

'What happens if the weather turns foul, though?' quizzed Susan. 'Wouldn't we need some coastal anchorages too?'

This was a fair point, but the Pilot had already cast up all kinds of portents. Admiralty publications are noted for an atmosphere of pessimistic caution, but the warnings set out for the Gulf of Finland and the Baltic were of a type I'd never before had to grapple with.

To begin, it warned that Admiralty charts are based on relevant national ones, whether Swedish, Russian or Finnish. Russian charts, however, allowed only for navigation via defined shipping lanes to the main ports of entry. The implication that coastal information could be in short supply was very soon confirmed:

CAUTION: Mariners should bear in mind the possibility of uncharted boulders of glacial origin . . . least depths over shoals and banks may always be doubtful due to many large boulders that may easily have escaped survey . . . It is therefore prudent to maintain a generous underkeel clearance.

And how to do that? I wondered, when it was obvious that our normal long stop, the echo-sounder, would be nearly useless over such bumpy terrain.

Skipping over details of the sea bed muds (one being 'very soft, slimy and malodorous, between green and black' . . .) and descriptions of heavy magnetic anomalies off the Swedish coast, the observations on 'Sea Level' provoked only further obfuscation.

'The surface level of the Baltic Sea is entirely unpredictable,' it stated with commendable clarity, 'being governed by a combination of wind, barometric pressure and the amount of water brought down by the rivers.' But the level could definitely be up to six feet more and five feet less than usual in certain large and loosely defined areas. The surface currents caused by wind were equally unpredictable, and the Pilot suggested it was best to determine the sea's movement by fixing the boat's position regularly; but there among the graphs of depression tracks and winter ice cover were some for fog and mist, hinting that eyeball navigation could be impossible too.

This was all startling news. Here were five levels of uncertainty – limited charts, incomplete surveys, depths, currents and occasional poor visibility – stacked on top of each other. But there was still more to come: where the weather gods left off, mere humans piled in with extra difficulties of their own.

Large areas, mainly along the Estonian coasts, were closed to foreign shipping: the whole of the eastern Gulf of Finland for 50 miles west of Leningrad was marked, 'Fortified area – under Naval control' and, from there on, apparently, old mine-fields took over. Here the book outdid itself: the risk was mainly from magnetic mines in the Vyborg and Leningrad approaches, although:

> The risks . . . are considered to be no greater than the normal marine hazard such as striking an uncharted wreck. [What a relief!] Within the danger areas there is also the additional danger from uncharted wrecks and shoals as the mine danger will have inhibited surveying.

'Very nice,' I snorted. 'No one need worry because no one has dared to discover what there is to worry about!'

Recommendations for evading the hazards included sailing only by day in certain waters, and keeping a good look-out after stormy weather. Nor did the Russians have a monopoly of excitement: Sweden had modern defensive mine-fields, which were liable to fire off unpredictably in thundery conditions.

A vision was emerging of the sort of ultimate nightmare that Hammond Innes would have been proud of: sailing fast before a building gale in thick fog, with unknown currents and depths beneath, keeping a sharp look-out in the spray and steep waves for floating mines and invisible boulders and wrecks. For good measure there might be other shipping.

It certainly sounded as though an electronic navigator would be a useful item, to provide us with accurate positions.

The need for intermediate anchorages along our route was, if anything, accentuated by the dangers, but at least the out-of-bounds zones along the coast reduced the area of search, and by combing the main text we ended up with a list of about a dozen coastal bays or fishing harbours on the rocky Estonian coast with beautifully sonorous, almost Indian-sounding, names: Bukhta-Surkyulan-Lakhti; Haapsalu; Narva Yyesuu Sadam. From the very different exposed and sandy shores of Latvia, Lithuania, Poland and East Germany, we selected seven or eight ports, including Gdańsk and her neighbour Gdynia in Poland, and a detour up the Odra river on the East German border, allowing six or seven weeks in all to visit the communist countries.

For a while the project faded in prominence.

In late November, Eric Healy telephoned. 'Roger, I met my friend in London last week. She's Polish and much involved in sailing. You should contact her. The answer to your question, she says, is "possible, but difficult – very few boats visit Poland, and it's difficult for even the Poles to sail to Russia".'

At least it wasn't a closed door. A week later, a letter arrived from London. The Cruising Association had contacted the Russian and Polish Embassies direct, with gratifying results.

The Russians had said there should be no problem in cruising in their waters, provided we adhered to entry regulations and gave a full itinerary; for Poland, we should need an invitation from within the country.

Glasnost, it seemed, really existed for yachtsmen!

I backed in through the front door and made for the kitchen at speed.

'Look at this, Sue,' I said, plonking the letter down on the marble slab where she was making bread.

'It looks as though we have a bit of work to do.'

Our work for the last month of 1986 was exploratory – turning over stones to discover what connections already existed between Britain and Ireland and the Eastern bloc countries. Susan and I had dual British and Irish nationality, and the crucial diplomatic procedures turned out to be a similarly mixed bag. For Poland and East Germany, we worked direct through the embassies and consulates in London, but the Russian paper-work was handled by the Irish Department of Foreign Affairs. It was their first such application, they warned; it would have to be routed via the embassy in Moscow to obtain a basic authorization, before it could be dealt with by the local Russian embassy.

Other, less formal encouragement was soon forthcoming. The Ireland–USSR Friendship Society, which had links to sister societies in Leningrad and the Baltic Republics, was keen to offer help with recommendations. John de Courcy Ireland, the country's foremost maritime historian, was the author of a recently published book which provided a wealth of information on connections between Ireland and Russia over the previous 250 years. Many Irishmen had served in the Russian navy ever since Peter the Great had recruited sailors from all over Europe in the early 1700s. One had been Commander-in-Chief of the Baltic fleet in Napoleonic times and others, in the nineteenth century, were as much distinguished by their magnificent hybrid names – Michael Iosipovich O'Rourke, Nikolai Iosipovich O'Rourke – as by their exploits.

'One of the early recruits was an officer by the name of Delap,' John de Courcy Ireland told me. 'He was appointed in 1714 and served as a lieutenant on Peter the Great's flagship, *Ekaterina*. On one particular occasion, Delap distinguished himself by volunteering to bring the Tsar ashore in a ship's boat during very stormy conditions: he took responsibility for Peter's life and probably saved him from drowning.'

Delap, he told me, had been from Kerry – an unlooked-for link, which added an extra piquancy to our project.

Success, however, would depend on making a good case, and Christmas 1986 found us dodging between the typewriter, the goose-house and the drawing board, laboriously assembling brochures and itineraries for each of the communist countries. This forced us to nail both the overall route – northabout via Norway was the shortest and most obvious – and the starting date. Determined to avoid a battle of wills on the proposed return with an autumn gale in the southern North Sea or in the plughole of the Dover Straits, we continually adjusted the itinerary like a tailor's dummy, darting in extra safety days for passages here and stop-overs there. This had the unwelcome effect that the departure date, comfortably invisible from the viewpoint of 1986, jolted ominously closer in the New Year, like a fixed point on the horizon that turns out to be a ship on a collision course. Less than five months to go! With sudden desperation we despatched an application to Moscow in early January, listing the places we wanted to visit.

South Kerry is a stunningly beautiful reclining nude whose limbs, strewn carelessly out to sea, expose a thin taut skin of herbage, relieved by the odd tuft of hairy trees only in the most secret places. Perhaps it's really a pair of lovers, entwined, his rocky ribs showing through where softer landscapes fail. It's a landscape to inspire love – landlocked bays, silver beaches, vivid sea – but also terrible turbulences and retractions.

In winter, the pulse of life slows to an occasional hiccup and heave, as long winds moan through dark valleys and short days. Our particular corner is undeniably remote: the nearest railway is 50 miles away, the county library 60, and an airport nearly 100. It takes an effort of will even to get up the first two miles of switchback cul-de-sac to the main road which, in places, can only accommodate one van at a time. If Russia looked distant, it was at least partly because we were looking through the wrong end of the telescope.

My first call in London was to Janka Bielak, our Polish contact, who was the Public Relations Secretary of the Sail Training Association. The Association organizes the annual 'Tall Ships' rallies and races, which bring together sailing yachts and ships from all over Europe, and in some of which I had participated as a volunteer.

Janka lived in West London, but when I telephoned to arrange a meeting she was in acute distress: her husband had died only a day or two before, and she was making funeral arrangements. Despite this trauma, she wouldn't hear of a discreet withdrawal, and insisted I should visit.

It wasn't at all easy to do: London was succumbing to its worst winter for years, with snow piled feet thick against fences and in railway cuttings. An imposing lady with grey hair and eyes, gaunt and hollow with strain, greeted me beneath the icicles of a red-tiled porch in suburbia. There were yet more icicles indoors – thickets of triangular burgees points downward formed jagged friezes everywhere, framing barometers, ships' wheels and scores of other sailing mementoes.

Quietly, unflinchingly, she told me a little of her history. Her father and mother, brother and sister-in-law, had all been lost in the war, to one side or the other; she herself had been sentenced to eight years in a prison camp and had served seven. Now, she repaid these wounds with love: the STA activities, the bringing together of young crews from various countries were her great reward in life.

'Now, how can I help? I would really love to sail with you, but I'm busy all summer with the Association rallies. All the boats will be in Kiel at the end of June, you know. Can you meet us there? After that we race to Sweden.'

I promised to keep it in mind as I took my leave, deeply impressed by her courage and kindness, and the spring-steel spirit of the Poles; but I had no idea how significant her suggestion was to prove in a few months' time.

Another facet of Polish spirit flashed out at me next day when I visited the Embassy to make soundings about visa applications. The Counsellor who greeted me was a man of medium height and age, alert and quick of movement, with dark brown eyes. He was immediately open to the idea.

'There should be no problem,' he murmured, leafing through our proposals. Suddenly he turned rigid and pale as he stared at an itinerary map. The offending sheet flew back across the table and his finger jabbed after it.

'Is not *Stettin*,' he snapped, pointing out a black dot and label indicating the sea-port near the East German border. 'Szczecin, that's *Polish*.' His eyes were alight. 'Stettin is *German* language. If you will visit Poland you must say in Polish, *Sh-che-tsin*.' He emphasized it phonetically. I got my tongue around it as soon as it would go, and apologized.

'I have the same difficulty with some American magazines, and others,' he said, calming a little. 'Look, if you write one city name in Polish,' (indicating Warsawa), 'you must do *all*. Is Poland. You understand?'

I understood only too perfectly, realizing with disquieting suddenness that we would need to steer a very careful course between the sensitivities of all the Baltic countries. By the time he showed me out, though, the storm clouds had cleared.

'For you, I think no problem,' he smiled.

It was very encouraging that one man could say so. The Soviet Embassy in Notting Hill Gate was my next port of call; it was to be a sort of dummy run for Dublin. I was in luck – the Head of the Consular Section took my papers in hand straightaway. 'If you go as seamen,' he said, 'strictly speaking you don't need visas – and perhaps the captain can go ashore. But if you all want to go onshore you must apply for authorization.'

He glanced at the route map again as he passed it back.

'Yes, I think it is all correct – if you will get permission.'

His momentary detention of the papers, the steady look as he spoke the phrase, warned of uncertainty and hard work to come. I collected a few newspapers on the way out and, in laborious slow motion, dragged through snow-drifts to an appointment in Belgrave Square.

The contrast could hardly be greater between the superb crescent sweep of stone and stucco overhead and the East German Embassy beneath. Squeezing down basement steps, I found myself in a sparse cubicle replete with cameras and a bullet-proof window. The official, a Mr Krebs, formal in a suit and tie, was kindly and very courteous, but embarrassed by the need to keep a voice amplification button depressed. That left him only one hand to flip through our papers, so in the end he abandoned high-tech and yelled through the layers of glass instead.

'It is the first such application,' a grille on the wall crackled. '*The first I've seen*,' he shouted.

He didn't know how it ought to be handled. We should write with very full details – he would put it to Berlin.

The last of the daylight fluttered to the roof-tops with the starlings as I left in thoughtful mood.

Obviously, the eastern bloc was not girded by a seamless wall, but perhaps by a series of mansions standing shoulder to shoulder with individual quirks and entrances. What I needed was to track down yachtsmen who had sailed through those doorways before.

The Cruising Association occupies a mezzanine under the brick and iron vaulting of the old Ivory House warehouse in St Katharine's Dock near Tower Bridge. From the comfort of its library I could look down on dour Thames barges and flippant plastic cruisers swimming in a little dark water and a lot of ice.

The stream of information about sailing to Russia seemed to run in reverse. Most of it sparkled through nineteenth-century logs and books: amazing accounts, some of them, of gentlemen's yachts accompanying the British fleet, for the fun of it, right under the Russian coastal guns in Crimean times; but the most recent account of a voyage to Leningrad dated from 1862. In the twentieth century, the trickle had dried up, apart from one or two voyages, by Arthur Ransome and others, to the Baltic Republics between the wars, during their period of independence. Over the ensuing 50 years until now, silence seemed to have fallen, as profound and unnatural as the white hush outside.

There were just three articles describing a voyage from England to Tallinn, the Estonian capital, in 1977. Bernard Hayman and his crew had stayed at the Olympic Centre prior to the Games. A photograph caption read: 'The first British yacht to fly the Russian courtesy flag' – presumably meaning 'since the Revolution'.

At last, a thread back to the land of the living! Yes, the author confirmed, he'd been well entertained, and enjoyed his time there; but had found the visit rather tense, perhaps partly because, as he'd mentioned in the articles, it had taken two and a half years to secure the visas. Also, he had arrived *early*. The Russians liked one to be on time!

The channels of personal contact were very short and no one, it seemed, had sailed to the Soviet Union since Bernard Hayman, at least not from the UK. It was known there were sailing clubs in Leningrad, but no one had heard of anyone reaching them. There was a sort of hierarchy of approachability for the three countries: Poland should be accessible enough and welcoming; the USSR might be difficult; but East Germany, I heard to my regret, was definitely not recommended – the authorities were thought to be hard-hearted, the navy trigger-happy.

I was told of a young, lone sailor who, a few years previously, had strayed inshore in his plywood catamaran. He was imprisoned and the yacht impounded. On production of bonds he was deported to West Germany, the story went, to await the subsequent despatch of his boat to him overland – he wouldn't be allowed to sail it out. It arrived, sawn into pieces, in tea-chests.

In Kerry, a less sanguine mood had set in. Even the Finns, we had discovered, couldn't normally sail to Russia, and they were next-door neighbours.

We would obviously be gambling on change already having occurred in the official outlook, a chance to stick our foot in the door; but so far all the facts were negative, almost all the encouragement verbal or nebulous. Just one item, however, was written and unequivocal. Flicking through the newspapers picked up in the Russian Embassy, I reread it – a summary of a speech by Mikhail Gorbachev on promoting peace: 'It is the responsibility of every country and region, every organization, and every individual . . .'

'And isn't that exactly what we intend?'

'Right, we'll go then,' said Susan.

'Can we afford it?' I queried, prising my doubts into the open with one hand while concealing a stack of chandlers' invoices in the other. No, we agreed, but we'd do it anyway.

'It will have to be a charter cruise, like the rest of *Canna*'s work,' I warned. Susan started drafting advertisements for the 'Baltic Goodwill Cruise'.

In Ireland, it's easy to meet people, and the Russians were no exception. The Cultural Attaché, tall and urbane, seemed to be expecting my visit. He explained that the problem was a lack of any cultural agreement to give a basis for such visits. Might it be possible to arrange an exchange cruise? I produced photographs of Russian crews being entertained at Susan's home club in Cheshire, and suggested that that was just what we hoped to do. We'll support it, he agreed.

The Consul was youngish and, luckily, interested in sailing.

'I'd come with you if I could,' he enthused but, like his London colleague, warned that the application was highly unusual, and that the decision would be Moscow's. If we could get authorization, visas could normally be provided within a week.

'Which is a lot less than for a Russian coming to the West!' he called after me.

The same insistent *if* had now been sounded in both Embassies and, doubtful how best to make ourselves heard in Moscow, we decided to hit every note on the keyboard – there was no time left for anything else. Like monkeys on the loose in a satellite, we pulled every string and pushed every knob and button in sight.

I made myself known in the Department of Foreign Affairs, scoured the yacht clubs, sniffed out shipping companies with business in the Baltic and haunted them by telephone. We unearthed the names of Russian delegates to international yachting committees, arranged for recommendations to be sent, and followed up with translations in Russian. Cyrillic script, of course! Exotic but quite unintelligible. We'd had no time to think of language.

Susan charitably commandeered Russian, leaving Polish to me. While I grappled with impossible strings of consonants (*chrzaszcz* is a beetle) Susan briskly toured the house and grounds affixing labels to every conceivable surface. The dashboard informed me I was driving an автомобиль (ahv-tah-mah-beel) not a car; the ceiling become a потолок (pah-tah-lohk).

'What's this "*kookh-nyah*"?' I called, as I made the porridge. 'Is it a *wall?*'

'Don't be stupid,' she said. 'It's the kitchen; you're in it.' Every week or so, I telephoned the Department of Foreign Affairs.

'No, I'm very sorry,' came Carole's invariable reply. 'There's nothing yet from Moscow.'

The silence was alarming, we'd had not one reply from Russia. What more could we do? Was it time for a Letter to Gorbachev? While we had been anxiously waiting, however, his counterpart in Ireland had just been changed. The chief harpist and Prime Minister was now Charles J. Haughey, a long-running political veteran, and a veteran sailor to boot. We wrote to ask for his support.

By now it was March, and *Canna* had to be launched on the April tides. As light relief from the paperwork we spent hours fiddling, fitting, sawing, sanding; upside down in the bowels at night, feeding through rebellious snakes of wire for the new Navigator; aloft in a canvas cradle and a spring wind fiddling with rigging pins at the mast-head; on our knees at the gunwales, praying it wouldn't rain before the varnish dried. We had to pick up whatever charter income we could before June.

Berth reservations for the cruise itself were slow, not even enough to crew the boat, let alone pay its way; but already a local newspaper had splashed a front-page photograph, stating we were 'Baltic Bound' and setting out my worries about over-abundant hospitality and vodka.

'I wonder if we're going to manage all of this?' I mused aloud, with increasing frequency. Susan was blandly optimistic. 'Of course we'll get there,' she replied flatly.

Towards the end of April, when the DFA telephoned *us*, I had a belated premonition that, as usual, she was right.

'Good news,' they said. 'Moscow has advised that an authorization is being issued. Your crew must all apply to Inflot, the shipping agency, in each port, and detailed instructions are on the way.'

Panic followed the euphoria. We had six weeks to go to arrange everything, and perhaps only four or five days of that to fling a crew together.

Irish insouciance is the opposite pole to Russian regulation and, try as we might, no one on our side could be made to understand what possible urgency there could be about something due to happen more than a month or two ahead. The Irish sense of time is like a comet's tail – a few sparse minutes pushed ahead, whole centuries dragged behind. Arthur the instigator, since his reluctant agreement to an early departure, was now in an invisible part of his orbit, and it seemed unlikely he'd reappear. Only Maxwell McKeever had booked for the first leg to Sweden. Crew changes were proposed for Helsinki, Kiel and England, leaving a central leg of six or seven weeks taking in the Soviet Union and Poland. Here there was a yawning gap, with nibbles but no takers.

A week went by, ten days. A pilotage booklet for the Soviet Ports arrived; but no instructions. Finally, we routed a telex – 'Russia runs on them!' we were told – through a friendly eel-fattening farm in the next village. Reams of identical information clattered out to five Russian ports.

To our enormous delight, a reply popped up before breakfast next day: 'GOOD MORNING, INFLOT LENINGRAD. RYT NOTED. WE AS COMMERCIAL PORT AGENTS WOULD LIKE TO CONFIRM BERTH RESERVATION AVAILABLE FOR MENTIONED PERIOD . . .' and over the next few days, three more approvals came in. Only Klaipėda in Lithuania declined, on the grounds that they had no tourist facilities. Four out of five was fine, all systems go; but obtaining berth reservations was only one stage in the process. Authorization from Intourist, the tourist agency, and berth confirmation from Inflot had to be obtained before we could approach the Embassy for visas.

From then on, it felt as if we were trying to tune a ten- or twelve-tone balalaika. Quite apart from the Russian string, there were plenty of guts to screw to the sticking point – but could we get them all to concert pitch on time?

Sponsorship was one such string: without Soviet approval, we hadn't a strong enough case to seek it; but now we had, there was barely time to shoot off enquiries for assistance in kind. A practically-minded relative sponsored the loo-paper, which was to be a blessing later.

The East German application was looking doubtful, as an unlucky series of postal failures had almost demolished our chances of personal recommendation.

Charts new, charts second-hand, charts sponsored trickled in, but there were still huge stretches of blank water. Yacht insurance came through at the last minute – without an extension to our normal cruising range, we'd either have had to scrap the cruise, or risk a massive claim ourselves.

Photography was a chronically weak string. We had at first confidently relied on personal contact, then advertisement, but nothing had resulted except showers of comment, abortive rendezvous, telephone calls from love-sick students who would only work in pairs and weekends with talented youngsters shipped over from England who weakened at the sight of salt water. Shay Fennelly bit the bullet in the nick of time, offering to attempt both still and film for the whole cruise.

Our activities became more and more bizarre as geographical isolation began to tell. We drove two hundred miles to get extra passport photographs taken. They came late in the post. I drove another twenty to the local police station to get them witnessed, only to find the local police station locked.

The last three weeks began with a car crash – our own and a neighbour's front ends crumpled in a magnificent sequence of stills – and it went on from there like a runaway film. The opposing car, borrowed and temporarily unbent, jammed solid next day in an exclamation of black rubber, while making time on country roads. Due at a lecture on 'The Role of Women in Russian Society', and at a cash-and-carry company a hundred miles away, I made my dates with minutes to spare. The Russian professor and grandmother, and the warehouse manager, one large and the other lean, were equally generous in their specific fields, and I arrived back next day laden down with comment on Soviet morale and peering out from a fortress of shrink-packed tins.

All the while on the Russian front, telexes flew like ping-pong balls. A file built up as the agencies played a match. Regularly I drove down to collect the latest update pinned to the eel-farm door. The score was still stuck at twenty-all when I returned from a last foray around the embassies and picked my way through bulk packs of split peas, dried apricots and muesli towards the 'in-tray'.

'PLS ADVISE APPROX TIME ARRIVAL/DEPARTURE LENINGRAD PILOT STATION. REGARDS!' cabled Inflot, but at the same instant Intourist were still having terrible difficulty searching for a pigeonhole to stuff the expedition into; and still the visas which had looked within grasp seemed to slither away beyond our departure date. We took up the Consul's parting words and begged him to make the running.

But where for that matter was the boat? A charter group from England had taken her away. They'd been brusque and business-like and quite unused to the waters. As I'd explained all *Canna*'s foibles, they detected mine.

'Don't *worry*!' they'd said. 'We'll bring her back in one piece!' but the wind rose strongly as they left the harbour, and broke the spinnaker out. She had disappeared south-west like a speed-boat, and hadn't been seen for a week. Nightfall again, and still no sign!

In pyjamas and an early dawn I groped to the window and saw her swinging to her mooring. Suddenly the house erupted. Maxwell arrived with reinforcements, close friends and more distant ones. His barn-door frame shambled up and down the yard organizing gear. People were strewn around the floors; packets in neat stacks, thousands of plastic bags. An unknown girl stretching shapely limbs over the tennis-table ironing numbers on to spare sails and 'CANNA' in big letters on to the dodgers. Rupert cataloguing a stack of charts nine inches thick. I made lists of lists, then lost them. We chased the hens for missing eggs, and the bank for foreign currency. Susan orchestrated door and telephone and typewriter bells, and the buzzer on the cooker, which disgorged long runs of loaves and fishes.

D-Day was Saturday. On Friday 5 June the ant's nest had taken a direct hit – there were insects everywhere. Shay came down from Co. Mayo, dwarfed by monstrous maggot-shaped rucksacks and photographic kit-bags. David's car crawled in on its belly, heavy with apparatus; there was film, more film, tripods and camera boxes fit for a furniture van. 'Oh, no problem,' he breezed. 'They'll fit anywhere there's a bit of room.'

As the afternoon wore on, the condition of *Canna* neared perfection, while the helpers see-sawed to exhaustion. When we gathered in the village restaurant, Fenny, *en route* from the North, was the only man not to have arrived.

'Thank you all. Let's hope we can do it,' we chinked.

Something *had* arrived from the north, though, ahead of our missing crewman. I hadn't had time to bother with the weather all the week. Now, as the noisy preoccupations fell away and subsided to a warm social hum like an excited beehive, I felt the candle-shadows stir a flicker of unease. Outside, beyond the small blue panes, blue trees were leaning away from a blue wind. The trees, and the flames, were bending in the wrong direction.

CHAPTER 3

Rough Passage – Ireland to Sweden

Waking before the alarm on Monday 8 June, I flicked on the radio with one elbow, propped myself on the other and peered out. An uncompromising concrete road bridge stared back, panning menacingly across the saloon window. Trawlers leave early from Portmagee and we'd had to anchor off. The bridge had been standing by all night to crunch us if we had dragged as the tides swung us back and forth. There had been no temptation to sleep in.

Our lives now revolved around the fixed points of forecasts, and woe betide anyone who talked as we jotted them down.

'SHANNON, ROCKALL – Northerly 6.' Then for weather and visibility: 'Fair. Good.'

It didn't seem fair to me at all. A vicious depression, squatting on our first leg destination in West Sweden, was churning the winds around it in an anticlockwise furore. It was not a bit of good to us, unless . . .

'I've more than half a mind to run with it and go south,' I announced, as we clambered into our wet gear.

We used the forecast pad chartlet of Europe as a battleground for our council of war, covering it with arrows and whorls.

'The winds are from the north down the west of Ireland,' I indicated. 'North-west across to Scillies, westerly up the Channel. It's due to stay like that for a week at least, and we could be at Dover in less than three days.'

The temptation to stand the cruise on its head and ride the roundabout anti-clockwise to Scandinavia was almost overwhelming. Long, long days running before the wind were what we'd need to settle the crew, and the mere fact of going with the wind would cut its strength by half.

'Against that, we'll have further to go. We'll lose 150 miles of northerly latitude, which we'll have to make up in the North Sea, and if the winds turn against us there we'll be in dire trouble. There's nowhere much to shelter.'

'We have to make northing sometime,' gruffed Maxwell. He was obviously keen to stick to our plans and, as senior crew and mate, his opinion carried weight.

'We'll go north,' I said. 'The wind's supposed to back west for a while tomorrow, which will help. If the forecasts don't confirm that today we'll turn about and go south.' But as the anchor chain rattled in and we picked up a little speed over the bright rippled water, I knew we would hardly turn back. It was a one-way gamble. I offered no thoughts on our next landfall, and nobody asked.

Within half an hour, we were fighting the Atlantic again. Valleys and hills of silver, blue and green bore down against us, lifting, lurching, slamming, breaking. Three big ones, a lull, a broken pitch, then more again. Every one had to be judged, fenced with, countered, defeated, every inch to windward disputed. Even so, we were crabbing far to leeward on starboard tack, heading away from the coast toward mid-ocean.

The next five days were a wearing, tedious hell. Our one intention was to get north, to reach the crucial turning points in Co. Mayo and Donegal, far up the exposed and rock-bound coast. Once there, we could hope to bend east and sail free with the wind we had, and we'd have a chance to achieve our deadline in Sweden; but to do it against a head wind meant we'd have to sail much further than the crow's course of nearly 250 miles. Every incident in the long grind was judged by whether it helped us forward in the struggle. The mountains of water were more menacing but less elusive than the mirages of land. For the first day, the Dingle Peninsula and its broken string of beads, the Blaskets, slanted across the starboard horizon, inching and crawling, getting no nearer. The sun crawled and crept to its summit, and painfully eased itself back down. A dark night with stars came and went. Starboard tack, sail a bit, port again. The land had followed us, stuck to us, tailed us like a kipper on a bridal car. Try as we might we couldn't get clear, and at dawn on 9 June it still hailed us over our stern, with a mocking smirk.

To force the pace we motorsailed, furling the foresail and running the engine at cruising speed, with the mainsail still hoisted. It didn't aid *Canna*'s speed as much as the angle of attack, allowing us to sail more north than west. The blessings, though, were badly mixed, and it was hard on the boat and the crew.

Each of the three others was on watch for three hours, asleep for three, then up for three more on stand-by, in case the helmsman needed a hand: a nine-hour cycle. With a four-man crew that meant I floated – doing most of the navigation between scattered snatches of sleep. It worked well when we sailed: the self-steering did all the hard work, and the man on watch could prowl around as he pleased. With motor-sailing all that changed. The self-steering couldn't always hold a straight enough course, and the watch-man was tied to the tiller. The stand-by was called out more often. The saloon was filled with the roar of the labouring diesel instead of the lulling gurgle of bubbles; the motion became short, hard and brutal.

I worried for the engine, keeping an ear cocked for any change in its note or any new edge to a rattle. Every so often I checked the gauges – the cooling water intake was close to the waterline on a port tack, and sometimes sucked air.

I was anxious for the crew. Shay, against advice, had bunked forward where the motion was worst. He was being hoisted and dropped inside his low cubby-hole with all the insistent regularity of a steam-hammer. One drop every 6 seconds, on average, 10 a minute, 600 an hour, nearly 15,000 a day. I hoped he'd survive it. I groped my way toward him in the gloom. 'Shay, your watch in ten minutes!'

As I spoke, there was a falling feeling, my head hit the deck, and an almighty bang shook the boat from end to end.

'Christ, what was *that*?' he asked anxiously.

'She's pounding,' I said, 'that's normal.'

'I've never been so glad of a strong boat,' he grunted wearily, burrowing out of the rat's nest of newspapers he had fashioned to combat condensation.

Dawn was breaking coldly as I went aloft. *Canna* had a low freeboard and, in these conditions, was a fairly wet boat. The small spray-hood over the companionway gave only moderate protection to the open cockpit.

'How's it going, Maxwell?' I asked.

'OK,' he answered firmly. 'Wettish, no traffic that I can see.' At least Maxwell seemed to be in his element. He sat stolidly for hours in one, unvaried, energy-conserving hunch. Repeated drenching seemed to make as much impression on him as a lawn sprinkler on a garden gnome, as the rain and sea ran off his glasses and down his generous folds and rolls.

I guessed, however, that someone or something was bound to fail; and on that second morning, we lost the first crewman. Fenny succumbed to his pain and sickness while cooking bacon and eggs. Maybe I shouldn't have insisted on routine so soon. Probably I should have suppressed a slight frown when three full breakfasts landed on the cabin sole for the second time in an hour. I certainly shouldn't have asked how he felt.

'Roger, I'm hanging on here by my toenails,' he said with unusual force and feeling, 'and when we next land I may have to leave you.' It was plain that he meant what he said; a bleak, hollow, ebbing mood filled the boat, and our efforts seemed even more fragile.

We put him ashore that evening on the remote Galway island of Inishbofin, staked out to the west by a rock like an upturned cheese; and, on the morning of 10 June, we left early without him, under a lifting sky. It was the worst of the sequence of delays, alarms, and minor disasters that was to dog the whole of our first two weeks at sea. I hadn't wanted to use heavy pressure: he knew, and I knew, that if he became seriously ill much further from land, across the North Sea, the penalties could be very high for him and for the expedition. It was a blow. We'd liked his muted twinkle of humour, and it was a bereavement to lose nearly half of the crew. The reduction from four to three had that effect; the luxury of a 'float' no longer existed. We all had to do the same work, and there was no more company on watch either, not much more than a peremptory collision in the companionway when one's stint was done.

My worries were now fewer but stronger. We were leaner and harder, and even more determined to get there – and we would, I thought, as long as we don't lose anyone else; but on the third day out we nearly did, in a way I hadn't foreseen. There was an awful thundering over my head, and someone calling my name.

'Take a hold of me!' yelled Shay from the bows. 'Dolphins.' He was trying to hook his ankle round the forestay and film them under the stemhead as he leaned right outboard, whistling and clicking as they breached, teetering on the edge of the pulpit regardless of all danger. An observer would have diagnosed a suicide attempt. He had no harness on. I braced myself around the furled genoa and grabbed him as the prow reared up with the speed of a lift.

There had been about five or six of the creatures, rubbing themselves on the hull, swerving and rolling, displaying cream-coloured curves on their sides, looking up at us with steady, curious glances, but they soon knifed away. Capable of outstripping a 30-knot ship, they had obviously found our halting four knots perfectly miserable.

So did we. No, I said, we wouldn't put in for the night. We'd head on north-east for Donegal, for Bloody Foreland if possible, the vital north-west corner, before the weather got worse. It did get worse. It flung down long grey showers. It was black, wet, cold, bleak and windy. Not another boat in sight. All night and half the next day. The Foreland failed us, so did the tide. We couldn't even quite make the small fishing village of Burton-port until it rose. Having sailed more than 300 miles so far over a route that was barely 200 direct, we eventually anchored off in blue water, cooked up something disgusting from tins, dropped sodden pullovers on anything to hand and dropped in to torpor where we fell.

It was a very low point. I had had to change the engine oil, and had grease to my elbows. We were out of water, out of diesel; out of luck, too, I felt. Leningrad was a fading vision, someone else's daft idea, as I rang home from a bottomless coin-box in a tatty, mock-timbered bar.

'Don't worry!' said Susan, from one of the outer planets. 'Things have improved. I've got the Russian visas.'

'They won't be much use if we can't get beyond Scotland next weekend,' I continued, oblivious.

On the fifth day, 11 June, it was gear failure. The mainsail leech failed just above the boom where it had been flexing for days. We reefed it down.

Bloody Foreland! Would we ever get clear of this coast? It wasn't even bold enough to get angry with, only a half-baked, low, shingly affair, but still we needed another grain of determination, still we couldn't sail free. Out to the most northerly point, the Gods of Erin dragged us, right out to the last, tiny fulcrum between the winds.

Tory Island lies six miles off the northern shore of Ireland. It crouches in a foetal curve, its high protective back pushed out against the cold, its lower southern slopes toward the land. Two miles long, but only a few hundred yards wide in places, its umbilical cord of ferries is often cut in winter; but now, beneath the sun, it gleamed with life and purpose. Everything was chiselled, cleft, and sawn; gem-like, emerald, rocky, white. Cliffs, stone walls, a little church; the two villages were clusters of newly-made sugar cubes, throwing shadows like shards of jet. Awestruck, we glided far in to the bay, a circle of uncompromising clarity; only when a few expectant figures marked the doorways did we swing away, skirting the sheltered scoop of shore.

'Amazing!' we marvelled. 'What a life!'

Once, the islanders had either fished or starved. Even now, every time a storm threatened, all their boats had to be brought to the mainland for shelter. There were no half efforts, no second chances – and somehow their determination breathed a waft of second wind toward us over the gap.

Wham! We're through a tide rip at the eastern end, out past the cliffs and into the wind. As *Canna* heels and forges ahead, I lean forward to the compass on the saloon doghouse – it's showing NE for Scotland – and peer up to the wind-vane. At last it's backed off from the bows; the wind's north-west! A bubbling wake astern. Tory Island is disappearing fast. I surface after a pent-up week and blow a vast spout of moist relief as we kill the engine.

'What's the matter?' Shay asked, polishing lenses again.

'Look,' I said, swinging a dramatic arm. 'Listen, we're *sailing*.' It's what we've been hoping for for a *week*! He glanced round, frowning.

'Oh. Yes,' he said, and went below.

I stayed on deck for hours. Separated by deep inlets, the huge headlands of Horn, Fanad and Malin sprawled out from the northern coast like the paws of a recumbent lion. Glowing tawny-red in the late evening light, they slid away astern as purple deepened in their folds and claws. A herring gull followed, gliding, soaring. My spirits rose with it. Maxwell smiled a small private smile.

Our boat was a mixed bag. She was built in England, bought in Wales, based in Ireland. Our crew was a mixture too; and both English and Irish had ploughed this route before us. That night, 12 June, we crossed the track of the *Oriana*, 128 years too late to keep her company. She was a yacht of 60 tons, two-masted, schooner-rigged and very swift, heading north from Kingstown in Dublin Bay out through the North Channel between Ireland

and Scotland. She had five crew on board, and two gentlemen; and she was
bound for Leningrad, then called St Petersburg. Both the owner, the
surgeon William J. Martin, and his companion, W. J. Corrigan, who
described himself as a hairy law student, were less than twenty-five years
old. Martin already had a thriving practice, and Corrigan, too, had strong
medical connections: his father was Sir Dominic Corrigan, whose illus-
trious career is now best known for his identification of ailments (such as
Corrigan's Pulse), and for his appointment as Queen Victoria's Physician-
in-Ordinary. Martin used the schooner as a sort of bachelor chariot,
heading north to Iceland one year, south to the Mediterranean another. On
the Petersburg cruise, Corrigan had kept a log, which circulated privately
among their families for more than a century, until it was at last published
in part in 1987.

The abbreviated log landed on my desk in mid-January, when Moscow
had already been notified of our departure date. *Oriana*'s had been the
same – 6 June. It was a remarkable coincidence, a wild chance that gave me
the same feeling of lift as catching a favourable tide. Her route had been
broadly similar, too, and her powerful rig and long waterline had, by dint
of fairly continuous sailing, taken her company to St Petersburg and back, a
distance of 5,400 miles, within two and a half months.

Martin had been a member of the Royal Irish Yacht Club, which is still
housed in one of a string of decorous pavilions overlooking the harbour of
Dun Laoghaire. His great-grand-nephew, Clive C. Martin, himself an
officer of the Club, had published the shortened log; and on hearing of
my interest, gladly sent on a copy of the full one. It was enlivened with
Corrigan's own sketches, which he'd pasted into the original, small,
leather-bound volume: line-drawings of Norwegian wooden houses, of
anchors, of the *Oriana* and her enormous bowsprit, dwarfed by the stem of
a Russian man-of-war with two lines of gun-ports; coloured facsimiles
of ensigns and burgees, scattered among sheets of his regular, legible hand.
The text was ripped off in a dashing style, full of young blood and hot
temper, peppered with appreciations and acid comment on those things
and people that did or didn't pass muster: 'Now if my Readers imagine I'm
going to write "nice" they had better give up reading . . . I'm not addicted
to swellism in any shape and if people don't like my writing they may go be
d . . . d for all I care,' he warned and, as we prepared our twentieth-century
revisit, Corrigan's record kept us amused, sustained and ecologically
horrified. He found the Norwegian coast by turns grand, beautiful,
devilish queer, and infernally wet. He and Martin made beasts of themselves on beer and strawberries in Copenhagen, and made amends by
attending church. They were hospitably received in Revel by a Colonel,
fared less well in St Petersburg, were nearly lost in a storm in Danzig, and
were becalmed with hosts of other sailing ships in the Danish Sounds.

Corrigan fished and hiked, and shot at anything that moved so long as it wasn't human or another boat.

With time on hand for once in a while, I hauled him out from under the chart table to see how they had fared in the early stages.

Their departure had been very different from ours:

Slipped our moorings 3½pm Dublin time June 6th, 1859 and after firing 4 guns left the harbour of Kingstown in gallant style.

    Tuesday, June 7th. This was an awful hot day and didn't scorch us a few – my neck is about the colour a well-boiled lobster would be if it got scarlatina . . . And 'my Readers' might guess a long time before they would guess how M and I were dressed to-day. Well, M sported a grey flannel shirt and cloth trews and india-rubber boots – no stockings – and a tarpaulin hat. I had no boots or stockings, only a white flannel shirt, blue flannel trews, red belt and a scarlet flannel cap and I looked like a returned gold digger as I've a fizzing red beard.

'And it's a terrible damned shame we weren't wearing flannel shirts and nothing on our feet instead of sodden stiff oilskins and safety harness,' I commented to Maxwell at dawn, as Ireland faded and, off the west of Scotland, the island of Islay hove in view. 'Do you know, if that bad weather hadn't delayed us, we might almost have collided with the *Oriana* just here!'

'I thought the weather had been fairly good, myself,' he riposted, still avid to sample the Minches, north Scotland and Orkney.

I had been just as keen. Canna, the idyllic island of our christening, lay only 60 miles to the north, but the wind was funnelling out of the Minch like a gale through a subway, and we'd had enough of running up a 'down' escalator. I wasn't on for tempting fate again. 'Sorry,' I said. 'We can't risk losing any more time. A short cut through Scotland is the better chance.'

The *Oriana* had continued north-west; we crossed her track north-eastward, and led her twin, the *Ierne*, toward the Firth of Lorne and the Caledonian Canal. The *Ierne* was three years behind the *Oriana* – she sailed to St Petersburg in 1862 – but she had not passed through Scotland until early July. Her skipper, S. R. Graves, was then Commodore of the Royal Mersey Yacht Club in Liverpool, and had published a book recounting the ten-week cruise the following year. He and Corrigan were to weave a sort of braided Minotaur thread for us from there on, between them touching many of the places we hoped to visit in the Baltic, sparking strange assonance and discords across the centuries.

One of the discords, I thought with bitter envy, was that Graves had begun by cheating; instead of a tooth-gritting slog against the wind, he had travelled luxuriously by train from Liverpool to collect *Ierne* in Oban, consuming quantities of sturgeon and salmon en route.

Ierne and *Oriana* both had stewards and skippers and other professional crew aboard, too; but, even so, Corrigan implies that decorous society still considered it faintly mad for gentlemen to eschew their creature comforts in pursuit of travel and curiosity in such an uncomfortable space. No doubt, compared to the splendour of a Georgian ballroom, a 70-ton yacht seemed hideously cramped, but what would Corrigan and Graves have made of our strange craft, one-tenth the size of *Oriana*, and its three bedraggled and weary characters, clad in plastic and nylon?

It hardly mattered to us now what reactions we got, so long as they helped us over our hurdles. Mainly they did, provided we were persistent. The weather soon became contrary again, and bitterly cold, but the humans were warm and obliging.

In Oban, while purchasing extra warps and fenders for navigating the canal, we collected telephoned directions to a sail-repairer a few miles away.

'Anchor off the wooded head, under the tower, and make for the caravan park,' she had said.

If we hurried, we'd get done by dark.

We nosed into the wide, empty bay she'd described. There were two other yachts, both untended. To my horror, there were also two caravan parks, both miles away and miles apart, receding deeper into the evening as we stripped the mainsail and launched the dinghy. I dithered to and fro as we puttered inshore, first heading towards this one, then that. The yachts shrank to specks. Maxwell and I staggered up through floury dunes, humping the heavy sail bag like Crusoe and Man Friday. Over a barbed-wire fence, a septic tank, through some prickly gorse. A few tents, boys kicking a ball, shaking their heads and staring. This couldn't possibly be right. As we sweated and our oilskins squeaked, we stumbled into a gaggle of suave and scented young couples in full party dress, piling out of a mobile home and into a limousine.

'Is there a sailmaker here?' I stuttered.

There was. Diana, a lovely Yorkshire girl, squatted on the floor of a most unlikely modern loft, picking at the mainsail seams with her fingernails.

'They're beginning to rot,' she said. 'For where you're going, we'd better have them right.'

For hours she picked and stitched and folded and taped, until the big windows began to turn blue.

The seams held out until the last day but one of the cruise.

Our passage through the Caledonian canal started badly. It was Sunday, it was not supposed to be open; it had been, and we'd missed it. We tried to force an entrance when the bottom lock opened mysteriously at sunset, found ourselves in front of a silent, unnoticed ship, piled high with timber, and backed out of her way in a hurry. She didn't slow down, and we didn't dare look in case she rammed the gates.

Next day, we missed the first big flight of locks too. There were already two yachts half-way up. Two trawlers came down, and the morning was gone. The lock-keepers made to break for lunch.

'We're going to Russia!' we explained, 'we're in a slight hurry.'

They winked knowingly. 'Well then, ye'll no want to hang around here. We'll put ye through fast,' they said, accepting the double trouble of an individual lift with good grace. They did put us through fast. Their cauldrons seethed with extra malevolence as the sluices opened wide and, missing our warps in one lock, we ended up jammed across it; but their co-operation saved us almost a day. We squeezed past the ghastly gates one by one, some so strained and twisted they had to be flushed into place with torrents of water and heart-rending shrieks and groans. I had been warned about them: they looked as if they might be the nineteenth-century originals, fitted by the canal's engineer, Thomas Telford; collapses were not unknown, and we were desperate to get through before they happened.

There were other more quaint delays – a hand-cranked swing-bridge blocked with baa-ing sheep; the driver of a wider one to be parted from his porridge – but the closing hours of the canal couldn't be helped at all. The resulting idleness, however, gave us a chance to get better acquainted. On the night of 16 June, just a month from our appointed rendezvous in Leningrad, we eyed each other speculatively around the saloon table by the mahogany glow of the oil lamp.

'How is it going, Shay?' I asked.

'It's OK,' he said, with a grimace. 'I'll survive!'

Not only was he managing to survive in difficult conditions that were entirely new to him, but he was contriving to get his work done too. Privately, I'd been sceptical about whether the electronic cameras would function beyond the first few days of flying spray, but now I was beginning to have hope. All his equipment was handled with love. Volumes of heavy diaries piled up on the bunks were used to record his shots. I realized after a while that we had the right man for the job: Shay was single-minded to the point of obsession, sometimes taking minutes to find the exact words he needed to express a point.

Maxwell provided a leaven of humour, slipping easily into a groove of stories culled from his esoteric world of cattle-dealing, of farmers and agents, and 'blockers' and 'whackers' – their go-betweens.

'It was the custom at most houses, when a deal was done for the landowner, to seal it by offering the agent a tot,' he told us. 'One particular lady was renowned for being close; and on this occasion, after making a sale, she sets out the usual miserly toddy. The agent reckons it's time to make a stand, raises the small tumbler, and studies it for ages most intently.

'"Would there be something wrong there, Jamey?" she asks.

'"No, not at all, ma'am," he replies. "You done the very best you could. I was just looking to see who made the wee Protestant glass."'

Maxwell went off into vast snorts and chortles that shook the hull and sent fish darting for safety. He was often quiet, didn't like too many people around, but when he got going he gave full measure. Whether we were floating in freezing melt-water under white-capped Ben Nevis, or immured in the secret recesses of Loch Oich, his store of tales brightened the enforced stop-overs like a string of bunting.

High morale stood us in good stead when we ran into trouble at the far end of the canal. The female customs officer who had welcomed us to Scotland had been in the pink of health, but the man who checked us out at Inverness was a yellow walking corpse, quite obviously an omen. Sure enough, in the mouth of the Moray Firth, near the breaking flank of the notorious Riff Bank, a strange sound came from the engine-room, like a small dog piddling. There was a continuous stream of water from the sump, and 30 seconds poking told me the worst.

'A burst muffler, men, I'm afraid. All the cooling water and half the exhaust are discharging into the bilge.'

We motored back flat out, keeping the bilge pumped, and the flooding current did the rest, getting us to the town dock just before the chandlers closed. The concerned cadaver reappeared and pointed me to a telephone. I hijacked it from a lorry driver. The inevitable Scots mechanic called Jock, with the aid of a Donegal man called Paddy and a bottle of home-brewed liquor, relieved us of worry and money in roughly equal amounts, but still it took hours to get the old muffler out, hours to get the new one in. Maxwell above, myself below, we heaved and grunted and clanged and swore. Unidentifiable noises off were traced to Shay, suppressing spasms of laughter as he filmed our backsides waving around. The night was quite black by the time we had finished.

We had not done as well as the *Ierne* had in 1862. It had taken us three and a half days to clear the Great Glen, but as we set ourselves to the North Sea crossing, the longest of the voyage, her crew would have understood our renewed preoccupation with weather. They would have recognized, too, the lines of the sail-training schooner, whose triple masts pricked the sky about noon as she passed us close, heading in, her elegant stern lifting hugely to a swell we had scarcely noticed. Only the radio call would have been novel: 'Yacht *Canna*, *Winston Churchill*, *Winston Churchill*. We were trying for Stavanger yesterday but the north-westerly became a full gale. It was far too severe for us, and we're heading to Inverness for shelter.'

The turmoil that had thrown her back was the death spasm of the violent low over Sweden that had plagued us from the start; but now, at last, the pattern had changed, and with it our fear of failure began to slip away. In west Scotland, both the weather and terrain had seemed severe and threatening, but now, for once, they seemed to be with us. The winds were already light, scuttling from NW to SW, gyrating aimlessly. We gybed and goose-winged, motored and cut, and between busy bouts we lay in the sun stretching and luxuriating, while Scotland slid by to starboard doing the same. Her long dusky swellings of dark-nippled moorland hung above bras of soft pastel green. Darker belts and swathes of forest were pinched by lurid garters of rape. The whole strip was freckled and sequined with townships: Lossiemouth, Buckie, Macduff and Banff. We feasted our eyes. We couldn't get away from her fast, even if we'd wanted to, so we hugged her close all day and well into the night. When she had winked her last and we were decently clear, I judged it time to telephone home. 'Come on over, and join us in Göteborg. Everything's going as planned,' I said. 'We're 20 miles north of Peterhead.'

Until now, I'd felt like a small bird hauling a worm from a lawn – the more of the route we'd gobbled, the further the rest of it seemed to stretch out. We'd only made 500 miles so far, there were 500 more between us and Sweden, but now the wind was with us. The new breeze came in, cool, steady and firm, and we had nothing harder to do than sail east. Full sail, five knots. No land in sight. The feverish affair on home ground had finished, and a foreign idyll had now begun. Perhaps, I allowed myself to think, everything might work out. Perhaps we actually *would* reach Russia . . .

'Aren't you afraid to be going to Russia?' a youngish neighbour had asked.

'Strange people,' commented a younger lad, about to emigrate for lack of work.

'Mind you stay on the right side of the pond and don't get caught as a spy,' came from an American.

Everywhere we went in the course of preparations, the Siberian jokes had come jerking out like Pavlovian reflexes. When thought set in, faces might fall to a more considered demeanour, and an amount of common humanity might be allowed; but the gap in personal perception still yawned. Certainly, the official Russia had been frostily sensitive in the past – Bernard Hayman's articles on his voyage to the Estonian capital had, we heard, unwittingly caused considerable offence – but that didn't come near to explaining the problem. The more knee-jerk prejudice we encountered, the less it seemed to match with the Russians we met, and the more we wanted to make the journey. If only we could get all the way, and do what we'd set out to do, perhaps we could probe this twentieth century bogey.

'No,' I had said. 'I'm not afraid of being in Russia, as long as we don't cause offence. My worries are all about getting there.'

That was still the case, I thought, as I drifted into an off-watch dream. It wouldn't do to relax too much – we were now beyond the limits of my previous sailing world, and there were bound to be problems to come.

'Roger, you'd better look at this.'

I struggled into cold consciousness. It was 3 am. Maxwell sounded concerned, which was highly unusual. Above in the dark was a boat, a ship maybe, a cluster of lights on the starboard beam.

'It's been getting closer,' he shouted over our surging wash. 'I can't make it out.'

In the binoculars danced a flurry of reds and whites. A fisherman, I supposed. We watched and waited, held our course. It was still closing, edging in, bit by bit, towards our bows. There were thickets of lights now, two masts of them, the after one strung with a double tapered row like a Christmas tree; the hull invisible, a dark suggestion of power. It was certainly no trawler.

'Give way!' I called. 'To port! We'll haul up hard north-east.'

'It's a tow,' yelled Maxwell, smacking his fist. 'Damn me, I thought it was!'

A blinding blue flash strobed him at the sheet winch. The ship's searchlight had the brilliance of a welding arc, pinned us against the blackness like a moth in flight, threw sail number shadows on the spray. We were reaching fast away to port but, apparently, not far enough. A flashing orange light began. We wrenched away due north. Slowly the strange hull drew past. Twin lights low down, backward staring eyes, gave us a glimpse of twin hawsers, thick as bridge cables, dragging through the sea.

He didn't answer on the VHF. I didn't go below. He veered away, but arrived again at dawn, crowding us further north like an articulated truck squeezing a cyclist against the pavement.

Other ships pursued the maverick through the airwaves, and we listened in.

'Special operations vessel here,' came an unidentifiable foreign accent. 'Don't cross less than three miles from my stern.'

A two to three mile tow? Maxwell and I exchanged quick looks of disbelief, and felt the first pricks of a cold sweat. Next day we encountered another which confirmed our guess.

'Yacht *Canna*. *Zeiss Mariner*. We have a cable two miles long with a red buoy and reflectors. Our course is 063° for two miles, then 90° to port.'

Probably they were engaged on seismic surveys, and I insisted on a very sharp look-out. Obviously obstructions to our progress across the North Sea were going to be physical rather than mental, and sure enough, we weren't finished with them yet.

*   *   *

Zero degrees! That day we achieved a quarter of our easterly distance to Leningrad when we crossed from west to east, into a new hemisphere, beyond the Greenwich meridian. The Buchan field sits smack on the line and smokes. It was a useful check on the Decca, which blinked its information out in LAT. and LONG. Three platforms sat isolated in a waste of sea, tended by three service boats. The rigs glowered against the glare to the south, their huge cylindrical legs plummeting down more than 300 feet.

Manipulating a lens like a coffee-pot, Shay as usual wanted to get closer. Helicopters clattered in the distance, the rigs glowed blackly, the air crackled with traffic, and he soon got his answer.

'Yacht *Canna*. Our accommodation rig has anchor cables extending one mile, marked by buoys.'

I shrug. 'What an amazing amount of clutter there is out here. Two decades ago there was nothing.'

In the grey evening, the leaning fortresses of the Forties Field marched past, their squat superstructures propped up in mid air. Like six siblings, they ponderously rearranged themselves as we passed, sliding behind each other to get a better look, with six pairs of thin fingers poked up in stark salute. As the dusk thickened, flames lit the clouds with a bloody halo, and the platform lights twinkled and gleamed beneath it on the last of the fixed obstructions.

Midnight, 19 June: after 724 miles, we were almost two weeks out, although it had felt like half a lifetime. 'Border crossing!' remarked the log. 'One hundred and sixty-one miles to Norway.'

The 20th became a sunny day, and the crew began to recover their spirits. The scarlet vane of the self-steering wagged against a blue sky; the cruising chute – an asymmetrical spinnaker – billowed in brilliant azure and scarlet stripes, making even the sky look dark, and that night, midsummer's night, the sun threw a ruby afterglow on the midnight clouds due to the north. By the 3 am watch, we were lolloping through a bubble of blue sea and sky. As I peered intently ahead, scanning for the Naze, our landfall on the southern tip of Norway, a pinprick of light suddenly appeared instead. The gleam grew strangely, erupting steadily from the horizon, as if a white hot scimitar: first the point, and then the whole curved blade. It finally lifted clear off the water, and transformed itself into the crescent moon. The lit segment implied the whole sphere in all its unimaginable bulk, hovering hugely beyond the edge of the earth. The pristine light lit a bright pathway toward a low dark thread, our destination on the coast.

Our voyage seemed tiny, and very grand.

Praestö and Sjursö, islands in Kristiansand harbour, are a tiny pair of rocky castanets with an anchorage between. Three and a half days out from

Inverness, we nosed in through the entrance in mid-afternoon, circled around like a settling dog and anchored. The water was perfectly still. The cliffs sheltered us from the unaccustomed roar of motor cruisers charging to and fro in the bay outside. From here we could go ashore, clamber through heather and aspen and pine, bruising sweet smells with our knees, and spy on the city, two miles away, which sprawls among a grizzled landscape of low hills and forest. I had no doubt the natives were friendly, but that was one of my problems. Those on the island watched us discreetly through the foliage, waved when their elders weren't looking, and came and went from miniature, planked, sienna huts and houses perched on rocks beneath trees. Mostly they had long blond hair.

'The women here are hideous and are only equalled by the men in ugliness,' commented Corrigan, unkindly, from Bergen. I wondered if he'd actually been in the same country. We seemed to have got our navigation only too right. The only ugly thing I could see were ferries like shoe boxes on their sides, which came and went from the city at high speed. Shay, returned from crashing through the bushes, was wistful. Maxwell was fidgety. I was still anxious about time and weather.

'We can do without the bother of a customs entry,' I said, and cursed the burst exhaust in Scotland. We set sail again before the sun went down, for the hop of 100 miles to Sweden.

We had stolen a march on the *Oriana*. As we approached the moonlit Norwegian coast on the night of 21 June, they too had been awake, delightedly checking the echo of a quiet Norwegian fiord to the north of us with a cornet and a shot-gun. Corrigan mentions that the eagles and gulls had found it somewhat offensive. A few days later they crossed our track, heading south to Denmark. Somewhere near the intersection, the crew had tried for fish.

> Wednesday June 29th. The skipper called me and Martin at 5 o'c am. saying there was a great take of mackerel, and the watch on deck had caught up to 40. Up we went and found it true. The fish continued taking very fast until 8 o'c when we had 150.

The gentlemen got tired of it, set the watch to do it, and ended up with 300 and more. The *Ierne* had much the same fortune three years later in the same spot. We tried with feathers, but got nothing. *Something* was reaping the waters though.

'Will you look at that?' said Shay, as we swerved around two trawlers. 'They're *vacuuming* the fish.'

Indeed they were. Elaborate pipework dangled over their sides as they sucked up whole shoals from their nets. We wondered how long it could last. For years now, European fleets had been hitting their heads against ceilings for certain species, while their catching capacity ballooned out like a mushroom cloud. Russian factory ships were regular visitors to our home waters, purchasing from local boats, and I was intrigued to know how they managed to despatch ships so far from their base in the Baltic.

The thought of the Baltic urged us on. We were anxious to get there. At first, it seemed my impatience had served us ill, and we made a slow night's progress, rolling and banging across the Skagerrak from Norway toward Göteborg. Now, at dawn, we had a following wind, and how we deserved it! Everything was going for us at last – wind and tide and swell, and good visibility. The Skaw, the northern hook of Denmark, came scything toward us, sprouting a stubble of aerials and pylons, giving us a close shave with its cut-throat profile.

Sweden showed up in late afternoon, but if south Norway had been less mountainous than we'd expected, this coast was even more surprising: very low-lying, with no prominent features, but painted spars and beacons and vards. A few yachts scuttled home between rocky islands, as the sun sank lower, glowed richer. Under an ice-blue sky, the reflections turned cream and marigold and amber. Past the Vinga light, we turned to port, then to starboard round an orange look-out hut, flaming like a bush-fire in the light. Rocks sent back our hollow chug as we stowed sail in a narrow gap. We were all snugged down as we rounded the marina's breakwater mole, and the sun ducked twice and died. The first leg was over, and we were up to time.

Drifting to sleep, I replayed an incident that day off the Skaw. Among the thicket of traffic manoeuvring through the crucial right-angled junction had been a Russian ship, old and black like a widow in weeds. We'd correctly held our course; she had carefully steered around us. I'd been glad to see it. Then, as her stern passed our nose, all the bare-armed crew on the afterdeck broke off from shaking blankets and waved. It was the very first welcome we'd had from a ship at sea – from Russians, and right at the mouth of the Baltic. It seemed to bode well.

CHAPTER 4

Sweden

The *Varangian* was a small double-ended yacht, clinker-built to a Shetland design. She was remarkably well-balanced and sea-kindly, running sweetly on trains of air-bubbles trapped in the lands, the V-grooves between the planks.

Luxuriating in the unaccustomed stillness of the boat, allowing myself an extra few minutes of doze, my mind drifted back through a curious circle of events. Twenty-two years before, in Scotland, *Varangian* had carried me to the island of Canna, the very first anchorage of my first long offshore cruise. Now our sloop, *Canna* (by chance bearing the name when we bought her), was carrying us to the ancestral home and haunts of the Varangians, one of the original Swedish Viking tribes.

The Varangians, or Rus, as they were also known, didn't confine their influence to the Shetlands, however:

> They travelled bravely
> Far after gold
> And eastwards
> Fed the eagles

From 800 AD onwards, the Rus had fed their enemies to the eagles all over the Eastern Baltic, beginning at the trading posts they established at river mouths from Leningrad round to Lithuania. Via the inland water routes, they had pushed expeditions as far as Byzantium and, well before the turn of the century, provided on request the very first Russian Tsar, who established an extensive Ukrainian kingdom based at Kiev on the Dnieper. Thus the Rus, so their modern descendants claimed, had actually named and founded Russia, although from the very start it began to develop quite separately from Sweden. The Swedish Tsar, Hrörekr, was quickly renamed Rurik, and the process had started.

For about 150 years, in the sixteenth and seventeenth centuries, Sweden had pursued massive territorial ambitions under successive kings, and attempted to secure boundaries encompassing the whole of the Baltic. She very nearly succeeded – by 1661 the Swedish empire included all of Lapland, Finland, Karelia and Ingria (the lands to the north and south of the Gulf of Finland, including the site of Leningrad), Estonia and Livonia (modern Latvia as far south as Riga). Sweden also ruled substantial sections of what is now East Germany and, as if that wasn't enough, sporadically dominated much of Poland by force or diplomacy or dynasty as the occasion served. The Poles knew the Swedish incursions of the 1650s, when Warsaw fell more than once to the invaders, as 'The Flood'.

Fifty years later, Peter the Great made his crucial move, biting through the Swedish encirclement to establish Leningrad. It was a very vulnerable bridgehead, however, and the Swedes viewed it as a more than unwelcome intrusion. Charles XII of Sweden made one grand final effort to wipe the Russians off the Baltic map, and shunt them back into their eastern fastnesses, once again sweeping south-east into the Ukraine with the intention of subsequently invading Moscow. As others after him, he was defeated by bitter weather, by ill luck and by Peter himself, at Poltava, north of Crimea, in 1709.

'Now, by God's help, are the foundations of St Petersburg laid for all time,' pronounced Peter.

The reverse was indeed final: Swedish influence in the Baltic declined by fits and starts over the next two centuries. The worst wound came in 1808, when Finland, West Lapland and the Åland Islands were all wrenched away by the Russians, due to the gross ineptness of the Swedish King Gustavus IV. The resulting treaty of Fredrikshamm of that year confirmed the amputation, and caused heavy trauma: everything that had been fought for, eastward, for over a thousand years had been lost; all that remained were modest gains to the west, away from the influence of Russian pressure. A millenium of effort had given way to superior power.

How did Sweden react to Russia now? I wondered.

It was an urgent question, not just a matter of curiosity. Having cleared the hurdles of the Atlantic and the North Sea successfully, we couldn't afford to fall foul of nationalistic sentiment or residual hostilities *en route*. Sweden, I knew, still had a dispute with the Soviet Union concerning fishing zones in the Baltic, and was extremely sensitive about her territorial integrity. In the past, some visiting yachts had been asked to keep a look-out for 'foreign submarines' in Swedish waters. That was the very last thing we would want to happen. We had also to negotiate our way through customs which, by all accounts, had become ultra-strict.

Our first contact with the modern Varangians was partly reassuring. A sharp ping on the pulpit announced the arrival of the marina outdoor staff, who had had time to mistake our ensign for that of a Central African republic, discover their error, find or make a 'green, white and gold', and run it up with the other visitors' flags. Amused to find us the colour they expected as we popped up in the cockpit, they conveyed the startling but welcome fact that the customs did not wish to visit us at all. Reactions to our Russian destination were, however, gleaned as we went about our business over the next few days.

Långedrag marina was one of several very substantial ones on the south side of the Göta river, a few miles downstream from the city centre. The tidy pontoons, like long grey jawbones, were two-thirds studded with shiny white teeth: baby motor-cruisers, mere bath-tub toys; rows of medium-sized molars like ours; and a few alarming incisors, gargantuan, sharp-ended racing yachts, filled with masses of gear, whose masts disappeared up into the morning haze. Beyond the blue clubhouse, which stood on piles, a few workshops and derricks lurked under low granite cliffs and, above them, timber houses perched this way and that, brown and yellow with white gables. They looked across the wide river mouth to a mainly industrial panorama of cranes, shipping terminals, islands, and distant rising ground, cut into strips by the forest of masts as if by a bacon slicer.

Canna fretted gently at her mooring lines. We had a few days to wait now until new crew joined at the weekend. Together with Susan and Rupert, our 15-year-old younger son, there would be Terry Rogers, a Dublin man whom I hadn't met. The break was an essential part of the plan, for shore duties as much as for rest. Most of our clothes were rigid with salt; there were gas refills to find and stores to repack. Stacked beneath the bunks were sufficient basic dry and tinned stores to last for most of the cruise but, even with only three people aboard, loose kit and cameras and wet gear seemed to invade the accommodation with the inexorable intent of Triffids on the loose. Now, with a full boat imminent, we pulled up the floorboard and bundled every last tin into the bilges to make more locker space. Maxwell scrubbed the hull. Shay recharged his batteries, and struggled desperately to get the better of the recalcitrant video camera. The smaller of the two was for use under way, in a waterproof casing; the one which was giving the trouble was a much larger tripod model, and absolutely essential for any future film. He eventually traced the problem to a missing recording tab.

'The tide is out, d'you see?' said Maxwell, as we strolled past the clubhouse on our way to town. It had dropped all of four inches on a big pebble we used as a gauge, even though we were still within line of sight of the North Sea, on the other side of which, amazingly, the tide ranges through 16 feet. It was already a different world, and the tram convinced us of it as it ground noisily and incongruously into the centre between sleek files of Volvos and Saabs.

'WELCOME TO GÖTEBORG – THE ♡ OF SCANDINAVIA' proclaimed a sign on a floating dock opposite, in letters ten feet high. It would not have been an appropriate slogan in earlier times. In the Middle Ages, Norwegian territory had included the land behind the dock, and the Swedes had managed to secure only a thin strip of this, the south-eastern, bank. It was curiously akin to the Russian scenario. Göteborg had been founded only 80 years earlier than Leningrad, in 1621, and for exactly the same reason: to control a vital trade outlet to the west, to the North Sea. Both cities had been 'back doors' of nations whose front doors faced east; both had become their countries' second cities.

Commercially Göteborg was now obviously lively and efficient, meeting all our requirements with ease; but the welcome seemed oddly restrained. Everyone was unfailingly polite, precise and thorough in their helpfulness, but almost devoid of gesture or jizz. The Swedes, like their tides, seemed almost unmoved and, after a while, I found myself falling into the same habit: staying still and talking only with my mouth. When, most untypically, a personable information clerk used both arms and half her torso, Italian-style, to give directions to the public library, I felt as though I'd been assaulted, and I edged away. The main streets were pervaded with quiet decorum. No one hollered, no one was raucous, even around a market stall. Children walked as if to Sunday school, and not one laughed or cried. Customers at pavement cafés and passing cars only whispered.

One day, just as I rattled my ears again to make sure the fault wasn't mine, a piece of performance art appeared, a wild provocation. Weaving extravagant gestures between the straight-laced estates and saloons came a period American soft-top car, letting everything hang out: a 'Chrysler Holiday' announced in chrome and creamy yellow, rolling on off-white Polo mints. Its sexy curves were quite outrageous. With the hood right down, the driver, with classic, slicked-back hair, was riding along in his automobile, his baby beside him at the wheel: she in a flouncy white dress, mostly missing. The jazz, billowing from the dashboard at high volume, was all of a piece, and rebounded from the stone and glassy-faced buildings in a palpable cloud of disapproval. I forgot myself and laughed, but no one else did. No one else waved or stopped and looked, or nudged his neighbour or winked. It obviously wasn't going to be easy to discover what went on behind these reticent facades.

'For one thing, Sweden "hypes up" paranoia about Russia,' said Peter. 'It's a means to keep the arms industry going, and provide a *raison-d'être* for the whole system.'

By an appropriate chance, it was in the original, most informal, part of the city that we began to sort out the contrasts between the private and public fronts of Sweden, and connections between past and present. We were relaxing with a friend from home and his young Swedish wife, Anna, at their apartment in the old town: a hillocky, higgledy-piggledy enclave of timber and brick under the shadow of an old church, patched with cobbled paths and lawns. Ferries from England and elsewhere sliced through the antique scenery from time to time and docked nearby.

There was certainly no shortage of fun and hospitality here: at very short notice a spread of beers and cheeses and pickled fish had appeared, 'including herrings in custard,' said Anna, pointing to something oily and yellow. She meant 'mustard'.

Peter and Anna were sailing enthusiasts themselves, or had been until caught in a gale near the Skaw, attempting the route we had just completed, but in the opposite direction. Anna, incapacitated by sea-sickness, had been lifted off by helicopter in a daring rescue which subsequently became a *cause célèbre*. Peter and his injured father had been forced far northwards by the storm and set on to a part of the Swedish coast for which they had no charts.

With characteristic resourcefulness, Peter had turned from psychiatry and sailing to teaching and writing, and his research topic was presently the 'politics of violence'. Some of the government references he had unearthed – treatises, for instance, on the effects of live ammunition on dogs, used as substitutes for human flesh – had fuelled his cynicism about the neutrality of his adoptive country. An Arab traveller in Viking Russia had remarked that every Swede always carried a sword, axe and dagger. Nowadays Peter reckoned much the same happened on a national scale, and what weapons weren't 'carried' by the armed forces were sold with scant regard to the morals of the purchasers. The traditional, prickly, defensive hunch of the individual was now heavily ramified in commerce and politics, he opined. Overall, it was a bleak assessment, which I hoped was an exaggeration, but it was at least partly confirmed in the course of our own encounters.

'What do you think – or what does the average Swede think – about Russia?' we asked the assistant in the chandler's shop opposite the huge sign of welcome, as he wrapped the essential charts for our onward journey.

'What you probably feel . . . a place of some fear and anxiety to approach,' he replied, putting words in our mouths. 'One would never know what the reaction might be – we don't think of going there.'

The marina diesel pump attendant, at other times an international charter skipper, echoed him. 'No one from Sweden thinks of sailing there,' he said. 'They all turn their backs and go in the other direction.'

Shay, however, revealing his talents, got a much more encouraging response from Sweden's first all-girl offshore yacht racing crew, whom he discovered at training.

'If you can find us an all-girl Soviet crew, we'd be delighted to race them,' they said.

It was time to go and do it: if most Swedes weren't keen to go east any more, we most certainly were. We had now been gone three weeks, and had covered just over 1,000 miles. There was nearly as much to do again, and less time in which to do it. Standing between us and the eastern end of the

Baltic was still a major uncertainty, the Göta canal. The whole system was 240 miles long, with 67 locks up and down, and about the same number of bridges, or more. It normally took at least five to seven days, I was told, in a quiet period, but the national summer holidays were just about to break, and much of the vast flood of Swedish pleasure boats would then be unleashed.

'There's one boat for every eight people in the country, the highest proportion in Europe,' Peter had said, 'and you want to be careful. There are a lot of boating accidents when people get drunk.'

I didn't fancy the prospect of being jammed in locks with convoys of inebriated cruisers. There would also be commercial traffic, which took priority: another possible cause of delay.

Already it was Friday 26 June. At the end of the day, *Canna* lurched gently once, then twice, and dipped her nose: Susan and Rupert had arrived dead on time. Terry, short, freckled, auburn and cheerful, whom they'd managed to lose at the airport, turned up on the following tram.

All aboard! Six people thickened the cockpit, with unsquashable thickets of gear.

'What a lovely place!' exclaimed the new arrivals, agog. 'Will we have time to see it? When are we leaving?'

'Not too early,' I said, feeling generous. 'How about half-past six in the morning?'

Everyone laughed heartily, except Susan, who knew me better. Susan had known me, in fact, for twenty years, and I was very glad to have her on board; she was steady, practical and buoyant, was normally up when I was down, and diligent when I was not. Her fuel was sleep, whereas mine was food, and she had all the habits of a beaver. Rupert gave me a knowing look – already she was setting things straight. Not least, Susan had been yachting since a toddler, having been used by her father as extra ballast in his racing boat; now, sailing came to her naturally, even though, since her teens, she had done little, and so far had not sailed offshore.

Of the others, Rupert was experienced mainly in dinghies, and Terry was an unknown quantity. I hoped the canals would ease them in gently.

In fact, we left well before six o'clock, and very soon were in phrasebook territory. A near gale from the south-west hurried us on under foresail only, more than counteracting the stream as we made our way up-river under snake-headed cranes and a cable-hung bridge; ahead of a huge white ferry, hooting and anxious to dock; past the masts and yards of a floating ship museum; past the city centre, with its crowding, reddish façades; on beyond the outskirt depots and docks, and out into the country.

Maxwell helmed, while I flipped through text-books to translate the instruction signs at the start of the canal. Whether by our radioed efforts or not, a vast, girdered railway bridge pivoted slowly, opening a channel each side. As we edged into the starboard gap, still preoccupied by language, a high-hulled black ship appeared from nowhere and charged the left-hand one from the opposite direction, sweeping through with only inches to spare, and pushing sheaves of water at us through a flimsy partition of piles. Within seconds her stern slid by overhead.

'I'm glad we got that right,' I breathed, squinting up, but the powerful throb of her passing propeller churned the comment to mincemeat. I felt the waft of potential disaster, as though I'd just driven straight through traffic lights while chatting to a friend, and belatedly noticed they were green. If we had taken the wrong side, we'd have been crushed like an egg.

'We'll keep well to starboard all the way,' I called out, for all and sundry to hear.

There was little else to do in the first flat river section of the canal, except negotiate one lock, and evade the odd wreath of exhaust fumes laid around the cockpit by the following wind. If we had but known the canal regulations, we could have sailed the first 50 miles. The crew took watches and settled into watching the landscape unfold.

Slender yellow booms, all numbered and lit like lampposts on their sides, hung inwards at close intervals, defining the channel and nudging traffic well clear of willow stumps and shallow banks. Green meadows pushed long curves into the water from one side; gentle scarps and granite cliffs bulged in from the other, raising a vast road bridge like a children's slide.

Beyond the menacing bastions of the old Norwegian fortress at Kungälv, the land began to heave and undulate. Ribbons of pale green sauntered by, interrupted by clusters of brown farmsteads and stands of racing green forest which sometimes pushed in to the banks like a crash barrier.

The arable land was a curiously cool shade of pastel, a faded viridian, insistent and haunting, not at all like the lurid yellow-greens of Celtic Britain and Ireland; Maxwell, anxious about his own acres of barley, didn't care for it at all. 'Very backward,' he growled.

'It's the worst spring they've had for twenty-five years,' I said, repeating the comment we'd heard everywhere. The ice had melted late in the Baltic, and the chill winds had still been littering Göteborg with pale streamers of lime and hornbeam flowers. To our uncharitable relief, the weather seemed to be deterring the holiday boaters too, who had begun to despair of a summer. Occasional groups of three or four yachts sped brightly downstream, but there were none going our way. A few ships passed too, one a sizeable Russian vessel. I wondered what the weather would hold in store for us at the far end of the Baltic.

The canal system itself had been mooted even earlier than Göteborg, but it had taken 300 years of deliberation and about 30 more of construction to make it a reality in 1832. Fifty-eight thousand men, many of them soldiers, had built the eastern part by hand. The whole link ran for 250 miles.

As in the Caledonian, Thomas Telford had been ultimately responsible for design (for which he received a Knighthood from the Swedish King Charles XIII, and his portrait set in diamonds), and both the systems linked four main lakes; but here the scale was very much grander. This first section, the Trollhättan canal, lifted ships up to Vänern, a lake about half the size of the Irish Sea, and the biggest in Europe, excepting only Lake Ladoga to the east of Leningrad. Beyond it, the Göta canal would climb on up to more than 300 feet.

The system had given Sweden a very significant economic boost, and laid the foundations of her engineering expertise. In fact, it was a Swedish engine that was pushing us now – Volvos are built in Göteberg – and the business still seemed to be thriving so well that the main dealers under whose noses we were parked in Långedrag hadn't even been able to spare two minutes to check whether I was maintaining their offspring in a manner it was entitled to expect.

I had agonized a bit about this. I had been very keen to grab the chance of a factory service before we were completely out of range in Russia and Poland.

'It works, so I'm not going to wait to fix it,' I decided at length, and Maxwell had concurred. We put up with the smoke, and I kept my fingers crossed.

Much of the impetus for building the canal was the imposition of Sound Dues by the Danes. The minute bottle-neck of the Baltic – the Sound overlooked by Hamlet's castle at Helsingör (Elsinore) – was barely half a mile wide, and the Danes exacted money for the privilege of passing through even after they'd been confined to their present-day islands on the western side. Countries had schemed and fought for control of the gap for centuries; Nelson had deployed his blind eye there to gain the upper hand in a related dispute. Only in 1857 had Denmark struck a canny deal with the rest of the maritime world and sold her rights for four million pounds, (which would have gone a very long way at that time), and even the United States chipped in its share to buy them out.

There's no mention of the Göta canal in Corrigan's log when the *Oriana* passed by only two years later in 1859, but it's not so very surprising. The gentlemen were intent on sampling the delights of Denmark; even if they hadn't been, the canal would scarcely have suited their schooner. Parts of the lakes couldn't be sailed, as we were to discover, and without an engine she would have needed a tow. Oxen came fairly cheap, but a steam tug cost £50 for a 100-ton yacht: a very considerable amount, on top of £10 dues; and with her cruising speed of about 11 knots, she would normally make a faster passage around Sweden rather than through it. As the canal led us steadily north-east through deep country, Corrigan and Martin had been pushing their route south from Norway toward Copenhagen. A day or two later, they had gone ashore in the capital and whooped it up on the money they'd saved by avoiding canal tolls and Sound Dues. We left them to it. We hoped to catch up with them later.

'Have you seen what's behind us?' called Terry urgently.

By now, the writhings of the land had given way to rocky gesticulations. The river, previously a hundred yards wide and more, was squeezed down to a narrowing canyon overhung by pines, where turbulent currents and our throbbing exhaust hurtled and echoed between hard elbows and knuckles. The marker beacons now were almost on the cliffs, perched on poles at the outboard end of miniature bridges. Only one boat had passed us in the day – the *Juno*, an old-fashioned fancy gateau filled with holiday-makers in layers – but now as we approached the fabled Trollhättan locks, the nose of an enormous dark blue ship was closing the channel, the creamy masts above making the pines look like matchsticks. As we twisted round headlands it momentarily vanished, only to appear again each time wider and closer, its white moustache bulging and twitching. Our sturdy boat shrank to the size of a dinghy.

'Only one more corner to go,' called Susan from the chart table and, in the nick of time, a triangular pool opened out, with the ladder of locks rearing tall in a sunlit corner. One half of the outer gates swung closed to warn us away.

It took almost a week to complete the passage of the canal, which fell into three distinct sections, as if we were crossing a mountain.

The long first day's river section had culminated in a frantic scramble up through the steep gulley of the Trollhättan locks: four oversized, dripping wet cellars, each of them deeper than the height of our mast. We had surfaced from them, near to exhaustion, in the early evening.

Next came a high and dreamy plateau. Gales and torrents had vanished, and for a while on Lake Vänern we had been completely alone, sailing across still water, faintly surrounded by thin strips of forest tailing off to infinite horizons, anchoring at dusk off a remote island where water lapped bare rock and ospreys flew.

Beyond, the eastern canals had transported us to new heights through avenues of sycamore and violent shifts of colour. In the narrow waters, the west wind returned, more urgent than ever, churning the long landscape into a green kaleidoscope shot with fleeting flecks of yellow. Streaks of sunlight hunted down a keeper's cottage, a stand of lupin or of meadow-sweet; and once, a walking buttercup, a lock-girl with a blaze of tawny hair, waving and smiling against a gloomy forest. The upper lakes, each different from the next, shook off all constraint, shifting through chromatic keys with wild abandon.

Vadstena, on the eastern shore of Lake Vättern, which we reached by the end of June, had been the highest point of all. A small town, almost central between the east and west coasts of Sweden, low to the water, irregular and wooded and studded with historic buildings, it had been in a particularly evasive mood when we approached in a late golden evening. Its fragile silhouette at first seemed to sink beyond our grasp but, as we gave chase across silky water, folding to rose and mauve, it dissolved into a fractious mirage. Copper-green spires mocked the beacons we passed. Orange roofs smouldered at long flames of cloud. A blue and red castle scoffed at brown houses in nests of turquoise trees.

'Where are we? North Africa?' asked Susan, just up from her bunk.

'No. Bulgaria, I'd say,' came a puzzled reply.

The dream deepened. Beyond a gap and two dark moles, a channel led towards the castle, flanked by lines of yachts and masts, like old retainers bearing staves, and vaulted ranks of taller trees. The long carpet ruckled to puce as we passed, the battlements reared up tall. Dusk had bruised the towers and domes and turned the purple moat to ink. Yellow and silver spilled on deck from latticed windows and faint stars; and we nosed very quietly in by the drawbridge, trying not to wake.

'You should have heard the clatter it made!' gasped Susan, in horror, describing her own sudden arousal from an anchor-watch reverie the previous night, when a late-arriving yacht had collided heavily with a reef. I too had held my breath that day on Vänern when, cutting a corner just as the sails began to draw strongly, I realized I'd misread the depths.

There had been other occasional eruptions of reality, even before we arrived at Vadstena. The immigration officials who checked our papers at Trollhättan were armed, we had noticed with distaste. Vättern itself had been carved up like a dressmaker's pattern by firing ranges, which we had had to check were not in use before crossing, and the further east we went, the more often low-flying jet fighters ruptured the skies with cataclysmic bursts of sound, destroying illusions and reminding us of Peter's comments in Göteborg.

Now, we had also to avoid ruptures between ourselves on the third and last section: the long, hard-going descent, where the lakes tailed out and banks of locks and canals took over.

Shay was very strong on publicity.

'I've stolen your thunder, I'm afraid,' he said, standing on the bows, a bit shamefaced, against the backdrop of the castle gate. We'd agreed he should offer an interview with me to the local newspaper, but he'd been talked into giving it himself. I was vexed and apprehensive. The last thing we wanted was to have our enterprise broadcast to the eastern bloc countries through a possibly unfriendly press, or an editor who distorted our intentions.

If some errors resulted from an excess of enthusiasm, others were due to a slight lack of it. Shay found Maxwell's well-meant advice on boat-handling exasperating, and Rupert's dead-pan manner did the same for me. Maxwell shied away from Shay's curries at a hundred paces, and Susan objected to the unique split level bunk I had devised for her by storing all the spare charts beneath one end, the only place where they would fit. At least, I pointed out, she had the choice of a high or low shelf for her head, a privilege none of the rest of us had.

Such minor strains on a completely full boat were only to be expected, and were mainly more amusing than aggravating. There were no mutinies, nor even flashes of temper. Committed to making progress, bit by bit we rubbed comfortable grooves into each other.

Terry, unsubduably cheerful, and a mine of useless but entertaining information, was easy-going to a fault (especially in the galley), but out of his element at night. In vain we warned that we were now abroad; in vain he scoured the grid-iron streets of towns in central Sweden, looking for a pub that sold porter, or indeed any pub at all, with all the determined optimism of an English matron tracking down a cup of tea.

'There's not a soul,' he'd complain, bewildered and disconsolate. 'The town's completely quiet.'

'And isn't that just what a town should be at night?' huffed Maxwell, eyeing him firmly. We had come to love his puckish, reactionary bent. 'Proper order, a bit of peace and quiet. Especially after a man's done a full day's work,' he continued; which indeed he had, and the lion's share of it too.

The usual system for the uphill locks was to nose alongside at the bottom and put one or two people ashore, who manoeuvred *Canna* in, keeping as far away from the top gates as possible to avoid turbulence from the sluices. Restraining her with taut lines on bollards or rings as she rose, when the top gates opened they jumped aboard for the next stretch of canal, or hauled her into the adjacent lock. It became a hypnotic sequence. Everyone went into suspension on the level sections, until the call came again.

'Next lock, all hands!'

We'd been very lucky on the way up: we were alone for a hundred miles or more; all the lock gates seemed to open for us; the lifting bridges, rolling bridges, swinging bridges – even a pram-like ferry, wound across on a rope – mostly responded as if by magic. But it had still been uphill work, and Maxwell had strained and hauled up the steep banks like a towpath cart-horse. On the descent the equipment became more primitive, and Maxwell insisted on winding the geared handles, round and round like a donkey at a cider press. No doubt he enjoyed it, but some of the crew enjoyed watching and photographing him too, peering at him critically from different angles until they got it right. Others, even more detached, took film of them doing it.

We were falling all the time now, edging toward the east coast. Motala, Berg, Norsholm – the towns were bigger, more frequent, giving off more of a holiday mood. By night, we gladly relaxed with other transient crews – a Norwegian sculptor and his family, a German engineer, Ann-Marie, who worked as a guide in a Loire chateau – but by day the increasing traffic slowed us down.

Even the boats moving with us were sometimes more hindrance than help. For two days we were ganged up with a crew of aggressive Norwegians, who made it a point of honour to let no one else get ahead, even if their propeller dropped off in the process (which to general relief it eventually did). *Shalom*, a huge reconstructed naval boat, carrying deck cargo of a small host of accordion-playing latter-day saints pounding out a numbing round of hymns, leap-frogged us *ad nauseam*, taking an infuriating precedence in the locks. We grew more frantic with the increasing delays, as our progress dwindled to less than 40 miles a day. Hoisting every stitch of sail and gunning the engine, we raced to clear the last man-made obstacles before the canal closed for the night, and to sail the next lake. Even there, we weren't in the clear. Smack in the middle of one was a speed-restricted channel, barely the width of two boats. To either side were stepping stones, and bollards like overgrown thimbles. The weird features were centuries old, erected by sailing men who'd previously had to haul their boats against the wind by hand, wading through up to their chests.

Against that, we had nothing at all to complain of, except perhaps tiredness, I reflected, as I watched Maxwell sleeping upright on a towpath bench. The sunlight and breeze slanted across him unnoticed as his head lolled first this way, then that, as if determined to drop off too. Others had collapsed across the saloon table, or mumbled drowsily in the cockpit. We were berthed alongside at Söderköping, the last main town on the canal: the transit had taken us nearly six days, and there were only two more locks to go.

'You're telling me this is the *Baltic*?' queried Maxwell, alert in a trice and incredulous.

It certainly didn't look or smell like a Sea. There was no wave, no weed, nor smell of salt. I'd expected something choppy and grey, but this was still and landlocked, spiky trees reflecting perfectly above golden rocks in the unruffled margin of blue water. It was hard even to see the way out from the tip of this long finger, the Slätbaken fiord. Beyond lay the broad palm of the Baltic, with its life-line of shipping sweeping across to Leningrad, barely

500 miles away. But already it was a wonderful relief! We'd escaped from the second canal and the Varangian's penthouse unscathed. Once more we were on a level with our furthest destination.

In the late afternoon, *Canna* swanned serenely east before the following breeze, her sails akimbo. We watched in wonderment as the Scandinavia we'd seen in tourist posters arranged itself in liquid panoramas of rock and forest and islands. A few miles on, at Stegeborg, it crystallized into a pointed round tower guarding an old ford and a reedy marina under a pointed moon.

'I've been checking,' said Shay. 'You know the Tall Ships are all due in Norrköping by 4 July? That's just two days from now. Where is Norrköping?'

'Two left turns, at the very top of the next fiord north towards Stockholm,' I said. 'About a hundred miles extra.'

'There are bound to be Russians and Polish boats too. Wouldn't the diversion be worth it?'

Preoccupied with reaching the Baltic at all, I'd scarcely given it a thought since my visit to Janka Bielak in London. She would probably already be there. Our next main port was to be Hanko, two or three days' sailing away, on the south-west tip of Finland. After that we would be changing crew in Helsinki, which was only 70 miles further east direct, but which might take us as long again due to the complications of the coast.

'We can spare just 24 hours,' I decided. With luck and good weather the crew could rest *en route*.

Swedish efficiency had been staggering: along the canals we could happily have picnicked in all the public loos, and one town even provided the wherewithal, by stapling samples of cheese and caviar to its tourist brochures. Now, true to form, radio operators connected us to the unlisted temporary race office number without so much as batting an eyelid.

'*Hello!*' we yelled.

'*Guten tag!*' came back faintly, as three or four spiders waved from a web of netting stretched tight under a huge black spear. Dark against the sun they were stowing sails on the bowsprit of the *Grossherzogin Elisabeth*, a German sail-training ship. Having finished her race out to sea, she was idling through the limpid waters of the Braviken under bare poles.

It had taken another pre-dawn start to get us this far, weaving between specks of rock on which stood a dozen trees and a cottage, all with a tiny pier and a boat. Now, as the open fiord narrowed, and Norrköping's oil tanks popped up like mushrooms, other visiting yachts converged. The entrance channel was simple and straight.

On the radio, I'd misstated my request.

'May we berth with the racing fleet?' I'd asked, when I should have said 'nearby'. We were visitors, not an official entry, and all the racing vessels were bigger than ours. 'No,' we'd been told, 'but look for a berth far up on the starboard side.'

To port there were grain silos and quays, already jam-packed with masts and bunting. We took it slowly, scanning for our spot.

'There are the Russians to port,' called Susan.

In three or four ranks near the tail of the fleet, the back-to-front lettering on their rakish hulls stood out a mile. Even I could read 'МИР' or *PEACE*. Then we noticed Poles, big and small, a dozen or more. Bulgarians, Germans and Dutch . . . We sheered away reluctantly to our allotted spot.

'Yacht *Canna*. Harbour Control. The other quay please. Somewhere near *Forward* and *Audra*.'

We needed no second bidding – they were the first two Russian yachts. Circling slowly, *Canna* came alongside; but as we made to pass warps, a familiar head of wavy grey hair rose gracefully into view.

'How did you do it?' said Janka Bielak. 'Come and meet my good friend – the skipper of *Forward*, Boris Khryaschev.'

Out of the 120 boats in the harbour, we'd chanced to tie up to the one she was on.

The Rally was a rendezvous in a series of races between Denmark and Sweden. For half a mile towards the town, the docks were lined two and three deep with sloops and schooners, yawls and ships, arranged in national groups. Music and hot dogs and a dozen languages mingled on the air as I pushed among toddlers in push-chairs, and skippers in reefers. Young crews sprawled on sun-soaked decks, or squatted on the dock among piles of kit. A brown girl sported a small white bikini, a swarthy ship's officer in full starched regalia bared only his fingers and face. I couldn't afford too many of these distractions as I prospected for cooking gas and new contacts, in that order. Gas was a crucial problem – our supplies were well down, and we were moving into territory where no one could guarantee replenishment – but it was quickly solved by a British boat which, on hearing of our itinerary, very generously donated enough to last us well into Poland. Meeting the Poles and Russians took a little longer. We scanned their boats with surprise and fascination. Of the Russian ones some were glass-fibre, some timber, one aluminium, between 40 and 55 feet. *Audra* and *Forward* were each about 40 feet, both with extremely sleek modern racing lines, both equipped with a full range of gadgetry. They had come first and third in their class.

There was *Solovki*, a weather-beaten timber yawl: she came from Archangel on the White Sea, not far from the Arctic Circle, and one of the destinations of the wartime convoys.

Tormilind, the 'Stormbird', a 47-foot sloop from Tallinn in Estonia, was a
very special case. She had been one of the visitors to Liverpool in 1984, and
was famous for an amazing feat of seamanship. Between Norway and
Scotland, a gale had carried her rudder away, causing severe damage
and leaving her out of control. With enormous effort, the crew had
manufactured a jury rudder from a stainless steel drinks tray and the
spinnaker pole, and had sent one of their number over the side to pass the
contraption up through the hole in the stern. Instead of turning back or
calling for assistance, they had carried on around the North of Scotland,
and down to Greenock. In a particular way, it was her visit we were aiming
to reciprocate. The same professional captain as then, a dapper man in his
fifties, received me with great courtesy, and presented his card, which was
printed in Estonian on one side and transliterated Russian on the other –
Tiit Noo, Tiit Nÿu.

The Polish fleet numbered more than 20, almost the biggest national
contribution, ranging from *Iskra II*, an immaculate navy square-rigged
ship of 170 feet, down to modest timber ketches like the *Dunajec* from
Gdynia. Her skipper, Adam Długosz, a young fresh-faced man with a
blond moustache, came aboard that evening and relived his race with the
fleet from Denmark, a distance of 350 miles or so.

'Eighty boats in our class,' he said, 'and thick fog. We could hardly see
our bows. A strong wind, so we sail fairly fast. We have no radar, so I have
no sleep. I sit in the cockpit, with flares in my hand, for more than a day and
a night. Looking. Is there a shadow beyond the bow? I can't leave that
question at all to the crew.' He shook his head at the memory, his eyes still
dark from the strain, and I was very glad indeed that we hadn't been
tempted to follow *Oriana*'s route south.

Adam was very surprised at our permission to visit the USSR: it is not
always sweetness and light between communist bloc countries, he said, and
confirmed that Poles themselves found it difficult enough to get permission
to visit. He also warned of a border dispute between Poland and East
Germany, giving advice we were to find very useful later.

Activity around the docks had still been hectic next morning, as stragglers from the race arrived amidst horns and sirens, cheers and straining
tugs and hawsers, but by noon we were on the move again, taking
advantage of the improving weather. Now, as we retraced the long groove
toward the open sea under motor, and the low coastline opened up once
more, we could begin to compare notes.

On shore we had scattered in all directions. In one Polish boat, a young
Russian, who'd come to claim on a wager, stayed on to chat about our
cruise, and urged us not to skip his home port of Riga. Shay had spent time
with Valiery Stepanenko, the skipper of *Solovki*. I had met him briefly, too,
an impressive man with slightly Mongolian features who, under his vest

and denims, was of a piece with his boat, a lean bronzed veteran like a knuckle of sculpted hardwood. He and his crew of eight had had a hard voyage around the North Cape of Norway, he said, which seemed more than likely, as it was a distance of 2,000 miles or more; but other Russian crews I mentioned it to later snorted with derision and confided that *Solovki* had been brought around on a ship. Whether this was fact, or a joke at the expense of the ice-men from the far north, we never discovered.

Other Polish and Russian crews had heaped up offers of help and hospitality at most of the harbours of the South Baltic, backed up with addresses and 'phone numbers and sketches showing how not to miss their favourite clubs and the essential immigration checkpoints; but best of all was the contact with our immediate neighbours.

That morning a delegation had arrived – Boris Khryaschev, the power-fully-built moustachioed skipper of *Forward*, in short-sleeved shirt and fashionable mirrored sunglasses; Sergei, the skipper of МИР; and a heavy-framed man from *Audra*.

My aide-mémoire of queries amused them.

'Is it coffee with questions or questions with coffee?' they laughed. 'Now, which ports are you visiting?'

They puzzled about our refusal from Klaipėda, *Audra*'s home port in Lithuania, but surmised it might be due to its substantial navy presence. Boris and Sergei were soon deep into explanations about Leningrad, where *Forward* was based, while Shay entertained their colleague, who spoke no English, with photographs of salmon fishing.

'When you get close, the canal is narrow, it's shallow outside. You can go just 20 feet *outside* the buoys on the wrong side, but not here at Kronstadt. Is simple. But probably you will have pilot anyway.'

All of the bay west of the city, they had showed me, was shallow and infested with weed. To get to their club there were special channels, and we'd certainly need a pilot for that, as well as approval from the authorities. That was something we'd have to attend to ourselves.

'Mines? Only a problem for steel boats, normally,' they confirmed. Most mines were magnetic and weren't much attracted to plastic.

We had asked about Gogland and the Estonian coast, and ended up fishing out the Russian courtesy ensign. This had been a frantic headache in May and June, being specially made for us at the last minute and ending up tiny. It looked even more minute in Norrköping against the vast ensigns the Swedes all wore.

'Will it do?'

'Oh, yes. Is good. Is clean. No problem. Have a good time!' they called. 'We send you an invitation to our club.'

A little later, as Shay swarmed up a mobile crane to film, and the Estonians entertained me with a video of Tallinn in *Tormilind*'s comfortable saloon, Susan was handed an invitation to the Baltic Shipping Company Club in Leningrad, whose Commodore was Captain Pannin. Like others I'd met already, the Russians had done as they'd said.

We had not been at all composed when leaving: I for one was suffering from a gross excess of vodka, coffee, *sliwowic*, and tension brought on by a shortage of language. I'd been disgusted to discover that much of my hard-won Polish had dissolved in the oceans and canals *en route*, and only scattered phrases were left. It had been very hard going to dredge them up.

'Come on Sue, your turn, do your bit!' I insisted.

'Спасибо большое, до свидания.' 'Thank you very much. Goodbye!' she called as we cast off, and 30 Russian heads swivelled our way.

'Oh, too much Russian, too much, *too much!*' they called back, across the widening gap, grinning from ear to ear. Susan always has a good colour, but she looked particularly well just then.

By now, Norrköping was only a faint smudge astern. The sun was steady and warm. Out to sea, 50 miles away, we were promised ideal conditions, and every hour we were making good five or six miles, away from western Europe towards our destination in the East.

Our only regret, if we had one, was not to have met more Swedes, not to have got behind their cool, green reticence. Close contacts had been only Peter's wife in Göteborg, and a pair of brothers in a yacht on Lake Vänern who'd been sailing round Sweden in a genial haze. We seemed to have met more Russians than natives.

CHAPTER 5

Helsinki

At noon on 5 July, *Canna* rounded the Landsort light, 40 miles south of Stockholm and, two hours later, the last specks of Swedish soil had disappeared on the horizon. The departure was in some ways the most exhilarating of the whole voyage. We were already 17°E of Greenwich, 27°E of Ireland; we had only 13° more to achieve. The wind was a perfect moderate south-westerly, and we ran before it under spinnaker and poled-out genoa, steering a dead straight course of ENE. The sea was gentle under a high-clouded sky, the motion easy. For half the crew, it was their first venture out of sight of land but, in the favourable conditions, away from the strain and hurry ashore, they had settled well. Susan spread oil on culinary waters by bringing more order into the catering, at the same time relieving me of the problem, Shay of his role as galley martyr, and Maxwell of Shay's spicier offerings.

She had also sprung a midnight alarm, reporting a lit, conical buoy where there should have been nothing at all. We couldn't possibly have closed the coast – the nearest feature, a lighthouse under construction, should have been way off our course – but, sure enough, there was a green light and a dark triangular shadow beneath, running fast across the grainy blue sky. Perhaps a newly marked wreck? Or had a magnetic error set us badly astray? It had turned out to be a yacht, a forerunner of a fleet of more than a hundred competitors in the main annual Swedish sailing event from Sandhamn to Gotland. We ploughed right through the race like a clumsy bird through a swarm of bees. Some had passed so close we could hear their winches grunt and grind, snatches of tactical talk from the crew, and waterlines swishing by at twice our speed. If only one of the pack had misread us and failed to give way when they should, our voyage would have ended with a catastrophic collision. I had waited up until the last of their red and green lights went to white and were swallowed up in the rising dawn.

Another day, the sails gently pulling, a gentle lullaby roll. The off-watch crew slept for hours on deck. Arms and legs turned brown, and washing hung drying around the rails. Rupert played cards below. Away to port, unseen, lay the Åland Islands, home of the Eriksson square-rigged clippers which had traded on into the 1930s. Too far away for us now, we had already traded Åland for Norrköping.

Another night, with the main boom preventer slowly creaking, lifting and dropping past the moon. The muffled tread of crew overhead, changing over the spinnaker pole. A hurried stop in the harbour at Hanko, where scented roses grew in the cracks in the granite, then on again through the coastal channels, eastward again toward Helsinki. The passage through the lace-like waterways was intense and beautiful, claustrophobic, and very hard work.

The newest Swedish charts had been perfect masterpieces of precision, printed in blue and yellow on paper as stiff as a vicar's collar. The Finnish charts looked like a bad case of measles: endless splodges of bilious green, strewn with blood-red pimples. There were scatters of double arrows, and tramlines too. The hundreds of scarlet blots were lights or leading marks, each arrow, of which there were thousands, a beacon, and each fragment of cow-splat an island or rock, of which there were ten times more. The beacons and tramlines marked two or three channels, roughly parallel to the coast. The inner ones were often narrow, overhung by trees, and sometimes just too shallow for our draught. The middle channel, where it existed, was usually the main one, weaving between inshore islands and the small ones further out, carrying traffic of every kind and sort: day boats, half-deckers, tugs, fishermen, punts and the dreadful cruisers. These last roared by in both directions like dragsters on a motorway, kicking up wash and rolling everything else. We could have done without their help – every beacon, every lighthouse, every slatted pylon with white stripes had to be laid for, looked for, passed, ticked off, and a new course laid. It was hard going because it required total concentration from at least two people, one reading the chart and one conning. If we made a mistake we'd certainly run hard aground. Even worse, the wind was astern and very light, so the chute was pressed into use and continually gybed. The skipper sprayed orders around like a Bren gun. 'To port ten degrees now, haul over the main.'

Terry, his hands as usual incapacitated by the camera that lived on his modest paunch, acted as an involuntary ship's telegraph. 'That's right, yes, bring her to port,' he announced, stepping aside in mild surprise while someone groped for the sheet he was standing on.

Eventually every sheet on deck was pressed into service, and Terry as well, to keep the boat moving. It ended with the chute wrapping itself round the forestay while I cursed loudly and Shay scrambled aloft to release it.

'To hell with it!' I roared. 'Get the bloody thing off. Half the time it ends up that way. More trouble than it's worth.'

The claustrophobia lay in the lack of an open horizon, and the continual roar of traffic. To sail clear outside the islands would be more relaxing, but longer and slower – there was usually less wind outside – and the passages out were often intricate and unmarked. The beauty came when we stopped.

The first anchorage, recommended by Finns at Hanko, was the perfect lagoon of Modermagan, surrounded by low cliffs, birches and pines. A few other yachts had nosed right in and tied up to the rock, but – *Boom!* we stopped far too suddenly.

'I'm very sorry about that,' said Maxwell, as he threw *Canna* quickly into reverse, and everyone else forward into a heap.

We'd obviously just encountered one of the erratic boulders the Admiralty Pilot had warned us about. A few minutes later, when I dived overboard to check for damage to the keel, I remembered another of its predictions – fresh water. A bag of bones at the best of times, my reduced buoyancy was nearly the last straw, and I just about surfaced again in a panic, to general amusement. The boat, too, was looking strange. With her cruising load of a ton or more, and floating in less dense water, her water-line had completely disappeared and she was drawing a good six inches more than usual. All the more cause to beware of boulders.

The others, gazing and prowling, had no complaints until the morning.

Terry was looking particularly puffy and swore.

'Those mosquitoes were as big as badgers!' he claimed.

Susan said she had seen their droppings in among the rocks and lichens, so it could possibly have been true.

'I think we might get the main down, and go in under jib.'

The entrance to Helsinki harbour was narrow and blind, and we didn't want to embarrass any ships coming out in a hurry. It turned out well. It gave us time to glide slowly in, and pick up the beacons one by one, as complex as ever; to turn the city slowly round on an icing stand, and examine its white fortifications and swages and domes and spires; and to adjust to jumping straight from the depths of the country (we'd had an anchorage to ourselves the night before) into the very heart of the biggest city so far.

The HMVK marina, the Helsinki Motor Yacht Club, was the most central and convenient. On one side of the square harbour lay a rank of ice-breaking ships with undercut bows; to starboard stood a coaling station, beyond a vestigial island with trees. Dead ahead, a wall of variegated offices and flats fronted the town proper, and away in the left-hand corner, reminding us why we'd come, was a dark red bustling babushka, grand and tall, her hair done up in gilded buns: the Russian Orthodox Cathedral stood and beckoned at the end of our pontoon.

It was the most exquisitely bare-faced pick-up I had ever seen. Across the table from us in the outdoor café, Rupert sat quietly by himself, casually stylish in whites and greys. A girl in a white dress, a few years older and extremely pretty, leant across from the next table, stretching out a slender hand to ask for a light for her friend; and her unbearably charming turned-up nose, peeping out from a golden waterfall, steadily edged closer to his.

The café seemed to have everything – an indoor section in a classical pavilion with pediments and statuary and, outside, bright green shrubbery, white balustrades, red umbrellas and a shoal of white tables and chairs, where harassed waiters squeezed through with grooves in their thighs and big mugs of beer jostled fragile chinas of tea.

Rupert was lucky to have a seat at all, let alone one complete with a lovely girl crouching beside it and gazing up into his eyes. Her friend slewed around towards me. She was dark-haired, but quite certainly none the worse for that. Good Lord, I thought. I sensed Susan beside me beginning to buzz, and three blocky men at the girl's table began to take an interest. Surely, not here . . . ?

It was Kirsi's 21st birthday tomorrow, said Paula, in a delectable accent, and they would all celebrate it in style. This was a sort of after-work getting-in-practice party. The men were their friends; but Kirsi by now had made a discovery.

'Oh, this is your *son*?' she shot at us, her blue eyes terribly wide. 'And how old?' she asked, glancing between the three of us.

'Fifteen,' we said.

'Oh *shit*,' she exploded, in perfect English, flumping down backwards on to her hands. Everyone else burst into laughter, and quickly we pushed the two tables together. Rupert, delighted his taciturn ploy had gone down hook, line and sinker, was grinning fit to burst, but Kirsi took a second or two more to recover. She was a cook in a commercial bank, she said. She prepared lunches and receptions. She had a fiancé, but he was a fireman and wasn't around at the moment, otherwise she might not have been tempted to recruit more guests. She wanted Rupert to come to the party, they were hoping to go somewhere special, but . . . with his age . . . They fixed a rendezvous for the next day, anyhow.

And us? From the folder of cruise information that lived with me, I showed them where we were going. In a moment the men had muscled in, competing with each other to explain their country's politics, her independence, the wars with Russia. My small map collected the odd beer-stain as they transfixed it with strong fingers between beer glasses, explaining which parts had been lost, and which retrieved.

'Very strong fighting here,' they said, stabbing at the middle of Finland's eastern boundary. 'Very cold, much ice. Now Mannerheim, you know Mannerheim . . . ?'

I did, but one of the three in particular wanted to make quite sure that we understood everything *he* felt and knew about his homeland's status and standing. Eventually he had to be genially quietened by his friends.

Something remarkable was happening here, I thought, as we pushed out through the prehensile queue, which seemed to have grown even bigger and jumpier. I felt as though I'd just had my brain stretched. A week ago, Terry had at last managed to find a kind of alcoholic concert hall, where he paid to get in, and had been obliged to savour each drink before buying another; but here, by the time we'd finished, the glasses had been struggling for a toe-hold on the table. Far from making the running ourselves, we had been hoisted into the city's bosom on our very first afternoon, provided with five new friends and an al fresco tutorial. And whatever it was that was happening to us was going on all around.

The wide 'Esplanadi', the heart of Helsinki, has two well-separated short rows of shops, two pavements, two streets, two lines of trees and, down the centre, a promenade. We were scrunching it now with the world and his wife. Some of the already well-dressed women were clustered at windows displaying expensive crystal and clothing, ignoring the world behind them reflected in the glass: workmen in nothing but overalls, the blue straps crossing bare shoulders, sitting cross-legged and upending minerals; a girl lying flat on the grass; couples parked on benches; families with prams. Older ladies in florid hats took tea in a glazed gazebo, oblivious to someone relieving himself. He was exhibiting a bare minimum of decency by peeing against a tree. Big Havis Amanda, exhibiting so very much more that she'd caused a scandal when first erected a hundred years before, was also grossly more prodigal with her fluids, which gushed from water-spouts in all directions into a pool of pinkish stone. A demure woman perched on the rim was soothing herself with the sound, while opposite the buxom bronze a lean metal man, his face painted silver, was calming the sobs of a child he'd frightened. Most of his other spectators were laughing. Next minute he stretched a robot's arm toward a more likely girl from the crowd.

Out beyond the trees and the fountain, where the Esplanadi turned square, the President's palace confronted the harbour and the market sat in between. The bustle was enormous: snaking trams, cavernous ferries to Estonia and Sweden, launches to the inner islands. Old people in punts pulled up to the quayside with serried ranks of fish for sale, market stalls were piled high with strawberries, and pyramids of peaches and plums. Music filtered through the sunlight, pervasive, wistful, sad and courageous: an accordionist and a balalaika, a violinist or a guitar; and even, once, a grey and white army band with tall chestnut outriders, marching past. It wasn't clear if the musicians were working. Almost everyone else was not and, from the sound of the crowds, they were nearly all Finns.

The Mayor himself was already on holiday from the civic offices overlooking the scene. This was a pity, as we had brought him formal greetings from Dublin.

'Perhaps half the city is going to go to the woods,' said his deputy, pausing from his own headlong preparations to receive us. 'It's a bad time to be meeting people at work.'

But the books he presented to *Canna*, and others which we gleaned from the tourist office while Maxwell nodded off under a rubber plant, started to make sense of our new surroundings.

'FINLAND – what it is not!' ran a bright red heading, attacking her stereotypes head-on with numbered rebuttals:

'1. Finland is not a small country, nor is it close to the North Pole,' it began.

'2. Finland is not awfully cold all the time and polar bears do not roam the streets of Helsinki.

'3. Finns and Lapps are not the same thing.'

Shay might be sorry about No. 2, I reflected, and I was well aware of No. 3. As for No. 4: 'Finland is not the country of unlimited sex that it is made out to be . . .', which warned of the distinction between sauna and sex, I had yet to discover serious doubts as to which was the more exhilarating experience.

Most of the remainder were political or historical, pointing out, for instance, that Finland and the UK were the only two Western European countries involved in the War which were not under enemy occupation, and that the 'majority of Finns are not communists and the Government is not communistic.' Perhaps these pithy points were aimed mainly at tourists who insisted on sweeping through the whole of Northern Europe in a week, like the man in a coach party who we thought at first was parodying a Yankee twang: 'Have we changed countries yet? What thing is this we're going to see?' – only to find that he wasn't.

But disclaimer No. 5 was the most intriguing of all:

'5. Finnish is not a Slavonic language, and only a very few Finns speak Russian which, of course, is a pity.'

The elderly courier for our coach tour of the city immediately confirmed that the humour was intended. 'We have here no very old buildings,' she began, 'so we compensate with very old guides.'

When the squeals of the Italians, belly laughs of the Germans and the polite coughs and hawkings of the English-speakers had ricocheted into a merry roundabout, as the same joke was trotted out in three languages, she got into her stride. More than half the next two hours' wisecracks concerned the eastern neighbours.

'You will see nearly every car has a label SU. This does *not* mean Soviet Union, but SU, Suomi, Suomi, Finland,' she insisted. 'And here now, in this very expensive suburb,' as we slewed through the residential area of Otaniemi in our monstrous fish-tank on wheels, 'all the most wealthy capitalists live, including his Excellency, the very charming Soviet Ambassador.'

Finland did a roaring trade with the Russians, the white-haired sparrow chirruped, indicating a half-completed nuclear ice-breaker in the docklands on order from the USSR.

'Because, you see, they are our brothers. Your brothers you get, your friends you choose.'

'Whew,' I winced to Susan, 'that's a bit sharp!'

'Thank you for your commentary,' I said during a walkabout. 'Do you look after Russian visitors too?'

'No,' she replied, taking the point like a flash. 'They come together in large groups, and they generally have particular hotels and their own guides. There are quite a lot of them.'

In fact, Russian tourists are big business for Finland, coming a very close third in numbers after Swedes and Germans.

We soon found that, even though the courier had served up a particularly piquant hors-d'oeuvre, the Helsinki Finnish seemed to live on a strong diet of national pride, largely defined in relation to Russia. It was very close to the surface, a recurrent topic that cropped up early in almost every social encounter, whether we raised it or not.

There were other signs of the Finnish temperament. There was the minor fracas that resulted from an old woman getting her foot stuck in a tram door. The driver, with great single-mindedness, steadily unbuttoned and locked away all her cash-bags while the hapless woman continued to squawk, then, having released her, she faced down her angry complaints and harangued the other passengers into the bargain. She'd have made a formidable soldier.

There seemed to be a feeling of robust practicality and cheerfulness and open hospitality. People came on board unbidden at all times of day, making themselves known and offering help. There were also cracks in the social pavement through which things other than roses grew. People tolerated a bit of untidiness. They sometimes indulged in rather fast driving, and drink and drunks were an obvious problem. One day, passing through a small park near the marina, I came across two purple inebriates, rocking to and fro with bottles in their hands, like the arms of metronomes set for fast and slow waltzes. The bamboo background was also swaying in the breeze, so it made me sea-sick to watch them, and I was very relieved when one seemed to break his spring at the end of an arc and fell full-length into the bushes. The two of them were still horizontal when I came back several hours later.

But the strongest flavour was still the same: the insistent spice of being non-Russian. Its deep buttressings made the actual Russian presences in

the city – the decorative Uspenski Cathedral we'd first noticed, and the
Russian restaurants in the side-streets – seem almost discreet; our own
deliberate avoidance of contentious national comparisons seem positively
bland. Everyone was at it. Shay had brought us to Terry's newly discovered
Valhalla, a bar that actually served Guinness, an apotheosis after which he
would, later, leave the boat and return home fulfilled. One of the patrons
was an unusual Finn with black hair and long expressive hands, a public
relations consultant for an engineering company, who wrote books on
Finnish history as a pastime. He was writing the history of the Northern
War and the Continuation War of 1939–45, or re-writing it, rather. It had
never been properly told, he explained, launching into a broad exposition
of Stalin's invasion from the east, and the Finnish/German push in the
opposite direction.

On the way back in the small hours, through the slightly eerie, emptying
streets, ringing with the disembodied cries of other late birds, a figure
stepped out from the shadow of a towering pedestrian statue in the
cathedral square, and moved toward us. Again, it was nothing ominous.
He was a merry and melancholy art student, who'd spent a little money he
didn't have, and was anxious to show us around. In the 100 yards between
the Mayor's house (the oldest in the city, he explained) and the waterside,
he moved on to the same topic. His parents had been natives of Karelia,
formerly eastern Finland, the battleground of our author's book, much of
which was now within the Soviet Karelian Republic. His family, like tens of
thousands of others, had been part of a general exodus to central and western Finland. It had gone smoothly, he said, integration had been managed well, but it had affected most of the population directly in some way.

'Thinking about the braveness of our soldiers in resistance brings tears to
my eyes,' he said as he gripped our hands, and I noticed it was true. A little
wine elicited a lot of veritas. He was not much older than Rupert.

Confirmation of these truths came from more sober sources. Fortunately, the Deputy Mayor had been partially wrong, and there were still plenty
of people at work in their offices. I noticed them as I prowled the streets in
outright fascination. Like the sea-maze at the harbour entrances, the
streetscape led me on, holding me entranced by the variety and exuberance
of the façades. There were ranks of classical buildings in the central area
near the marina, some of them incredibly bold and mannerist, with
enormous exaggerated head-high plinths and cave-like window reveals.
Others displayed exquisite doorways, and details in a flowing and vegetable
Art-Nouveau style; some sported muscular torsos and busts bearing heavy
upperworks with grim determination. Even obviously modern buildings
pursued this delight in movement and effort within their financial constraints. Apparently architecture was a matter of public interest and display,
just like the woven tapestry and ceramics in the Esplanadi. Architects'

offices had models and drawings in their windows, as if they were tasty confections and pastries and, wonder of wonders, in a shopping arcade, on a Sunday, and tended by full-time staff, was a complete display of the city development plan, open all day to the public. Fascinated by the phenomenon, and with the subterranean idea of returning to Helsinki if we should have to winter in the Baltic, I followed our visitors' example, waltzed into some of the architects' cake-shops and introduced myself.

'What did he say to you?' asked Anja Turtola, the following day. 'Did he say *anything?*'

Anja, a vivacious brunette, was perched on the cockpit coaming, one of two or three visitors. The rest of the crew were handing up drinks. She had seen a newspaper article about us and realized I was the person her husband Risto had mentioned, who'd walked in from the street, unannounced, to meet him. I had to admit that he hadn't said much.

'Oh, never mind him!' she grinned. 'He's the original silent Finn. When are you coming to see us? We live there,' she said, pointing out a middle-aged reddish building at the water's edge. 'I could see you were here from the window.'

'We're in the same apartment block as the Prime Minister,' she had added, as an afterthought, and a casual indication of the egalitarian nature of Finnish society. It didn't seem to add to security requirements, as Susan and I made our way up flights of flowing terrazzo stairs, replete with dark inlaid tendrils of decoration and subtle irregularities of geometry. It was a grand, high-ceilinged apartment, floored with parquet and cork, and skins. The walls were panelled and painted in shiny black. Risto, stocky and wide-featured, occupied a sofa like a genial troll. All the pale, timber-framed furniture was of exquisite quality.

'I bought it without telling him when he had started in practice and had no money,' said Anja. 'He never got around to sending it back.' The quiet man smiled a slow smile.

Over goat's cheese pastries and slivers of smoked reindeer meat, they fleshed in a bit more of the skeleton we had glimpsed. Anja's immediate ancestors had had very direct connections with Russia. Her paternal grandfather had been the manager of a rope-works for the Russian Navy, and her father had been born in St Petersburg. He had brought up his family in Vyborg, the town set deep in the crook of the north-east of the Gulf of Finland, about 85 miles north-west of Leningrad. Anja's childhood playgrounds had been all along the coast, among the peninsulas and islands that fringed the Vyborgski Zaliv. All this area was now Russian territory. Whereas, before the war, the Russian boundary had been some 15 kilometres west of Leningrad, Stalin had carried it about 50 kilometres west of Vyborg.

I mentioned the Finnish historian's comment to the effect that Finland had now come to terms with the realities of its geographical, economic and political situation. Was that true of people like themselves? Yes, they confirmed. When Finns speak of Russia, they do so without overt rancour. They accept their situation and territory as it is, and are extremely proud of having secured it.

I began to realize that we were on shifting ground as far as our approach to the Goodwill Cruise was concerned. History was to play a much bigger part in it, particularly here, than I expected. We had wanted to deal with life as we found it and discover hopes for the future, without too much harking back to the past, but this was obviously simplistic. It just wasn't possible to truncate a personal and national consciousness. People were like members of a ship's crew, scanning astern as well as ahead; more familiar with where they had been than where they were going. We would have to embrace all of it.

For one thing, Helsinki owed its prominence to the Russians. The original capital had been at Turku, in the south-west. For a while, Finland had been like a doll being fought over by two angry children, Sweden and Russia, with other members of the European family being called in or interfering on one side or the other. Peter the Great had first wrenched off the arm of the Karelian isthmus, including Vyborg. In 1808 the Russians, under Alexander I, took over the whole of Finland and Äland. The fall of the vast castle of Sveaborg, spread over six fortified islands at the mouth of Helsinki harbour (which Maxwell and Rupert were exploring as we talked), was the key to their success, and in 1812, Helsinki, which had started life as a trading competitor to Tallinn in Estonia, became Finland's new capital with only 4,000 inhabitants. Alexander turned Finland into a Grand Duchy with moderate self-government, and reattached the Vyborg arm.

At the time of the Russian annexation, an English fleet had enlisted with the Swedes, harassing the Russians and firing on their shore batteries. The British returned in 1853–4, in Crimean times, to tug the Russian hair, bombarding their Finnish forts, including Sveaborg, in a desultory campaign that turned into a floating jolly; and only a few years later arrived in yachts to fraternize again. Commodore Graves, skipper of the *Ierne*, visiting in 1862, commented that, 'The Finlanders are thoroughly disloyal to the Russian crown, and given a chance would rejoin the Swedes', which was hardly surprising, as many spoke only Swedish anyway. Until the Russian Revolution, Finnish national sentiment increased. Successive tsars confronted it or yielded to it, including Nicholas II, (under whose statue we had met the art student). In 1917, Finland had at last become independent, under the brilliant leadership of her hero Carl Mannerheim.

All was well until 1939, when Stalin, citing a possible threat from Germany, requested concessions, including a lease of the Hanko peninsula, the loss of two islands in the Gulf and land in Karelia. The Finns refused and the Winter War of 1939–40 began. The Russians eventually prevailed, but not without enormous effort and cost, in freezing weather and against much smaller Finnish forces. Vyborg was again crucial as Russia pushed west toward Helsinki, holding out so bitterly the Russians were forced to bypass it across the Baltic ice, as the Finns bombed it in front of them. Karelia also was disputed inch by inch. When Germany attacked Russia, Mannerheim set himself to regain ground, but the loss of territory, including Vyborg, was finally confirmed between Stalin and the two western leaders in Persia. Stalin insisted on heavy compensation. Finland subsequently had had to live by diplomacy instead of war, and the modern Finns were very proud of that too. The last word in the official tourist guide comments about 'What Finland is not' concerned her talent for going it alone:

> '10. "We have noticed that we manage fairly well ourselves, even though diplomacy has been needed . . . It has been said that Brezhnev once telephoned Finland's president during the China crisis. Brezhnev asked, "Could you give me a good piece of advice as to the correct way to proceed in order to get along with a big Eastern neighbour?"'

My immediate task now was to find the correct way to proceed in order to get *to* Finland's big eastern neighbour, in a purely physical sense. Most of our main anxieties had already been gobbled up by getting as far east as we had, and on time. Now it was 11 July, and we were due in Leningrad on 16 July. But what route should we take? For the Russians at Norrköping, it hadn't appeared as a problem – we could simply join the main shipping channel twenty-five miles to the south and then head east for about two hundred – but there were several drawbacks. First, we weren't at all keen to keep company with a stream of commercial traffic in unknown waters for longer than we had to. Second, we mustn't arrive early, or late. The longer the leg from Helsinki, the more difficult perfect timing would be, the greater the risk of delay *en route*, and the sooner we should start. Also, it wasn't obvious from the charts where one moved into Soviet waters along the shipping lanes. As an unusual visitor, we wanted to get the etiquette right and avoid attracting unnecessary attention. If we stayed in Finnish waters as long as we could by heading east along the coast, the Finnish-Soviet boundaries became clearly defined and, from a suitable point in East Finland, the distance to Leningrad would be halved. But could it be done? Had it been done? Would the authorities allow it? From everything I had heard and seen, the sea frontier was bound to be sensitive.

I found I, too, needed modest diplomacy when making enquiries. Finnish sailors we had met had been incredulous about our visas.

'But I've been trying to get permission to sail to Russia for 20 years!' said one, and the comment cropped up so many times as to become embarrassing.

The main sailing clubs are scattered around the islands and inlets of Helsinki harbour. The *éminence grise* of the prestigious Swedish-speaking Nylandska Jahtklubben, a kindly old man with a limp and a stick and fierce blue eyes, hadn't been able to offer much help. He couldn't tell me about the east Finnish islands. Not many people sailed in that direction, he said; all the best scenery lay to the west. The question of sailing even further east, or to Germany, met with a dismissive wave.

At last, at the main Finnish-speaking club, I found a yachtsman with some personal knowledge of the east coast.

'Some of the eastern islands are very attractive,' he told me, naming a few.

'But what about the military restricted areas around them I've noted on the charts?'

'They're a nuisance,' he said. 'A neighbouring country starts the fashion, so we have to have some too. Finnish people can stay in them longer than foreigners. But some of them you can use.'

Combing the pilots and brochures minutely, I decided on Haapasaari, a tiny cluster of tiny islands, tucked into the south-east corner of Finland's territorial waters, 15 or so miles off the coast, and seven from the Russian border. No one had been able to tell me if we could cross from there – even the city police didn't know, but they mentioned there'd be coastguards. I decided it was worth the chance; decided on departure for 13 July.

'Where on earth are we heading for, Pekka?' I asked, but the driver of the big Mercedes only grinned quietly and put his foot down further. All the other traffic, coming and going, accelerated past us in the opposite direction on the luminous ribbon of motorway, and it was obvious that we were already well west of Helsinki's suburbs. Susan and Alan were the other passengers. Terry was already back in Dublin, and Maxwell by now had left the crew too. He had parted from us with typical lack of fuss that morning, with the intention of taking a roundabout route home via Sweden, Lapland and Norway. In fact, although, as we later heard, he trundled thousands of miles by rail and took a ferry round Norway's North Cape, it was by way of compensation: he had been very keen to sail on with us to Leningrad and fly back from there, but it had threatened complications if *Canna* should arrive in Russia late.

Reluctantly, we had scrapped the idea in May: in Helsinki he'd found it was also too late to organize a trip by train to join us for a few days in Leningrad. We had been particularly sorry to see him go, not just because of his enormous capacity for work – I had a favourite impression of him as a stripped-down Buddha, prowling around the water-line in the red dinghy

and his underpants, scrubbing-brush in hand – but for his steady consisten-
cy and his interest in the whole expedition. Maxwell's place was taken by
Alan Balfe, a cheerful, dark-haired research chemist from Dublin, roughly
half Maxwell's bulk and age, who was due to stay with us as far as Poland.

Our host, Pekka Kause, who was a regional health officer, had been the
mainstay of our Finnish planning. For months in the spring he had sent
barrages of invitations, coastal information and encouragement. We'd
been reconciled to missing him because he, too, had been away sailing, to
Denmark; but, arriving back earlier than expected, he had radioed us while
still on his way in.

'You must come out for a sauna,' he said, 'I'll pick you up in an hour.'

That had been 9.30 pm. Now it was nearly 11, but still the light hung on in
a pale purple overcast, above the speeding blur of forest.

'Oh, we're not going to our house,' smiled Pekka. 'We're going back out
to Porkkala, where the family and the boat are. We have a sauna there
too.'

I was aghast at his hospitality. Porkkala was the long peninsula west of
Helsinki, where we'd last anchored before coming to the city, but it was
about 30 miles by road. That meant 120 miles of driving for him in just one
night. He diverted the objection with a final helping of history. 'Porkkala is
very interesting. It's perhaps 12 miles long and very beautiful, mainly
woodland. The Russians held on to it after the war, you know, for years, up
until 1957.'

Russian interest had no doubt been provoked by the fact that the Finns
and Germans had managed to string an anti-submarine net from Porkkala
all the way across to the Estonian shore, a distance of 30 miles or more,
which successfully trapped all of the Russian Baltic fleet for the remainder
of the war.

'Why did they release it then?' I asked.

'We had very good diplomacy, I think,' he said. 'The Russians wanted to
show the world what could be achieved with good relations. It was good
propaganda. Almost the only land they ever parted with.'

We gave ourselves up to pure hedonism after that. The place was
certainly worth a lot of negotiations. The forests opened here and there to
small pockets of arable land and pasture. Small farmsteads crouched in the
twilight. The car branched continually on to minor roads, yet smaller
roads, tracks through the forest, darker and darker, until finally it abandoned all guidance, turned on to a carpet of scented needles, climbed over a
boulder or two and squeezed between huge trunks where there was barely
room to open the doors.

Down between the pines, by torchlight, were three wooden cabins. The
first was the loo, the second disgorged a flood of warmth and light and a
welcome from Pekka's family. The third, on the edge of the Sea (so calm

that I called it a lake), was the sauna. End on to a wooden jetty was the family's powerful yacht.

Only once more that evening did I raise the Russian question, when our turn came to sweat and birch and gulp scalding steam. Somewhere I'd heard that a visitor may insult a Finn's wife if he must, but he shouldn't query his sauna. I had no intention of the one – even now, at two am, Eva-Raise, a slim, alert, bird-like lady, was preparing a traditional stew – so I approached the other subject with extreme caution, fearful of burning my fingers or some other vital extremity.

'Is it a solely Finnish tradition?' I asked. 'Nowhere else?'

'No,' said Pekka, 'it's Finnish. The Russians might have something like it in parts, but they're not the same. There are several types of sauna, with smoke, without smoke, continuous or not. Now this one we have here is the very best of all . . .'

The night was total, blue magic. As we picked our way naked from stone to stone to the water's edge, by the light of small candles set on the ground, the full moon rose slowly, yellow on navy, lighting the entrance into the bay. It defined the outlines of wordless blue water. Like a ritual, only total immersion seemed right, although Pekka hung back and chuckled indulgently. The bed of the lake yielded soft underfoot. The shaggy pile of blue-back forest folded around as we surfaced again. Even when the glow of food and talk and intense relaxation and peace had warmed the logs of the cabin walls, the blue still pursued us, shimmering at the windows. I went and gazed out. Crowding tree-trunks burned blue brands into the sea and the sky and a few low, blue branches were shifting in the very faintest of breeze. Such peace.

We left as the colour faded and brightened. We had to sail that day, I insisted. In the dawn, drifts of mists still hung in the hollows, on pale green fields with tinges of brown. Something darker suddenly stirred.

'Over there, see! Six or seven moose. If we keep going they may not move.'

Pekka drove on, but so did they. Their improbable, front-heavy, reddish-brown heads and powerful shoulders lumbered through crops in the unfenced field alongside us, then veered away from the car as if in a rodeo. We could see just the ears of the young ones at the very tops of their bounds. Our cup ran over, and so did our frustration – not one of us had brought a camera. A blush began to brighten the mist and the gable ends of barns.

By six am we were back in the city, by six pm we were gone.

'Ru, will you put on top the big chart of Helsinki harbour!' I called down to the chart table, as I showed Alan how to start the engine.

As always, it was a relief to be casting off ties but, as always, it had been a breakneck rush to finally do it.

I had hauled the crew out of their bunks shortly after our cat-on-the-tiles return, and Rupert was no less peeved by that than by having missed the midnight carousals.

'Well, what did you have to eat, then?' he demanded through a mouthful of bran.

'Reindeer salami, and a lot of moose mousse,' I said, which had very nearly been true. 'Now hurry on, we've to go and buy a whole lot more of the same.'

Susan, who was more vegetarian than carnivore, kicked me under the table.

We had certainly been living higher than normal on the fat of the land, between the market and meals out – I could still sense the tang of *lakka* and *mesimorja*, golden cloudberry and arctic bramble liqueurs with which we'd chased some of them down – but now it was time to think ahead. A serious chandler had warned of restricted food supplies in Russia and, although it wasn't clear whether his information was up-to-date, we decided to play it safe. He had also commented that the Leningrad water supply was often infested with parasites, so I had scoured the town for purifying tablets, and at last feeling safe enough, against all normal caution, to invest in smart footwear in which to meet the Mayor of Leningrad, I had ended up with a grossly unsuitable pair of Portuguese white plastic shoes, which the crew promptly christened my 'pansy pooftahs'.

In the midst of these important matters, the immigration police pointed out that it might be helpful to Russian officials if we had formal clearance stamps from Finland, which they provided. Other friends of a few minutes' standing offered temporary buoys and fetched weather forecasts. Their kindness was only balanced by the thrill of live water chuckling under the forefoot once more, the throb of the deck, new wind in our hair, and a small group of well-wishers waving us away.

Out again past the black and cream ice-breakers, huge idle layabouts biding their times. Motoring out in calm quiet weather, slowly getting ourselves together. Under the portals of the old Sveaborg castle, a moment's brief panic as a small ferry ignores the Collision Rules, as do ferries everywhere. Out on a different set of leading lines, keeping the white beacons, like policemen's traffic cones splashed with red, astern of us on the low rocky shore. There's not much traffic. Two big ferries have gone on ahead. In the gentle glow of evening, one of them turns to port, towards Russia. When we reach that next dark beacon, we too shall do that. We'll turn due east . . . nothing else does, I notice. I'm so lost in the romance of the notion that we belatedly avoid running *Canna* aground.

'We have to give the marker more clearance to starboard!'

Now we're round it, heading east toward the Kalbådagrund light, our next turning point on a sunken shoal, invisible 20 miles away.

CHAPTER 6

Haapasaari – The Stone in the Stream

As the light gets duller, and the last beacons astern fade to uncertain pencils, we're carrying our own world with us again. There's nearly no wind, the water's still, and so again we are motoring. It was a time for reflections, and for enjoying a sense of thrill. At this stage, things were going far better than we had ever dared to hope. We were up to time. Ahead of us lay our destination with only a few more stiles to cross: already we were east of Athens, although less than six weeks away from home, and the stormy Atlantic was far behind. Sometimes I found it hard to believe. There'd been no disasters and no eruptions . . .

So far. Now, I realized, we had to remould our crew of five for the crucial six or eight weeks ahead. One man at a time was taking the tiller while the rest made up for lost sleep.

'Happy, Alan?' I queried.

He nodded and grinned, alert and agog. A shock of hair fell over his forehead, and his white teeth flashed infectiously. Alan had managed to make a break for the cruise between a post in a Dublin pathology laboratory and an appointment at a children's hospital in the USA, but he was also a keen sailor and sail-training enthusiast who had voyaged on traditional square-rigged ships. Once he'd been shown fire-extinguishers and flares, and how not to get chewed by the engine fly-wheel while opening the cockpit valves, I guessed he would find his own way around. A naturally pleasant and easy disposition had already made him an asset on board.

After his various excitements ashore, Rupert had already relaxed again into unobtrusive competency, raising inscrutability to an art while waiting for something else to happen; Susan, on the other hand, was in a mood that matched my own, in which future and present and past all mingled. 'Remarkable people, the Finns,' she murmured, as the coast rolled by on her twilight watch. We had been as much impressed by their art as their pride. For its own sake it didn't seem much in evidence. As well as putting art up on the wall, they *did* it, and put it to use. They wove it and wore it, blew it and drank from it, designed and lived in it. It was nearly all practical and saleable. This strong, independent business bent made them quite as happy to build ships for the USA as for Russia, or for themselves. It also explained why the godsend who'd taken Susan on a shopping expedition in his car had quickly sketched in the possibility of turning our boat into a floating emporium, and the Goodwill Cruise into a successful commercial enterprise, by pointing out what goods were now in demand in Russia and Poland. This was something we'd set our faces against from the start.

'There'll be no black market trading, no shading the fringes. We'll do everything by the book,' I had sternly warned the crew. We weren't going to damage a precedent, whatever happened. I began to wonder if monetary killings might not be a potent source of aggravation between countries. We already knew that some Finns were persistent offenders in Russia, and were sometimes briefly jailed for their efforts.

Shay, for slightly different reasons, was beginning to feel apprehensive about photography. He had already put in an enormous effort; now he was checking his gear again, which comprised half a dozen cameras, including the videos, and elaborate lenses and film. Expeditions often carry a 'carnet' to cover their photographic equipment, a document indicating to customs officers it is intended for use *en route* and is not for sale. Shay and I had discussed this warmly and at length, but eventually I vetoed the idea, pointing out that it would force us to clock in and out of particular ports in every country to do the paperwork, which could cause us fatal delays. We'd travel with elaborate receipts, I decided, and not a drop too much duty-free. To date we hadn't been queried, and perhaps it would stay that way. We had also enquired from the Russian Embassy what onshore rules there would be, and were told: 'None at all, it's a free country' – except for possible security items, like bridges and docks, which we mustn't photo-graph – but nothing had been set down in writing. Over the last few days, Russia had come to occupy a lot more than half of our physical and mental horizons, and was due to peer out from the summer night any time now. Squeezed between its imminent appearance and my own repeated admonishments, Shay began to wonder '*what if?*'. Might his gear be confiscated; might the customs object? Too late to do owt now, unless we were going to leave it on a Finnish boulder.

To port, the last of a low red sunset glowed fitfully between the coast and an overcast sky. As the wind began to breathe coolly from the north-east, from the direction of Russia, and we hoisted all sail, it seemed to me that a thin blue shadow on the horizon, a long slit eye, opened a shade on the starboard bow. Was it really there? The night darkened and we saw no more, except the quadruple flash of the lighthouse we needed.

Through the short night hours, I thought of the hundreds of thousands of sailing vessels that had passed that way before us; the long aggressive galleys of the Scandinavians; the modest and sturdy planked fishing boats from both sides of the Gulf; the trading barques hauling away essential naval supplies of timber and tar to ports all over Europe; and, in turn, the awesome, terrifying warships, with overbearing masts and several storeys

of gunports, like coastal fortresses suddenly put to sea; and the sleeker lines
of gentlemen's yachts.

The warships and yachts had made some strange combinations. *Oriana*
had gone ahead of us, and Graves's *Ierne* was for now our notional
companion. She had followed us through the Caledonian Canal, and
veered around Sweden, but on this leg she had hitched a tow, along with
another yacht of similar size, from the *St George*, a 72-gun ship with Prince
Albert aboard, part of a British Baltic fleet and, like us, engaged in a
goodwill visit. I imagined the trio forging through the night alongside us,
the two yachts dipping their long bowsprits, their sails furled, like
greyhounds at the heels of the heavy man-of-war, the dirty black pipe
puffing clouds of smoke up to his mast-head caps; and the three helmsmen
at three big spoked wheels, scarcely concerned by borders or passports or
visas.

Which was better? I wondered. Their systems of pilots and introductions
to Consuls, or ours of charts and bureaucracy and paperwork? When Susan
had arrived in Göteborg, she had brought with her the long-awaited letter
from Mr Krebs, head of the East German Consular Section in London,
concerning our proposal to visit.

'Within the framework of the Goodwill Cruise,' it ran, 'there is no
possibility for this. We were informed by the GDR authorities that
such entries are not allowed on principle.'

The flat, deflating 'no', seemed somehow to strengthen the links to our
sailing companions of more than a century ago, and to lend extra significance and warmth to our invitations from Russia and Poland.

'Land ahoy!' came the call to my slanting bunk. We were making well up to
windward in the early day.

It had been Russia; it was Russia looking at us quite clearly now: the
lens-like profile of Gogland island, blue-grey, mysterious, unblinking. It
was a curious nostalgia in reverse. For weeks and months, we'd pored over
the charts on firm tables, in known surroundings thousands of miles away,
peering wonderingly at the small yellow outline shaped like a key-blade,
which deflected the shipping lanes around it. Even on the large scale charts
it showed no details, no village, no features. This enigma, we had guessed,
would be the first of Russia, but now here it was, still mysterious. Bolder
than the Finnish shore, a rising eyelid, it was thickly wooded, the pine-trees
draping the steep slopes. Even through binoculars it gave almost nothing
away. Some rocks at the bottom, a tower or mast near the top. All five of us
lined the rails as it pivoted slowly a few miles away.

'Are we still in Finland?' asked Alan, aiming his camera.

I wondered. The island hadn't known the answer itself, as it yo-yo'd during the war, and even now the boundary lines seemed slightly am-biguous, complicated by Finnish fishing zones on the Russian side. We may have clipped a buoy a few hundred yards on the wrong side. Correcting the error, we stayed carefully in Finnish waters, flying the blue and white Finnish flag. It was probably as well we did. We'd been watched by a white patrol boat last evening, certainly Finnish, and now a grey counterpart appeared from beyond Gogland, aslant to starboard. It showed no ensign, and didn't come close.

Soon we could see its manoeuvres no longer. The breeze had stiffened, an expected watch-tower came into sight marking our destination, and the narrow end of Gogland watched us zig-zag away north-east toward the fractured scatter of Haapasaari. I hoped we'd find refuge there. After three days with nearly no sleep, I badly needed it.

'*Tassa!*' the other yachtsmen called, waving wildly. '*Here*, over here!'

'*Kiitos!*' we called back. 'Thank you. Is there deep enough water?' Our echo-sounder showed we'd be aground any second.

'There's enough. Two metres,' they said, as we squeezed and squealed between their boats. 'It may drop a metre, but not today or tomorrow.'

The ominous predictions of the Admiralty Pilots were beginning to come true, especially in this toy-like harbour. Nearly everything was tiny – a tiny cut blasted through rock for an entrance, a minute lagoon sur-rounded by toy wooden houses perched on pebbles and boulders. In the middle were four, full-sized navigation beacons marking sunken rocks, looking like moon rockets in the Lilliputian surroundings. We hadn't seen the pier for the boats, it was that small. We tied up to it with some misgivings. The last thing we wanted, 1,800 miles from base, and only 100 from Leningrad, was to get stuck indefinitely in a shallow harbour by one of the Baltic's unpredictable lapses.

'No problems!' said our neighbours, who were all Finnish.

Things hadn't looked quite so welcoming an hour before. Even this diminutive harbour slashed the half-mile long island almost in two. On the approach, a forbidding tower dominated its highest point, all grim brick-work and concrete and slitted windows of a peculiarly nightmarish type. The whole group of islands lay within the most extensive of all the restricted areas, extending right up to the Soviet border, and was also overlapped by a firing range. Access to the group was by defined routes, but the pilotage diagrams matched the scale of the islands, and we had found ourselves in an even smaller harbour on the western side. Fishermen had looked up from the stern-decks of their trawlers without acknowledge-ment. There was nothing else but coastguard boats.

'This doesn't look quite right,' said Susan, as I called to a uniformed guard with a platinum crew-cut stalking sternly down to the pier. He had made a telephoning sign and disappeared.

'Is OK,' he said, after returning to check our documents. His English was laborious, but quite precise.

'Is permitted for you to remain for not more than 48 hours, but in the civilians' harbour . . .'

So here we were on a stepping stone in mid-stream, able just to maintain our balance for a few seconds, it seemed, while we shifted our weight and looked around to resolve the last few uncertainties, if we could. We must either then go on or go back.

To see the island should have been easy. Beyond the pier was a single tap, a small wooden church, a mildly odious earth-closet, one shop, sparsely stocked with tins and postcards. There was a single glass telephone kiosk perched on the summit of a bare sweep of rock, a pimple on somebody's cranium.

But for all its small scale, there was a bewildering variety of scenery. On the sheltered eastern corner, beyond the boarded chalets with vividly painted windows, even more lurid dragonflies flitted among green reeds and patches of sun. Two hundred yards away, a disused grass-covered bunker lurked beneath pine trees. This was the windward side, looking over to the Finnish mainland. A cool breeze drove wavelets on to bare rock. Tufts of moss and purple stands of larkspur sprouted in crevices further back. Pine trees moaned and stirred with faint unease. In the distance a single yacht manoeuvred between endless stretches of forested islands.

The humans were an even more unlikely mixture. Among the burly fishermen in their working clothes and the yachtsmen in designer gear and boob tubes, a pair of uniformed chimney-sweeps raided a motor cruiser for something they'd forgotten – two small men with black stove-pipe hats and crinkly boots, loopy rods and spiky brushes. Other landlubbers in over-bright shorts wandered between timber frames, where orange fishing nets were drying. Stiff, grey guards clicked up and down, clattering on the rock. They took their turn with everyone else to stand in the little glass box for a few minutes at a time, surrounded by a glinting sea and a million spears of pine, talking to another galaxy.

I thought I'd been transported there myself when I bumped into Shay on the end of the pier, grinning widely under his gold-rimmed spectacles, and clutching a very big man with a microphone, and a very thin one without.

'Why not?' I thought. 'All we need now is Laurel and Hardy and the picture will be complete.'

'Roger, meet Jaako and Olavi,' he said. 'They're on one of the boats here, on holiday. But they're with Finnish radio, and would like to do an interview.'

Jaako's incredibly brilliant dark brown eyes gleamed even brighter, and in no time I too was talking into a black gadget to a disembodied audience. I told about our route, the difficult weather, the *Canna*: 'She is a very conventional, rather old-fashioned cruising boat, just about ten metres long. Her width is less than three metres. She was built in England about 15 years ago.'

'Why to Leningrad? You mentioned the *Glasnost*. Is that so very interesting from your point of view?'

'Yes,' I explained. 'It was encouraging to see a Russian policy of greater welcome to people from other countries. We wanted to see if what had been possible for sailors from Britain and Ireland in the nineteenth century was still possible now.'

'And I hope fervently we haven't blown any of our chances of being well received,' I thought, coming up with a jolt as I remembered the Swedish newspaper. When it had caught up with us in Helsinki, I hadn't liked what I'd seen, and then there had been Finnish editions of it too.

'*Glasnost – risteily*,' it began, under a picture of Shay and *Canna*. 'A *Glasnost* cruise.' Then in huge type: '*Mitä. Eikö NL: ssa ole pubeja!* No pubs in the Soviet Union!'

Oh, marvellous, I had groaned. Thirst is the curse of the drinking classes. Exactly what we need when First Secretary Gorbachev is trying to bludgeon all his countrymen into laying off the vodka. Undoubtedly their neighbours' papers would be scanned in Moscow. Finnish friends we'd shown the article to had giggled happily and said it was very well written, but knowing by now their talent for humour, the comments were no help at all.

Perhaps Stan and Ollie here could do us a good turn, I thought doubtfully, by giving us a straight professional opinion?

'Cheers, cheers.' We clinked tumblers in *Canna*'s suddenly small saloon, and Jaako's extremely generous rolls of good feeding wobbled in sympathy with his gestures as he embarked on a virtuoso performance.

'He was asking me what I was thinking about it,' he intoned in a lugubrious gravelly voice to his blond straight man, who said next to nothing. 'And I told him that there was something strange about the feeling having read the article. Something *odd*,' he emphasized, even more slowly and sepulchrally, turning to me.

'That article was written so that, in my mind, the person who wrote it had in his or her mind something odd or strange in your trip . . . because you are the first boat from say, the western hemisphere, which have sailed through Helsinki to Leningrad which *haven't* got anything odd in their minds. Because for instance *religion* is one very good reason why people are trying to sail in Leningrad . . .'

'Religion?' we echoed, completely lost.

'Yes, with *bibles*. Yes, believe me,' he growled. 'Yes. They have been flying for instance with ball*oons* over Finnish border, exporting bibles, and the Russian border guards . . . degga degga degga . . .' His elbows jerked heavily into his guts as he fought to control the machine gun blasting away through the saloon hatch at the offending blimp overhead . . . 'degga degga degga . . . whoooooooooooooooooo,' as he followed the whistling descent of its remains, 'whamn! Millions of bibles, good *Lord*!' he exclaimed, gazing around the saloon floor in amazement.

We nearly bent down to help him gather them up.

'Ha, ha, ha. *Ha, ha, ha*,' he roared, his spare tyres threatening to get completely out of hand as I flushed with a surplus of understanding.

'So what you're saying is it was strange because there was *nothing* strange?'

'That's *exactly* it,' he said.

What a charmer! He'd given us a fright, followed by precisely the assurance we'd hoped for, and had managed to poke fun at our overblown anxieties and those of the Russians all at once.

The hilarity was curtailed by the sound of a launch arriving and a call of 'Yakt *Canna*!' A serious-looking military man stepped out on to the pier beside us.

'Meester Fox-all. We have some news about your intentions for Russia.'

'Yes?' I said, tightly.

'You must cross the border between buoys 15 and 16 . . . there, and there. Then it will be quite all right.'

I felt tongue-tied as we briefly shook hands. 'Well, thank you for everything, Finland,' I thought. 'We're even more deeply impressed. You're spirited, practical, kind, efficient and friendly and amusing too. You've given us everything we could possibly have hoped for. You've passed us on to a place you can't normally get to this way, with the very best of goodwill. Would the Russian bear give as warm a hug? Should he do so, we shan't forget you.

As the guard undemonstratively turned away, the afternoon sunlight enriched the familiar shades of sienna and umber on the houses and boat sheds. Rupert and Alan staggered down the jetty with the last few containers of drinking water. It was very nearly time to leave.

Tomorrow we'd swing our trailing leg across to the opposite bank, to Russia.

CHAPTER 7

Crossing the Border

'Kotka Radio. Do you read me? Kotka Radio, Yacht *Canna*.' Other shipping traffic gatecrashed our call in a blast of static, and we waited for it to clear. The VHF station was on the Finnish coast, barely 15 miles away, but our system did not always transmit sufficiently strongly across intervening land. I signalled to Alan to shut off the engine to reduce background noise.

'Kotka Radio, Yacht *Canna*. We are now departing Haapasaari harbour by the east entrance. We are heading towards the southern boundary as directed by the coastguards. We expect to make a report at the Leningradskiy buoy to Inflot Leningrad at approx. 08.00 hours tomorrow 16th, Russian time.'

'OK. Standby, standby . . . ' came the response, urgent and clipped.

Before I even had time to consider if it were possible, the operator offered a call to the shipping agents in Leningrad. That would be a tremendous boon – we had had no contact with the Russian authorities since Susan's last telexes in early June.

I glanced around as we waited. It was nearly noon by local time, overcast and quiet, with a gentle easterly breeze I hoped would go round to the north. It would need to. In the end we had cut it a bit fine, having allowed just less than 20 hours to reach the pilot station nearly 100 miles away. If the wind went against us, we might not make it. Shay was beside me, cameras to hand. Alan, Rupert and Susan were above in the cockpit, expectant and eager. Beyond them, as the boat lolled, the horizon tilted this way and that, a green and grey-blue strip of islands overlapping interminably. There was open sea ahead of us, but across it lay the Russian border, barely five miles distant. Now was the moment of truth.

'Yacht *Canna*, go ahead please.'

A different voice sparked through the clutter, very heavily accented. It could have said, 'Inflot Leningrad.'

'Good morning, this is Irish yacht *Canna*, I spell, Charlie-Alpha-November-November-Alpha. Over.'

'Indeed.' A very long pause. Then slowly, 'Yacht *Canna*.'

They read us! By now everyone was crowding toward the saloon, leaning in from the cockpit.

'Inflot Leningrad, yes, correct. We are on a goodwill cruise to Baltic countries. We are leaving Finland at 13.00 hours today and entering Soviet waters at that time. We are expecting to make the call to harbourmaster Leningrad at approximately 08.00 hours tomorrow, over.'

'Understood. You expect to leave Finland about 13.00 hours . . .'

He sounded young and steady and pleasant, but it took about five minutes to sort out our time of arrival. As I was transmitting 08.00 they were hearing 6 pm. With patience and lots of zeros, we finally got it right.

'Yes, Leningrad, correct. As you may be aware, we have a berth reservation with you, and the necessary visas and authorizations.'

'Understood. You have all necessary visas . . .' he said, signing off.

'Well, we're definitely expected!' Alan laughed, and immediately fired the engine. Within seconds we were making our usual six knots.

'OK,' I called, 'let's sail her too!' but I needn't have bothered. There were already crew at the halyards and cleats. To starboard, the plain concrete pillar and white lantern of Veitkari lighthouse, Haapasaari's south-eastern sentry, motored by a cable away. A little fragment of land flew by to port and a bigger chunk, Kilpis, trundled behind it. The miniature archipelago shuffled away into the distance behind us like a motley herd heading home for the night, their fading brown humps turning slowly to blue. It seemed now that we might finally reap the reward of our nine months of effort.

We had already reached one of the geographical limits of the cruise – Haapasaari had been the most northerly point at 60°15'. Leningrad, assuming we got there, would be the furthest east. Now, as *Canna* heeled a bit more, Rupert set the self-steering, adjusting the pivoting vane to the wind and the engine was gratefully cancelled. We neared the border heading south-east; but at the crucial moment light rain fell, the first for weeks, shrouding the frontier buoys we needed.

Canna pushed on regardless toward the invisible five-mile gap; and at 14.50 on 15 July, we hoisted the hammer and sickle. In Soviet waters at last! – but there was nothing special, no line in the water, no fringe of boats nor even a change of light; only the rain clouds lifting all round and ripples as far as the eye could see.

We toasted ourselves with a bottle of wine, proud and elated to have got so far. There were only about 90 miles to go, and surely nothing could now prevent us?

Or could it? We began to puzzle as we pressed on further, and still there was nothing at all to see. We were trespassing in a tribal wood, and I'd expected to meet some natives. One mile, two, and not a thing stirred. An hour went by, three miles, then nearly four, and still no sign of the Navy. They couldn't be far away, but where? we wondered, scanning ahead.

'There's something behind us!' Rupert called out and ten eyes swivelled to encounter an apparition. He hadn't said 'boat' because two small feathers sped inward from the horizon, a white one beneath and a brown above it, keeping pace with a potent and tiny gap between them. We watched the unnerving sight in suspense, until realizing that the high-speed hen was going full throttle, and showing nothing but bow-wave and smoke. We held our course, and she held hers, closing in with us quickly. A mile perhaps, then a half or less, and a hint of grey appearing. I hoped some official had told them about us, and that we'd get our signals right. The engines roared a crescendo and died, her wash dissolved as she settled and dwarfed us, less than 50 yards away.

'Dip the ensign!' I called to Shay at the backstay, although I couldn't see hers. There were big black numbers on grey steel, a sharp overhanging bow, domed gun-turrets, sharper machine guns, and a high-flying bridge with grey-clad officers at the controls. A line of ratings leaned on the rails. We stood and waved, but no one responded. They gave us no signal to stop or to go, nothing came through on the radio. Through binoculars we found ourselves looking down theirs, and I swore I could see their eyeballs (blue). That did it, it seemed; we stared for long moments and then, soon after, with engines restarted, they sheered away.

'I hope they're more talkative in Leningrad,' burst out Alan, but at least the matter-of-fact inspection confirmed that we had passed muster.

Our last few shreds of apprehension were garnered by the patrol boat, and in no time at all they had vanished with her beyond the horizon. Soon there was nothing ahead of us except one or two groups of stiff little men walking flattened dogs along the sea's rim, the masts, cranes and containers of ships whose connecting hulls we couldn't yet see; and suddenly released, the sense of our unique situation, needle-sharp since Haapasaari, seemed to widen and deepen and take in all our surroundings. In that early afternoon, sights and sounds leapt out at us warmer and stronger. The bows rose and fell with a long-legged lope, and a luscious and endless gurgle. A steady wind moaned and whined round the forestay, filling the bulging genoa with power, and as the pulpit leaned and lunged onwards the stanchion-tops fluted a two-tone song. I lay on the foredeck a few extra moments, soaking it up and gazing into the sky.

Sailing is an ideal way, I reflected, to make the transition from country to country. It gave time to get one's thoughts in order, and here, particularly, it was as though the 200-foot depth of water sluicing under the keel was washing away any doubtful opinions of our destination gleaned over the last few weeks, and leaving our next hosts a clean slate to write on. I felt ready, now, for what we might find.

The rest of the crew sounded buoyant, too. Snatches of talk drifted forward from the cockpit as if from a neighbouring room. I sensed we were going to enjoy the next few hours and weeks, and would remember them for a very long time.

*   *   *

'That's far too darned close, for goodness' sake, Rupert! And I'd asked you to call me.'

The blue-hulled tanker was crossing our bows, only a few hundred yards away. There was no danger now, but there might have been sooner when either of us could have made a false move. She was westbound from Russia in the shipping lane, and it was we who had to keep out of her way.

My fault, of course. Bouts of euphoria had had that effect before. I'd only ever crashed a vehicle when I'd been feeling really happy. To do with loss of concentration, no doubt, and I had deserted the navigation a few moments too long. But we had to concentrate from here on in. We had left behind the graded scatter of Finland's myriad islands; now, beyond the brief interlude of open water, we were heading towards the rather different hazards of the Estonian coast's much larger, looser, more rangy islands, and the far-flung banks of shoaling ground, marked on the charts with a funereal clutter of crosses. Although the girth of this bulge in the Gulf was more than 65 miles, the widest gap between scraps of land was less than ten. Our route around them formed a series of dog-legs to bring us to Leningrad Bay. We had rehearsed it so often on the charts we felt as if we could walk it, and we soon found that *Canna*'s promenade on through Russian waters, through the late afternoon and the night, mingled all the vivid and graven impact of a child's first voyage to school with the enchantment of a pop-up book and the strangeness of a dream.

It took another half-hour to cross the ships' dual-carriageway; first the west-going lane a full mile wide, then the east, and the central reservation between them shaded in purple. We looked left, then right, then right again, avoiding further alarums, and turned to port on the further foot-path. The weather looked on kindly. As we struck our new course east, the wind backed north and allowed us to sail it and, just when the pilotage became tricky, sunlight and visibility sharpened. Now we were navigating between the scrapyards of shoals and rocks to starboard, some fenced out of bounds by dotted lines on the charts, and the clearway to port that pedestrian boats like ours were supposed to keep out of.

After skirting a watery roundabout, complete with a floating central lamppost, where shipping to Vyborg and Leningrad parted, we clipped the north-side beacon of the sunken Maschnye Bank, then the corner of a deep water prohibited area, throwing a tack of a few yards to clear it. By late afternoon, *Canna* was edging south-east down a tapering passage, with occasional shipping to port and another invisible bank to starboard, littered with dangerous boulders. I thought of the Pilot's warnings and shuddered, seeing it all in gales and fog.

'28°15′E,' stated Decca, but it had now to be read with a handful of salt. We had been getting spectacular results, to within 100 yards or less, with the instrument locked on to one of the groups of stations that are scattered over much of Europe, but there were none in Russia or Poland. The Finnish chain it was obliged to select had only two slave stations instead of the usual three. The further east we went, the narrower the angle between the signals, and the greater the inaccuracy. Already the gadget confessed it was uncertain of itself by 1½ miles, and steadily getting worse. It was crucial, instead, to watch out for the buoys, the bollards that marked the shallow water. We entered their details and time as they passed, together with the distance, read from the traditional spinner-type log trailing from our stern.

'21.22. North Cardinal. Bank Nagayeva,' yelled Susan. 'Log 99.6.'

'That's nearly 1,800 miles so far,' I called back, adding in the hundreds. 'But where's the next one? It ought to be there, black and yellow.'

Ostrov Seskar, low and wooded, crowded in on our starboard bow. It was foul all round, shoaling for miles in places, but the spot where the buoy should have been came and went. It was missing completely until, scanning for the reefs it marked, we found it aboard a maintenance ship far in under the cliffs.

Now, in the dusk, the alleyway narrowed all the time, as the outliers of the three-mile-long island edged us into turbulent water and squeezed us against the shipping lane. At the very end, on Alan's watch, a cruise liner passed us very close, her tumbling wash lit by strings of lights; and beyond her, the very last marks of the channel came up, as we shot out from our straitened tunnel into a broad piazza.

Here again we would head due east, picking our way in freedom across the 30-mile space, or following, if we wanted to, the straight line marked by the safe-water lampposts, almost exactly an hour's sailing apart. The light of Seskar's western lighthouse was already only a loom, and her eastern twin swung a slow double beam across us for a while, until that too faded, sinking into a bank of cloud.

That final night was memorable. It wasn't really night at all, but a sort of mystical mongrel. For a festival month in midsummer, Leningrad never goes dark, and in mid-July her White Nights still lingered on. Dusk thickened and hovered but dark never came. Everything swirled in a Van Gogh confusion, the sails and the sea and ripples and stars, the clouds and suspicions of distant land, playing grandmother's footsteps in the corners of our eyes.

Sleeping in my gear, I dozed on and off through the short half-night, always waking to the wide-eyed blue stare of the cabin windows, and the rolling crimson orb of the compass glaring back through the galley porthole as we checked the course. I was used to their baleful presences, and the yellow pool of light on the chart that kept them at bay as our track line crept forward from hour to hour, but we never knew what to expect in the twilight beyond. Nothing was ever what it seemed and nothing appeared in the same place twice.

Sometimes beacons reared alongside, nodding and ghostly in red and white stripes, their number momentarily visible. In an instant they vanished, leaving their flashing light pinned to the sky like a low-flying aircraft. Alan had watched a high green light gyrate towards us for minutes on end. An unlikely and very handsome yawl sketched itself in beneath, just long enough for the crew to inspect us and call over something we couldn't quite catch.

'Two flares, come quickly!' was Shay's last reveille but, by the time I was up, there was nothing to see. I returned to a solid and sensible dream of sunlit farmland and trees.

The thrill of landing on a foreign shore! There's nothing to beat the anticipation of that first glimpse and cry of 'land', the slow edging forward, the changing light, uncertainty and wonder and doubt all crystallized in a bluish outline.

And now, at daybreak, here it was! We were still close-hauled and heeling gently, heading straight for Leningrad Bay, the last bottle-neck in the Gulf of Finland, between the Stirsudden and Ustinsky headlands, barely 15 miles apart; and here, suddenly, where centuries before the Russians had valiantly held off the Swedes with light rowing frigates of 40 guns, there were now upended dominoes guarding the land each side and flashing a domino mixture of signs.

It was more or less as we had intended. 'ETA PILOT STATION 16.7, 08.00,' we'd telexed in the frantic days before our departure – a dawn arrival to locate the lighthouses before the low coastal landmarks were lost in daylight. Now here they were – but what were we to expect? Imagination was free to drift in the strange limbo between sighting and securing, before real life set in again, and it had had nothing much to guide it. All the previous day we had been agog, watching scraps of land drift past with insatiable curiosity. There had been the tiny knoll of Ostrov Sommers with a few blind-eyed, barrack-like houses on top; Ostrov Malyy far away; and Seskar, locked in a forbidden zone, which had turned a bland and wooded shoulder. Its church and villages could hardly be seen, its low cliffs and forests had darkened into a cool collusion and stealthily tiptoed away. Even their navigational marks of slatted timbers in iron frames had told us no more than the sketches in the pilot books. Was this, I wondered, what we would find? Everything transformed to three dimensions, but swinging past us imperviously, as remote and untouchable as if we were locked in a space ship?

By 3.30 am, the light was colder, and grey. 'Anchoring and fishing prohibited', stated the chart. 'West limit of Kronstadt fortified zone.' It all seemed lonely and bleak and chill, and I shivered, sharing the daybreak watch with Rupert.

'What's that?' I shot at him, pointing ahead at a shadow that hadn't been there.

'Yachts,' he said.

Two yachts, heading exactly toward us, and running before the wind! Reckoning we've an hour in hand in our schedule, we lean on the tiller in a fit of delight and swing *Canna* across in front of their bows, spilling wind till they come up astern. Two modern-looking cruiser-racers, sailing head to tail. They're closing and closing – we can see their crew, four or five men in each boat. *Ydaya*, reads the nearer one, but can't say much more over the gap of language and distance. Instead, they stand in the cockpit, giving us a triumphal, clenched, overhead salute, beneath the Russian ensign. What a welcome! We jump on the deck and shout and wave back, exhilarated by the reception. 'No photography till we're in,' I had said, but just can't hold back and break the rule, grabbing a camera from Shay.

But having finally wrenched away, and closed toward the pilot station, Susan, as seemed to be her wont, laced the drama with farce.

'There's something I think you should know,' she said, when we had the cockpit to ourselves. 'There's a dubious magazine below, and I'm wondering what to do with it.'

My God, here was a problem! The customs, I knew, would go mad if they saw it. Bibles by comparison would be very small beer. We had to get rid of it somehow, but how? Burn it in the stove? There wasn't time, it probably wouldn't, we'd arrive like a floating Vatican chimney. Overboard? It would probably stay intact for ages.

'Go and get it,' I ordered, like Captain Bligh.

There was only one other thing to do, and with grand irrationality I stood on the afterdeck, tearing off sheets and throwing them over the stern.

'Don't *read* it, for God's sake!' Susan stormed, assuming vicarious pleasure. Certainly, the acreage of pink and brown flesh was enormous. The more I ripped and crumpled, the more there seemed to be. But would the stuff soften and sink? Not likely! The more I crumpled, the less it complied. The printer had been just as liberal with ink as the photographer with his exposures. The assorted pudenda perched on the surface like a string of brazen birds, squawking and pointing back towards us. When the deed was done, we revved a bit harder and glanced around. Had anyone been watching? We were still several miles from the nearest land, but a livid orange ship nearby was steadily getting closer and closer.

'Good morning!' said a man in a smart brown suit, with a smile, a twinkle and a small black case. 'I am Andrej.'

It had been the pilot ship at anchor, of course, but very much bigger than we'd expected. Our final burst of speed had brought us to it by eight on the dot. At first I'd taken it for a small 'dangerous liquids' tanker waiting for a pilot itself, but the mistake became obvious from the permanent gangway down each side, and the sturdy launch with three men aboard, putting out to meet us.

We shook our first Russian hand very warmly.

Before the advent of detailed charts, it used to be common to buy local knowledge, as *Ierne*'s owner Commodore Graves had done in 1862:

'A prudent precaution is to provide oneself with a good pilot, obtainable at about £10 per month at Copenhagen or Stockholm. They generally speak English and are useful as interpreters.'

In fact, Graves had engaged a Copenhagen pilot for the whole voyage, who joined *Ierne* in Scotland. It seems to have been the best way to go about it; Martin and Corrigan, by contrast, had had perpetual difficulties from Norway onwards as they picked up pilots from port to port.

'Twenty-five dols = £6 or so, a good deal for his 3 days work . . . He said he could bring us no further than the entrance. We said we had agreed with him and would have no other . . . the beggar did not understand English very well . . . I wanted to heave him overboard at once,' fumed Corrigan, at last, in south Sweden, losing his cool completely. Perhaps his 'fizzing red beard' had been part of the problem. Fortunately mine was of quieter hue, and it certainly didn't look as though we would have any such provocation.

Andrej was a straight, sprightly, fresh-faced man in middle age, with crinkly hair, good English and an easy manner. I had never had a pilot on *Canna*, nor had Andrej been on a sailing yacht, but we soon sorted it out.

'A colleague of mine does much sailing on Ladoga Lake,' he said. 'This would be holidays for him' – although he seemed to enjoy it equally, firmly taking the tiller, from which he couldn't be parted for the next five hours and more, and agreeing with enthusiasm to our suggestion of motor-sailing. He refused bacon and eggs, accepted coffee, and occasionally rummaged in his case for spectacles, but as we heeled and picked up extra speed against the breeze freshening from the direction of the still invisible city, cooler now than at any time since Sweden, it was obvious he'd made one major misjudgement. His smart suit and polished leather shoes were nicely judged for a heated bridge-deck, but in our open cockpit, Andrej was turning blue. In between buoys and passing traffic, we loaded him with woollies and wellies and wet gear, until he had almost doubled in size. There was still a good distance to go – the pilot station is 25 miles out – and we didn't want to deliver a corpse to the agents.

*　　　　*　　　　*

We were now in very historic waters. Two miles away on our port beam was Tolbukhin lighthouse, a sturdy round tower more than 100 feet high, linked to a keeper's house by a gallery on stilts. Ahead was Kronstadt, Russia's principal Baltic navy base for nearly 300 years. It was here that the British expeditionary fleet of 1854–5 anchored, under the command of Sir Charles Napier, aiming to blockade the Tsar's fleet into harbour as tit-for-tat for the Russian campaigns in the Black Sea. The effort had had very little success, due to the Russian's new-fangled steam-engined tugs, used to tow their sailing ships out of trouble; and their invention of heavy defensive mines, weighing almost a quarter of a ton, which the British described as 'infernal machines'.

All the same, it was amazing that, barely four years later, the crew of the *Oriana* could sail in, be received kindly by Russian naval officers, and chat companionably about the Crimean campaigns and the cost of cannon-balls. Warfare was certainly a more gentlemanly procedure in those times, to the extent that some of Napier's officers even had their wives on board.

Commerce also played a big role in the turn-round. By the time *Ierne* arrived from the Mersey in 1862, the Russians had already struck a substantial deal with the English to upgrade their fleet. Graves reported that Kronstadt was then littered with timber ships, in a state of dismember-ment, and that: 'Messrs Mitchells & Co. of Newcastle upon Tyne have been instructed to convert the dockyards of St Petersburg. Steam engines and other machines of most modern construction have been sent from Manchester and London. Mitchells have also undertaken to build some of the armour-plated war steamers required for the Russian Navy . . .'

Less than 60 years later, the British were back again, to destroy or cripple the fleet they had previously built up. In 1919, it was a much smaller but more resourceful expedition, following on from the joint European, Japanese and American invasion which tried to throttle the Bolshevik Revolution in its infancy. At that time, a British fleet was attempting to secure the new-found independence of the Baltic Republics, Estonia and Latvia, and Lenin was having difficulty with pockets of resistance near Leningrad. The famous revolt of the extreme left-wing Kronstadt sailors had already been put down, and the fortress and the Navy were firmly in the hands of the Reds. In mid-June their battleships, including the cruiser *Oleg*, were bombarding the fortress of Krasnaya Gorka, held by White Russians a few miles away on the southern shore.

Captain Augustus Agar and his colleagues, working from a disused yacht harbour in Finland, near the Russian border, with small motor torpedo-boats, struck the *Oleg* and sank her. Over the few months before and after that action, his team made more than a dozen sorties, running secret agents to and from Leningrad by skimming at high speed over the breakwaters between the forts to the north of Kronstadt during the short nights. Finally they mounted a spectacular direct assault on the Russian fleet, in the harbours of Kronstadt itself. Seven MTBs were used for that mission, some of which were lost to collisions among themselves and to Russian shelling, but the result of the Baltic Raid was two Russian battleships and one destroyer sunk, and another cruiser damaged.

There were several extraordinary features to the whole episode. In his earlier activities, Agar had acted very much on his own initiative: arming his boats with torpedoes, although his initial instructions had been for intelligence work only; arriving in eastern Finland masquerading as a civilian, and changing into naval uniform when afloat; attacking the *Oleg* without specific instructions. His actions then attracted retrospective approval, and were so politically fraught that the details were kept secret for decades and not incorporated into any official naval history.

Now, in this teat-end of the Gulf, less than 15 miles wide, we were almost exactly where the *Oleg* had sunk. Krasnaya Gorka was away on our starboard quarter, marked by a 200-foot lighthouse on the low grey coast. Terioiki, once Agar's base, was just barely discernible as the township of Zelenogorsk on the opposite shore. Kronstadt itself, on its strategic central island, Ostrov Kotlin, was looming very close on our port bow. The tapered island, about six miles by one, was pancake-flat, bristling with masts at one end like a worn-out toothbrush, and heavily overbalanced by the town of Kronstadt at the other, with the sharp spire of its Cathedral rising above the dockyard buildings and banks of trees.

'The channel then grew very narrow and the tide ran rather strong,' commented Corrigan, who was forced to admit that here at least a pilot was essential. 'We had to steer between vessels only about double our beam apart.' Nothing much seemed to have changed: we too were being squeezed across towards Kronstadt by smaller islands and forts to starboard. And it was just as easy to see our route – Andrej was amused and amazed to find himself for once being threatened by the enormous, heavy steel buoys, green to starboard, red to port, looming overhead, instead of trying to pick them out as small specks from the wing bridge of a ship; and, as predicted by the Russian skippers in Norrköping, we had to keep carefully between them. There was less than four foot of water outside the buoys in places, a dredger tanker was overtaking us at speed, and a ferry launch nipped smartly across the channel ahead. The *Oriana* had rammed and half sunk a small boat attempting the same manoeuvre; we had no wish to recreate that particular incident, and were perfectly happy for Andrej to have the helm, especially as, between bouts of concentration, he still had time to point out the sights. All six of us crowded the cockpit, and *Canna* was down by the stern.

'Over there,' he said, indicating a tall, isolated warehouse, 'four war

research scientists were kept under very tight security. On starboard – yes?
Is right? – an old arsenal. It was shelled. Exploded. Everyone killed.'

The hulk of masonry yawned with gappy, brick-arched mouths and eyes
on several floors, a gruesome monument.

The distant town of Lomonosov poked out beyond it, the only place on
that southern shore not overrun by the Germans in World War II, being
under the cover of Kronstadt's guns.

A few minutes more, and we were passing the harbour entrances
themselves, close to port, where even now the basins, as they swung by,
were full of ships: grey, white and cream, studded with turrets, revolving
radars and satellite dishes, still packed in tight ranks under the arched and
slated stone buildings around the main square. One or two were on the
move. A patrol boat to starboard was grappling with lines to a mooring
buoy.

'We got up to the Russian fleet about 12 o'c noon,' recorded Corrigan.
'Passing under their sterns we dipped the Ensign to each of them. None of
them minded it altho' there were numbers of officers on all their poops,
except the Admiral's ship, a 3 decker. The officers on her poop clapped their
hands and took off their caps for us. I suppose they are not allowed to cheer
and then they dipped their ensign 3 times which we answered.'

'Should we do the same?' we enquired of Andrej.

'No, no, not necessary!' he said, flattening a deprecating palm.

We waved instead, and across the space of more than a century, received
a few waves and a volley of cheers.

We were now as far as most of the old sailing-ships had been able to go.
Somewhere here at this cluttered east end of Kotlin there had been a bar of
mud and sand, with a moored light-vessel displaying a depth board. A hefty
20-rouble fine was levied on any ships that stuck. The depth in 1859 had
been around eight feet, so the *Oriana* which drew 11 feet, couldn't attempt
it; but it was nine and three-quarters when the *Ierne* arrived, and she was
able to make it to St Petersburg with a few inches to spare. Corrigan
opined: 'I don't think Petersburgh or Cronstadt will ever be any good as
ports, especially after railways are made to Riga and Revel.' But he had
reckoned without new machinery. The Morskoy Canal, built 20 or 30 years
later is now regularly dredged to about 40 feet, and shipping of all kinds
goes right up to the city; we too sailed on, leaving our distant friends in the
Oriana at anchor amongst a forest of masts. But Agar's exploits, we saw,
would not be possible now.

As *Canna* set herself to the dead straight run of 14 miles, the old line of
fortresses north-east of Kronstadt opened up for the first time. Along with
a massive bridge, they were now mere incidents on a seven-mile-long
causeway: part of a flood barrier, Andrej explained, to guard Leningrad
from the Baltic surges. The work had been going on for years, and would

take many more to complete. In time there'd be a gate where we'd just passed through.

Now that we could again keep outside the beacons, which popped up every mile and a half, Andrej relaxed. He explained the traffic as it passed – huge strings of barges labouring into the city, carrying sand dredged up from the bed of the bay, for use in building work. Ice-breakers with up to 35,000 horsepower, which could demolish ice more than two feet thick, to keep the winter channels open. As he opened up to us more, spot-lighting patches in his career, the sky opened too, and shafts of sun chased across the yellow-brown water and the vermilion buoys. For years, Andrej had been a pilot in the Merchant Navy and, during that time, had once berthed in Belfast. For four months he'd served on a sail-training ship in the Black Sea. His family was from the Ukraine, where he went for his holidays. He liked it better there; he found Leningrad just too big for comfort. It took him an hour to get from home to the shore-base by tram; then he was stationed at the pilot ship for 24 hours at a stretch. For every day on, he had three days off (which seemed a fairly good deal); he had a daughter, a son training as a ship's radio officer, of whom he was obviously proud, and almost certainly a wife too, but enquiries in that direction were parried with a shrug and a smile.

By now we had nosed well beyond the piazza, and in to the porch of Peter the Great. His monuments of nearly three centuries ago were closing all around us, including the summer palace of Petrodvorets, which Andrej pointed out under the sun, its gilt domes gleaming over a fringe of trees. It was one of the Tsar's most outstanding creations, and a place we badly wanted to visit. Started as a resting place for him when waiting there in bad weather to be ferried out to supervise the building of Kronstadt, it had first comprised only a 'cottage'. This was reckoned to be not quite good enough and, in any case, he'd probably had enough of making do (his first three-roomed house in Leningrad he built with his own hands) so, over the next 20 years, Peter had erred in the other direction, and covered vast acres of the gently sloping shore with a wild profusion of nymphs and fountains, menageries and monuments, cascades and conservatories, pavilions and palaces, scores of them, terraced and gilded and painted on a scale which only he seemed to encompass. Now, it was a superb public park and museum; but, in his own time, Peter had become very fond of the main Summer Palace, and particularly of the Marine Study in his private apartments, from which he would direct naval operations with signals, or simply watch ships, where we were now sailing, by telescope. He had even installed a dock and canal for direct connection with the sea.

Activities at Petrodvorets had been spectacular: in 1834, anonymous sailors aboard their yacht, *Reindeer*, the earliest of any visiting British yachtsmen we'd traced, had gone ashore by invitation to celebrate Tsar

Nicholas I's birthday (they'd been presented a week before), reporting in a later account, 'immense crowds of people, a fine evening, plenty of bands playing.

'At about ten o'clock a rocket went up, and immediately upwards of 1,500 men were in motion lighting up the lamps. In an astonishingly short space of time, the gardens as if by magic were one blaze of light – the effect of the illuminations with the water works was brilliant – the gardens were as large as twenty Vauxhalls. After much doubting we decided not to go to the Bal Masqué at the Palace for which we were provided with Dominoes [costumes] as all the mob seemed there – from after twelve the Imperial Family drove around the Gardens in twenty Irish jaunting cars.' After this, the visitors made a suitably stylish exit by water.

'Could *Canna* visit?' we enquired of Andrej.

'Maybe,' he answered, 'but if not allowed, you can take one of these,' and pointed out the hydrofoil tourist launches.

Unnoticed, we had closed with the hydrofoils' diagonal track. Known simply as Meteors, they were soon hurtling past us fore and aft at 35 miles an hour or more, huge aluminium bullets about 100 feet long, standing clear of the water on wafer-thin legs like water-skiers, straining forward, their crew peering down from a raking windscreen as if from a supersonic plane. They were plying to and from the city in a continuous stream, kicking up huge sheaths of spray as their raking prop-shafts ploughed the water, jetting up plumes of dirty brown smoke, and leaving gallons of unburnt diesel behind them in the sky.

'A bit expensive,' Andrej murmured. 'Perhaps is better you go by train.'

In the last leg of the canal, between low, crumbling walls of stone, sprouting bushes and wiry grass, the city began to swell and grow. We began to see what Andrej complained of. Vague bluish outlines remorselessly lifted and startlingly jumped into scale. The ramparts of flats that stretched for miles either side of the bows were not the modest affairs they had seemed, but 10- or 12-storey giants, striped with stacks of balconies and gleaming pillars of windows. They climaxed right in the centre, over our nose, where older buildings pushed up cones and spires. Slowly they spread to engulf us; from the ground beneath, dockside cranes in various colours reared up like fern-stems, until their heads overhung us and we reached a final bifurcation under a concrete sign like a petrol station logo fifty times too big. 'ЛЕНИНГРАД' it stated in red.

Andrej made a dive for the radio. Something was obviously slightly amiss. A lot of shouting in Russian followed.

'I think we wait here,' he said, indicating a lay-by. 'Big ship coming down, no room.'

It passed almost as soon as we dropped sail, a white Swedish cruise ship lined with miniature passengers peeping down from twice the height of our mast. We were now obviously an object of some amazement. The crews of ships and barges that passed had watched until we were out of sight. Now, over the black and green and rusty flanks of assorted cargo ships, Bulgarian, Cuban, French, and Russian, with rudders as big as our deck, crews stopped for a moment or two, pulled off their gloves to wave, or just peered down at the unlikely white ant creeping under their flanks. We returned their surprise with apprehension. Painters' scaffold hung above us, cranes slewed wide, dangling grabs and chains. If anything fell from such a height, it would go straight through us from top to bottom. At least the tiny dockers had helmets. The safest bet was under a brand-new satellite-tracking ship, white enamelled like a piece of kitchen hardware, thick with revolving gadgets, but there was to be no lingering. Still two miles to go.

Tension began to build again. What would we find beyond this cluttered channel? To port was a half deserted strip of ground carrying an incongruous classical building set among trees and piles of coke. Where it tailed out, Andrej handed back the tiller.

'Do we have full speed?' he asked, assuming a stiff professional stance.

'River Neva runs out here, very strong current,' he warned. 'I want you to cross it – between those two beacons.'

The river splits into a short delta west of the city, branching between islands which form the docks. We were crossing the main branch, more than a quarter of a mile wide. The far bank crabbed towards us, complete with a power-station and coal-stacks; and beyond them stood a curious cubical contraption, with rows of grey mascara'd eyelids under a slender spire.

'The Passenger Terminal,' Andrej beamed, with the sound of a satisfied man.

I was totally horrified. Under the strange grey building were piles and a concrete wharf. A worm at the back of my mind had worried it might be something like this, intended only for ships, and the departing liner had left it brutally empty. The sheer concrete barely reached down to our decks, below it were sucking sheets of steel. Black fenders the size of ten garden rollers were chained to the wall at the height of our chests.

'We can't possibly tie up here,' I protested, my expectations gone suddenly cold. Two thousand miles, and nowhere to moor!

Alan, Susan and Rupert were already momentarily frozen with fenders and warps in their hands. Above us hovered a group of mainly uniformed men.

'Perhaps you go at the end here, Kapitan,' said Andrej, but the words were lurched from his mouth by the wash of a passing tug. He had to agree the walls were untenable, but could offer no other ideas.

To our enormous relief, the difficulty was resolved fairly quickly. Nosing into a small bay behind the wharf, we spotted a forgotten flight of steps.

'Right. Fenders to starboard. Rupert and Shay, stand by to throw lines.'

Everyone jumped into action. As we inched alongside, the officials clattered down, and a bronze-suited man leaned over to greet us, introducing himself as the shipping agent even before I had killed the engine.

'Gennady Khabarov,' he said.

The formalities went by in less than an hour, spun out only slightly by smokes and coffee and multiple layers of carbon paper. The khaki men were customs, the grey ones immigration. Obviously in a hurry, they had swarmed over the rails and down the hatch while the embarrassed Andrej was still urging me to sign his pilot certificate. They tapped their fingers, and shot a few sharp questions as he left. Then, crammed into opposite rows at the saloon table, they parked their caps and ploughed through the papers with occasional grunts and frowns of mild exasperation. Crew lists in quintuplet, stamped all round. Visas scrutinized. A list of cargo, which amounted to nothing. Lists of money. Alan and Shay were perched on steps and shelves, Rupert and Susan were blocked in the forward cabin. I riffled through hundreds of single dollars, the result of advice from a Polish friend. Gennady intoned the refrain 'no problem'. No customs search, no interest at all in the duty-free, no concern about Shay's cameras.

'What about film?' he pressed, amazed. 'Are there any restrictions?'

'You can bring in a million if you want to,' they said.

Gennady apologized for everyone else's procedures, and then produced his berthing report, which capped them and finally broke the ice.

'Ship's name, and length, no problem, all usual,' he said, as I diligently began to write in the answers. He snatched it back with a grin as soon as I got stuck.

'Question 5: How many tugs you need. Two? Maybe three?' The cabin dissolved into laughter.

'And this one. "How many tons of water?" I think with a few litres more you will sink,' he said, looking incredulously at our low freeboard. 'You don't bother. All these questions. We just put something sensible. You're tired now. We will give you all help you want later, tomorrow.'

The only thing that temporarily threw him was our lack of a de-ratification cert confirming that all *Canna*'s rodents were purged. We were to hear more about it later. For now, the thrill of clearing our last hurdle was overwhelming. Belatedly, as the officials clattered away, dazed with the effort and the whirl of the day's impressions, we entered the log for the last time on the eastward journey: '16 July: 13.41: 1,890 MILES: 1,025 MILLIBARS: BERTHED LENINGRAD.'

Apart from a few details on the dock, nearly everything was grey. Grey concrete, grey water. The hotel window-hoods above were sheathed in grey aluminium. Opposite, long anonymous buildings, all of concrete and glass, and panoramas of tarmac. But the sky was neither leaden nor heavy; the early evening was high and quiet, as if waiting for something to happen. Solitary, too: the rest of the crew had long since disappeared, except Susan who was sleeping. And beyond the immediate bounds was a suspicion of city noise and a hint of foliage.

Up and out and along the wharf; but in the Terminal building the passport guard had gone away, and the bank was already closed. Damn! I'd forgotten to change any money. The Intourist office was closing too, but Nina, a large lively lady in black, insisted on giving me kopecks. She wouldn't hear of me paying them back. Beyond another set of swing doors I voyaged solo across the pale grey car-park, steering for distant telephone kiosks. Nothing else moved until I reached the further shore, beyond the ambit of maritime life; and there, suddenly, transmissions began in sound and colour. I was on the edge of a busy road with a central lawn and beds of flowers. Far away there were blue and yellow buses approaching. A few trees opposite, people on foot. To the right, a warehouse and triple chimneys towered in bold perspective, glowing red, and turning a bend in the road. I followed the curves of noise around to where a small group waited: some men, a girl with a pony-tail, and a couple with a collapsible pram. A bus pulled up with a rasping and musical whine. A trolley-bus! I hadn't seen one for years. It was old and badly maintained and dowdy. The driver in mufti sold me a ticket. Five kopecks. Someone showed how to cancel it in a gadget fixed to a pole. The seats were half full, and I sat near the front, looking back. The bus surged on down endless tree-lined streets, each stop called on the intercom. I felt a small elation stirring. No one knew me. A foreign man in a foreign town among anonymous people.

Sitting opposite, stoic and quite expressionless, an older woman in raincoat and headscarf, her shopping bag handle mended with string. A man with a paunch in his pullover, staring fixedly down at his shoes. They took no notice of what swung by at the windows; nameless vans of a light army type, modest and softly-rounded cars, discoloured factories and apartment buildings, four or five storeys high. Side-roads joined at glancing angles, spilling in floods of light and people. There were many more people walking than riding. Crowds went steadily by under trees and stretched across junctions like melted cheese.

After a while, I got off and joined them, ranging from shop to shop; into a dairy stacked with wire-crated bottles, and enormous slabs of butter and lard. No mini-packs, no plastic bags. Down below windows at pavement level, a basement with oval tins and chickens, and three or four kinds of dubious fish. No, thank you, I shook my head, I don't want them. On the floor above was a chemist's parlour, with tall and elegant lace-trimmed windows, long bright-polished wooden counters, labelled jars, sparkling flasks and a row of starched assistants. There were kiosks with newspapers printed pale, and queues around open-air stalls for bananas.

By now I was branching toward the centre, drowsing through almost traffic-free streets. Under the eaves of a market, a few small trucks were jammed into archways, and women with biceps like barrels were man-handling goods into cellars from vans. Mostly, though, people were on their way home. A pair of nubile girls jostled by, trailing a waft of earrings and laughter. Along with the heels of well-dressed women, clicking from kerb to kerb, and the deliberate plodding brogues of spick and span military men, they echoed and faded by turns into their courtyards and doors.

I wondered what their flats would be like; but by then I was down by the river, leaning on its balustrades, looking along its walls. How strongly it flowed, and how wide! On the further bank were more endless ranks of faintly Venetian buildings, confronting those behind me, but the chim-neyed skyline was almost unbroken. I recognized nothing. To the left, a single gilded dome lifted over a distant bridge. And how long the bridge! It was creeping darkly with trams and people, like insects crossing an arching twig. Across the bridges, and along the quays and the streets, a tangled skein of tramway cables knotted and knitted the city together, and over it arched the muted sky as if seen through a macramé curtain. Starlings flew through the holes. In that moment, my worn-out postcard picture of Leningrad finally disintegrated, and came together differently – untidy, loose, extensive, grand, vibrant and varied and mobile. It came alive and so did I. A suffused and tingling thrill carried me onwards over the bridge, past a boy peeping down through the slots where it opened, on through yet more cobbled streets and dark and unsmart canyons, on yet again in search of the centre. When, at last, it opened up, the scale was even harder to grasp. In a magnificent boulevard, twice as long as I'd expected, lush trees, lining a central walkway, strode away to the vanishing point. People strolled beneath them more slowly, dotted like dreaming Seurat figures along the tapered path. Still there was no rush nor hurry; nor need, I felt, to look over the shoulder. I felt calm and secure and strangely unruffled and rested. Only the stone-vaulted eyes of buildings gazed from under the branches. Even a truckload of soldiers hardly altered the mood.

Decembrists Square, and its statues and lawns. St Isaac's Cathedral, with pillars 60 feet high. A glimpse, perhaps, of the Hermitage beyond, and roads as wide as football fields. They could all now wait for another day. I'd arrived through the back of the shop by mistake, and the window-display would wait for tomorrow.

A Number Six tram brought me back. It was disjointed and noisy and overloaded; there were at least a hundred and fifty aboard, with shoppers and sailors and all sorts still fighting to get on. The floor flexed and bent with the humps in the road. I hung on tight and was packed even tighter, but somehow the elation didn't diminish. The matron between whose breasts I was wedged looked impassively past me. Politely I did the same for her, and allowed my thoughts to wander. They went back to *Canna*'s arrival. At the moment of first contact, early that afternoon, Gennady had leaned down toward us all, his face delighted and glowing.

'Welcome to the Soviet Union. Welcome to Russia!' he had said.

Part II
THE
SOVIET
UNION

CHAPTER 8

Leningrad – the Big Neva

'I won't describe any more of Petersburg. I think it a most infernal hole,' fumed Corrigan in his diary, after his first day's sight-seeing. Nor did he: the *Oriana*, which had arrived in the city only two days before *Canna*, as it were, was about to depart again heading west, even as we were being checked in by customs. Why so soon? W. J. Martin's great-grand-nephew had been able to offer no idea as to why, after sailing 2,000 miles, his forebear had given the city such short shrift; and, although we hoped to do it more justice, things hadn't started too well for us either.

For one thing, there was an initial sense of disappointment that it was no longer possible to view the city from a visiting boat as it had been planned when founded.

The 'Strelka', the eastern tip of Vassilievsky Island that divides the Neva into 'Big' and 'Little', with its Bourse (now the Maritime Museum), flanked by twin Rostral Columns, originally bearing flames to guide ships in fog, had been the hub of shipping life; but although the Passenger Terminal was on the same island, it was two miles distant at the opposite end. Originally, Basil's Island had been linked to the mainland by pontoon bridges, so that ships of small enough draught could sail right into the heart of the city; but these inconveniences had been understandably replaced by fixed bridges, and the docks had been moved, so that the splendours of the city's frontage no longer spread to greet the sailor. The river, too, for all its width and grandeur, is now oddly dead and mostly trafficked only by a few launches for tourists.

Besides, first impressions are notoriously mixed; and on that first evening, while I had been floating through the back-streets on clouds of exaltation, other crew had been less lucky.

Alone on board, prey to a confusion of fact and fiction, Susan had been exploded out of apprehensive dreams by martial music blaring muezzin-style from the hotel looming overhead: the fractured electronic echoes of patriotic marches, presumably to climax its tourists' day, had bounded around like aural shrapnel. Shay, who burned his candles at both ends and down their sides, had arrived soon after: grey, depressed, displaced and hungry, furious at what he saw as a lack of facilities provided; and only Alan and Rupert had managed to season their mishaps with laughter.

The two of them made a fine pair: Alan somehow preserving a childlike

innocence into early middle age, with Rupert, on his first foray abroad, in
no condition to restrain him.

'I wanted a photograph of a tower . . .' Alan would hoot, '. . . so I was
lying down on the pavement . . .' Or, 'When I collided with the tree . . .'

People had apparently thought he was mad. He had also failed to master
the ticket-dispenser in the tram, causing it to disgorge coils and spirals of
four-kopeck tickets like a runaway toilet-roll holder. The pair had finally
rounded things out by ignoring a pedestrian subway. An official car had
run over their toes, its doors flying open like a priest's soutane as it
screeched to a halt. Uniforms galloped out and motioned them to get in.
For a minute, they'd thought they might have to oblige, until they'd made
abject apologies.

Various people had been transfixed. So, by now, were we: among our
five crew, all splitting their sides, there were already four different cities.

'Hello, *Canna!*' came a breezy call next morning.

It was Gennady Khabarov, more than a little dapper in a plum-coloured
leather-and-wool jacket and perfectly pressed grey flannels. Officially our
agent and mentor, we quickly came to like him for himself. Previously a
seaman, he had taken a shore job, he told us later, to be with his family more
often. Unfailingly thoughtful and attentive, his lively moustachioed figure
was to pop up once or twice every day.

'May I come down?' He had organized seamen's status for us at the
seamen's club, he explained. 'And about services; we've arranged nearly all,
but what about garbage? We could send you a lorry, but we have to charge
you for that.'

His eyes bulged when I explained we would hardly fill one plastic bag in
six days, let alone a pantechnicon. He was obviously having some difficulty
adjusting his notion of scale.

In fact, we both were. That, apparently, was why immigration and
customs men had been in such a hurry to clear us: despite our best efforts,
we'd contrived to be late at the Terminal. Gennady's office had assumed a
normal ship's speed of eight knots or so from the pilot station inwards, as
against our best of barely six, and I had failed to detect the discrepancy
during our radio contact.

'Not so important,' he said, soothing my apologies. 'We cleared the big
cruise-liner out before you instead of after.'

Whereas in most other countries one could wait for hours for official
clearance, it had been very impressive to have four or five uniforms lined up
to meet us, even if they had misjudged our boat.

'You are very small to have come so far. We expected something much
bigger,' they said.

We, in turn, from our very first telex, had been curious about the nature of Inflot. They acted as agents for all foreign shipping, we knew; and their offices in the various ports had telexed berthing charges payable which seemed, on the face of it, quite outrageous – about £250 for six days in Leningrad, not much less for four days in Tallinn, Estonia. Our mild and courteous remonstrations had caused the Dublin diplomats to throw their hands in the air, and a Russian professor, visiting Cork, advised the charges were 'normal'; so when Leningrad requested their full amount in advance, we'd paid in dollars before *Canna* had even smelt the Atlantic. What, we had wondered, would we get for our money?

As Gennady enlightened us, we were more than ever intrigued; as far as the Russians were concerned, we were a ship, and would get the full ship's treatment: pilots delivered on board; officials all ready and waiting; transport, telex and telephone to hand; a chandler's store to avail ourselves of; city visits laid on if we wanted, and all our material needs catered for. A day or two later, Gennady himself and an assistant lugged top-up diesel on board, and laundry was similarly fetched and carried. We began to understand the arrangement.

'We've been asked to look after you,' they said. 'Whatever you need, let us know.'

But one of the few things Inflot couldn't supply was a satisfactory berth. *Canna*'s lodgement was unattractive. Either side of the slot in which she was wedged, dripping piles stalked off into an endless subterranean forest; in the scummy water beneath lurked miscellaneous flotsam and dunnage, and a hefty steel raft that lurched with every passing ship and threatened to punch our nose. The situation caused Gennady acute embarrassment and curses under his breath, the more so as it wasn't even permanent. In a day or two, he said, our spot would be needed for a passenger liner.

'Don't worry, I think of something,' he said. 'You know, this is the first time for us and a little difficult. We have to find out everything.'

There had, apparently, been one other western yacht a few months before, flying the Swiss flag and chartered from Germany. But she hadn't been Inflot's responsibility, nor so much of a problem: she'd been big enough to manage the wharf for the couple of days she had stayed, and there hadn't been so much shipping then either.

'Very busy time now,' explained Gennady apologetically. 'Many ships, many tourists.'

Belatedly, on impulse, I dug out the sailing club invitation from the Russian yachts we'd met in Sweden, that we'd expected to have to deal with ourselves.

'Now why you not say this before?' he rebuked me. 'I'll see what our office can do.'

There was another difference between the Swiss boat and ours: her crew had lodged in the hotel. From the start, we had indicated we would live in our shell, being quite unable to cope with first-class room rates of a hundred pounds a night or more, quite apart from the pain of being separated from our boat.

And probably this was why, we suddenly guessed, Corrigan's impressions of the city had been so unfavourable – they, like us, had expected to get close to the centre (they had even bought special tea and coffee 'machines' in Tallinn for firing up on the quayside when they arrived, having heard they wouldn't be allowed to use their own stove on board) – but, having been forced to abandon the *Oriana* at Kronstadt and take lodgings in the city, they 'came up by the 9 o'clock boat' (type not stated) and 'went to Miss Benson's on the English Quay'. Rereading their comments, one could imagine chintz-covered armchairs and genteel china cramping the style of the two young bloods. It was probably why their spirits had barely lifted to the church of St Ivan, 'which cost £8 million. It has lapis lazuli and malachite pillars and is most gorgeous', and why almost everything else had seemed irksome.

'The Post Restante people are rather impudent. You're not allowed to smoke in the streets. If seen doing so, a couple of Babbuschniks haul you off and you are fined 1 rble 1st offence, 3 for 2nd,' frothed Corrigan, in a state of dudgeon sounding exactly like Shay's.

There would have been other drawbacks, too: water was still not piped then in many parts of the city, and the roads were diabolical. Cobbles in the Nevsky Prospekt had to be relaid every year; further out, the roads were planked with timber and, beyond again, very muddy and rutted. In winter, when the rivers were frozen, travel by horse-drawn sledge was much easier; but in summer everyone sensibly decamped, leaving the city almost empty, and the parks we had wandered through locked up.

Altogether, it was not surprising that they had already been upping their anchor in Kronstadt at much the same time as Gennady was dwindling away down the dock. But Gennady's problems, our problems, were really those of success – the achievement of a unique privilege, a semi-private visit by boat, for which facilities didn't yet fully exist. I felt we could live with problems like that. On the other hand, had we really grasped the lesson that the Russians treat everything that floats as a ship, it would have saved us some sharp excitements later on in the voyage.

The English Quay? Here was a fascination indeed. It's obvious that despite a very general dread of Russian distance and foreignness, a sizeable English colony throve in St Petersburg for much of the nineteenth century. Even as Mitchells revamped her dockyards, Coats of Manchester ran substantial cotton mills. Other Britons provided telegraphs, or replicas of Stephenson's railway engines. English governesses were an even more extraordinary export – although viewed from home by Mrs Gaskell as 'the

ABOVE: Canna *driving east through the Baltic towards Leningrad. Water temperature was a moderate 16°C, slightly less than normal.*

LEFT: *Locking down through the eastern section of the Göta Canal. Fortunately, the bridges and locks were often grouped together.*

LEFT: *Shay Fennelly, photographer. Self-portrait at the masthead.*

BELOW: *It is hard to believe Leningrad was built on a swamp - the scale everywhere is vast. Here the Lenin Museum overlooks the Neva.*

ABOVE: *Navy celebrations were due shortly after we left Leningrad. Here a crew of Soviet sailors in traditional singlets put in some rowing practice as Canna arrives in the Little Neva.*

RIGHT: *'Welcome to Russia!' Gennady Khabarov, of the Leningrad Inflot shipping agency, dealt with our unusual problems with unfailing kindness and patience.*

OPPOSITE ABOVE: *The gilded dome of St Isaac's Cathedral and Tsar Peter the Great on his 1500-ton boulder look down on a Leningrad pavement café.*

OPPOSITE BELOW: *The only remaining gable of the 15th-century St Birgit's Monastery overlooks a group of Estonian cruising yachts behind the Olympic centre at Pirita.*

LEFT: *The Church of Spas-na-Krovi in Leningrad has been under restoration for more than twenty years, and does not yet appear on tourist literature.*

BELOW: *Groups of gypsies appeared like vivid hallucinations among the staid city-dwellers of Leningrad.*

ABOVE: *The Latvian Shipping Company Club occupies a peaceful and convenient niche near the centre of Riga.*

LEFT: *Mikhail Eisenstein (the father of Sergei, the famous film-maker) was a Riga architect. This is just one of a remarkably individualistic street of houses he designed.*

ABOVE: *The city of Gdańsk, extremely wealthy in earlier centuries, was painstakingly restored after horrendous war damage.*

RIGHT: *Two beauties in one of the characteristic beach-shelters in Kołobrzeg, Poland, had no trouble inveigling our photographer.*

BELOW: *The maritime college and the masts of the 'Dar Pomorza' overlook the sheltered harbour of Gdynia. On the horizon, the low peninsula of Hel.*

ABOVE: *Tourist ships lie off from the tax-haven island of Helgoland in the German Bight.* Canna *lies in the enclosed harbour beyond the hospital awaiting a suitable wind.*

LEFT: Canna *in her winter berth at Derrynane Harbour, Co. Kerry.* (RF)

equivalent of taking the veil, or a ladylike form of suicide', hundreds of peripatetic maidens moved in often exalted circles, travelling with wealthy Russian families, schooling their offspring in the English language and dressing them in Norfolk jackets (French, the language of aristocracy, became too common, and Russian was viewed as downright vulgar). Some of these free spirits made highly suitable matches; one even reared a tsarina's children. In Petersburg, this English colony, as if elsewhere in the Empire, cocooned itself with all the essentials; with an English Club, and an English Church and Seminary, an English Shop in the Nevsky Prospekt from which to buy their Golden Syrup; with a badminton club, naturally, and, out on one of the Neva's islands, with tennis and with golf (which now, a century later, was just catching on with privileged Soviets!) – and yes, of course, with their rowing and their yachting, their boaters and their strawberries.

They even had their own area too: the 'Lines' of Vassilievsky Island, the historic parallel early streets crossing the Bolshoi Prospekt, down which I'd unwittingly wandered the night before (and to which, somewhere at the height of the Revolution, a Mr Oustinoff had come from Germany to look for his missing parents, and survived to father a certain Peter Ustinov), included the English Line, which no doubt debouched at the English Quay and Miss Benson's.

A self-sufficient squad indeed – certainly no less so than the expatriate Germans, French or Swiss – and, despite *Oriana*'s abrupt departure, they'd provided her with a big advantage.

Mr C. Eastland de Michele, Her Britannic Majesty's Consul, had called as soon as she arrived (Corrigan pasted his visiting-card in his log) and invited the gentleman-owner to visit him in the city. Now, for want of any such august presence, I entrusted our arrangements for official meetings to the dockside Intourist Office, and made instead for the next best thing – the Union of Soviet Friendship Societies, who have branches throughout the country. I wasn't disappointed. The Vice-Chairman, Verq Brovinq, whose name we had, turned out, like God, to be a woman, Vera Brovkina, ensconced in splendour half-way between the consular and the divine.

Not for the first or last time misjudging the scale of the city, I had cantered in the nick of time between the four equestrian statues guarding the Nevsky Prospekt Bridge, over the Fontanka Canal, and found the House of Peace and Friendship sprawled along its bank for half a block, its two huge storeys looking like four or five. As one small part of the incredible Leningrad legacy, the former Chouvalov palace, built in the eighteenth and nineteenth centuries, was an eye-opener. Huge wreaths and ramps of marble stairs swept up to gilt and mirrored and parqueted halls, the Blue Room and the White Room, and reception parlours the size of an average ballroom. Vera Brovkina exactly matched her surroundings – a very well-kept period lady, generous in scale and gesture and fringed with lace, but distinctly imperious and formal.

I was conducted on a brief tour of the splendours; and tomorrow, would we all attend to see a video of the city? – an acolyte would arrange it; and exquisite and aromatic tea appeared as if by magic. But the Director's eyes gleamed, I thought, a little too hard and official across the china, like those of the four bronze horsemen outside, or the crystalline glint of the chandeliers on the phalanx of mineral water bottles standing to attention on the polished table between us. For future visits by yacht we were quickly referred to Moscow, and queries about sailing clubs were bounced by 'phone to Gennady. After a while it dawned that Ms Brovkina was firmly stone-walling – and that Vera was on the further side.

'We've sailed a very long way to be here,' I said, at last, with a flush of warmth and exasperation. 'We would simply like to meet a few families and yachtsmen!'

She paused a little and, I noticed, her glance had softened and moistened. 'I'm very sorry we can't help you more,' she said. 'It doesn't really come within our duties, you know. The Society is part of a Government body, and we're just not organized in that way – at least, not yet, I'm afraid.'

For those few moments, as she leaned forward in her gilded chair, twisting her ring finger slightly, the official persona, the briskly efficient organizer and regal presence slipped sideways a little, and a shy potential for change showed through.

Shay, in inimitable fashion, had already made progress elsewhere and, with Alan and Rupert in tow, had arranged an assignation for us all under the Pushkin monument.

Iskusstva Square must be one of the most romantic spots to wait for girls who come late. Alexander Sergeyevich, who died in a duel, stands tall and dark on a plinth of blood-red stone; a decorous ring of gravel and benches circle his wide-flung gestures, and fringing trees filter the buzz of far-away traffic.

> A city new in pomp unmatched
> Of Northern lands the pride and gem
> I love thee, work of Peter's hand!
> I love thy stern symmetric form;
> The Neva's calm and queenly flow
> Betwixt her quays of granite stone
> With iron tracings richly wrought

But the only sounds greeting his declamations were the whispers and laughter of others waiting and watching, and the scrunch of pebbles as solitary people turned on their heels or took slow circuits behind his back.

The afternoon went well. When Shay's friends, Svetlana and Nastasia, finally arrived with the others, we repaired to a nearby hotel where, over a tepid lager, they unconsciously demolished any remaining illusions concerning the standard Russian. Stately Svetlana had overtones of something sultry and tempting that could have come straight out of Pasternak, but surely her friend was American? She had all the features of a Boston drum majorette: fair complexion, short fair hair, the skirt on the short side too, the lip line wide and well painted. When it opened, perfect American-English came out, and her responses were direct to the point of being alarming. But Nastasia too was Leningrad born and bred, she told us, as we queued for the buffet: her parents' flat was one of those overlooking our approach by sea. Her work as a tourist guide did often bring her into close contact with the 'Yanks', however – too close, sometimes, as this evening, when she would forgo her own time to visit some in hospital.

'Always they have the same problems. I must press their hands very kindly, and tell them that nobody, but *nobody* normally dies in Russia of diarrhoea – it isn't at all romantic, you know.'

'So is the water really a problem?' quizzed Shay, as we gazed at our gherkins and sturgeon in aspic with renewed respect; but no, she judged, just that they didn't get the same junk to eat as at home. '. . . and to think,' she snorted, 'my parents imagine I'm only messing around. How can it be a proper job, just meeting people and talking?'

There was no doubt she was exceptionally good at it. Like an expert canoeist, she shot the rapids of a party piece: a Pommy pun on effete English upper-crust plum, and a coarse Australian strine; slid through to the quieter pools of religion, commitment and career and took a quick spin around the meaning of life. It soon left only the problem of sex.

'Here,' she affirmed, panning a challenging look across our four pairs of eyes, 'the women do all the work, and the men have their three C's . . .' (Roughly translated, these were the sofa, the papers, and the TV, along with whatever nuances one cared to read in between.)

'Not what we've been told,' we laughed. 'Aren't there any reconstructed men? What about *perestroika*?'

'Not much. Not many,' she mocked, as we began to feel a bit shrivelled. 'And if there are, I don't meet them!'

'Why not? Where do you go for your holidays?'

'Usually south,' she said, and Svetlana nodded agreement. 'It's warm. I'm due there soon for a three-week break.'

'Do Intourist arrange that for you?' I asked, meaning only – can you use your office to fix it? – but she took it up quite differently.

'No. Why should it be to do with them? I arrange it myself,' she shot back, with an unmistakable note of assertion.

While thus engaged above board, Susan had wangled some sailors below and kept them all to herself. Four or five young trainees from the naval college opposite, among the trees, had materialized on the dock, egging themselves on with horseplay and dares until Susan brought them on board. The uniformed dock guard overhead, on one of his infrequent rounds, had looked doubtful.

'He wants to know if we're causing a nuisance?' they said, passing on his enquiry.

'Not at all,' she replied by the same roundabout route, 'tell him to come down and join us for tea.'

He'd declined and retreated, leaving the teenagers chuckling.

I'd already been guilty of cramping my expectations. On the first night, remembering the passport check when leaving the Terminal, I'd scrapped ideas for bringing friends to the boat. I shouldn't have bothered too much. There was no official when I returned, nor a single door unlocked. There had been nothing for it but to scale the steel fence round the side, under the gaze of a few gawky cameras, perched up on high like robots. But no bells rang, the others did likewise and, later, in other ports, we found similar harmless circumventions used by all and sundry – typically, a bent bar in a fence, or a pair of ladders that just happened to be propped nearby.

Two more friends turned up that night, both from the new arrival opposite *Canna* – a modest and beamy Russian cruise-ship with snub bow and verandah'd side-decks. There was Riho, a dark-haired schoolboy from Tallinn, whom Shay had already bumped into cycling around the wharf, the other was a bearded, white-shirted officer who needed no encouragement to join us on board for a nightcap. He turned out to be the ship's engineer.

'A Baltic cruiser,' he explained, smacking his lips on the Scotch. 'Tallinn, Riga, Vyborg, Leningrad. Russian people – 122 passengers, 16 crew.' Even a small swimming pool, he mimed.

'The captain? Yes – very good man.'

It was a good post for Yuri, too. Like other seamen we would meet, he had had a varied career, wandering much of Europe with the merchant and fishing fleets, including the odd visit to Belfast. Now, with a family in Riga, he cruised the Baltic for six months in the summer, and took it easy at home in the winter, while the ship was being maintained. He spoke in a mixture of Russian and English and signs, excusing himself when his English ran out, by claiming 'no practicum'.

He'd obviously had more 'practicum' at bending his elbow. And why not? It was his day off, he'd said. He disappeared momentarily, reappearing with mysterious, misshapen paper packages. Bottles of beer tumbled out, half a side of superb smoked trout, and – what was this? – a bottle of fine white port!

'Skipper's favourite,' chaffed Susan.

Yuri winked hugely, as I took a big sip and the top of my head blew off, to a circular roar of laughter. Vodka like volcano fire! Or lava, rather, scorching a path to my entrails. At last my fears had come true, as Yuri rang the changes all night to the chorus of '*Za zdorovye!*'

We began with formal set-pieces, knocking it back all together, with suitable dedications to the continued buoyancy of our boats and our health; continued in jocular vein with tumblers balanced on elbows, and ended (as far as I know) in intimate twosomes, linked arms and a mutual scratching of bearded cheeks. And, as the outlines of cabin, crew and companionway wavered, advanced and receded, I was dimly aware that the human landscape of the city, just like the built one, was stirring itself into life with the same wild extra dimension, the same strange blend of the vaguely foreseen and the unexpected; and our rigid framework of anticipation was bursting up into kaleidoscopic fragments and hinting at patterns more varied, warmer, and more colourful than any we had imagined.

If we had Peter the Great to thank for Leningrad in the first place, we had him to blame for most of our problems too – or so the historians would have us believe. He never got to grips with the organization of his country; for all his talent and efforts, establishment of colleges and ministries, he only made a bad tangle worse, like the reins, one imagines, of the 20-odd horses he used to pull his coaches. He then ossified the bureaucratic spaghetti by promises of nobility to the higher achievers (Lenin's father joined the aristocracy that way, and Lenin himself was therefore titled) and, since that error, the story goes, everyone else has suffered. Whatever his faults, it seems unfair, after more than two centuries, to pile on his grave the 30,000 million documents the Russian system now spews out each year, or blame him if a few of them land in an inappropriate place.

But gaps and discontinuities there were, as in the public transport. There were no plans or routes or timetables at the stops or on the vehicles, nor maps to be had at Intourist offices either.

'Don't you think that odd?' said a bewildered Shay to the girls at the Terminal.

'Yes,' they politely agreed, but placidly shook their heads, meaning 'no'. Obviously it wasn't a bit odd or, if it ever had been, it wasn't now worth the thought. Fortunately, the House of Friendship had plugged the gap with diagrams (in Russian only) that allowed us to cruise the red and green and magenta routes of bus and trolley and tram.

For a day or two, we didn't hear from either Inflot or Intourist concerning our less usual requests; and approval for our visit began to look even more like a benign aberration or a brand-new departure, or both, when it became obvious that Gennady was having great problems finding a bent paling, or a suitable ladder to scale the official fences.

'Is not easy,' he confided, apropos of the sailing club. 'I'm very sorry, but you will have to go to Commercial Dock instead. It's very difficult to find the right person, and difficult with the telephone too.'

This last was surprising. Whatever the city was short of, it wasn't telephones. Banks of rounded boxes, like the nests of oversized birds, were stuck to the walls all over the street. None were graffitied, all seemed to work, and most of my calls had responded. Gennady's blockage was, perhaps, as much one of protocol as of occupied lines.

The dock supervisors obviously had similar problems next morning when they espied us hurriedly topping up Canna's water supply before our departure. Under a manhole cover, Alan and I were struggling with an outlet that would have shamed a skyscraper's hydrant. With no provision to connect our garden hose, floods of water went everywhere, as we clumsily filled our medicine bottles from a vase-like hole in a yellow contraption with clocks on. When an overalled dock-hand appeared, threading his way through the legs of a crane, we could sense something wrong from his speed. Had we read the dials before we started, he wanted to know? No, we confessed, foolishly gaping. Tutting and fishing out spanners, he poked his torso into the nether regions and, seconds later, staggered away with the entire half-hundredweight meter tucked up under his arm. The outlet now gushed like a geyser, and even more gallons went to waste, but at least it wasn't recorded. Was it rigid officialdom, or the new flexibility? Maybe both, we decided. If our piddling needs weren't metered, they also needn't be charged.

But for all its bulk, the administrative system mainly worked. Another pilot turned up on the dot of 9 am. He was keen to get on, and regally unamused when the seaman, Yuri, none the worse for the night, appeared on the dock's edge, calling and cheering and supping a toast from an invisible glass on his elbow.

The Dock, unfortunately, was worse than before, and proportionately more embarrassing as, having crabbed again across the Neva, and popped in through the neck of a huge square basin, the appointed pier confronted us under a clump of dusty trees. It wasn't so much worn as worked to death, its legs wrapped in steel like cake-box cardboard, with a guillotine edge at the bottom – once again, too high for our decks.

Demurring, we'd selected a wall between a steel pontoon and a floating crane like the Eiffel Tower. As before, when we made fast, relief could be parcelled and portioned and, almost as soon, Gennady appeared, spurting gravel from the wheels of his van and a string of heartfelt apologies.

The Baltic, it seemed, as so long forewarned, had suffered one of its Admiralty lapses.

'I really did check the berth,' he explained, 'but the water level has fallen.'

It was just as well it had done it just then. The pier was abuzz with pilot boats 24 hours a day, nosing around like restless dogs, and shepherding ships to their pens.

The Commercial Dock turned out to be our most fascinating lodgement, especially compared to the Passenger Terminal. There, everything had been quietly restrained and formal; the galleries stretching around the six-storey hotel atrium were sheathed in grey marble, and its open stairways trimmed with brass. Banks and barbers and restaurants operated decorously behind ten-foot walls of glass. Few people had seemed to be moving in the wide and carpeted hush.

But in the Dock, we were head over heels in a rumbustious workaday world that lay far out beyond the fashionable part of the city, as Shay, who'd not joined in *Canna*'s move, reported when he later arrived. Within the red-rimmed noticeboards, commending dockers for feats of achievement, which framed the arched and gated guard-posts, the docks formed a secluded enclave that sprawled across several of the city's 42 islands: an area which, bit by bit, we explored. The steel and concrete pontoon under our bows was one-third of a new floating bridge, destined to tail us to Tallinn. Our lines were made on to its cow's head-sized pivots and heavy galvanized railings. A lad with a ladder and a bare brown top, who took elaborate care of Susan, turned out to be a sort of caretaker, lodged in a garden shed with bunks and a gas ring down at its opposite end. Behind the goods stowed for shipment, and a yawning brick and concrete warehouse, were ships loading plywood boxes, long indented quays and assorted blocks of offices, cobbled streets and tree-lined avenues, internal bus-stops and corners of green waste-ground, strewn with branching railway lines.

'Leningrad,' the official booklets boasted, 'produces 58 per cent of the nation's turbines, 60 per cent of its generators, one-third of its rubber shoes.' The evidence of it could be seen all around us, excepting only the plimsolls. Up on the dock were stacks and ranks of railway lines, with sleepers and without, slabs of steel plate several feet high, big crates of ventilation gear, much of it labelled for Cuba.

That it could be a dangerous place was obvious, even without the safety posters plastered around the walls. Ends of pipes and bars projected at eye height. Vast swiss rolls of steel were lightly wedged to prevent them making away, fork-lift trucks presented their prongs around corners, and over the plastic-helmeted heads of lean-faced men in dungarees and women clutching clipboards, chains and grabs and hooks clanked and clashed like empty skulls being bashed together.

We felt slightly naked and half surprised to be wandering around, bare-headed and unremarked. The main impression was of plenty of time and people. The Baltic Shipping Company employed about 32,000 people, mainly in Leningrad, of whom 8,000 were dockers. The pontoon lad seemed to have nothing to tend but one or two winches, and a small pile of timber and tools. In the warehouse offices, redolent of school classrooms, their walls and tall iron radiators gleaming dully with generations of gloss paint, one or two women at timber desks interspersed obviously none-too-pressing paperwork with liberal helpings of chat. From time to time a docker barged in with sundry comments or queries, once or twice a telephone rang; but the talk went on and time went by like the terminal meander of a lazy river, and the fact of our borrowing their telephone was of no more importance than the passing by of a gnat. No doubt we were just another variety of odd bod that had blown in on one of the ships.

The Inflot staff were a brighter kettle of fish. They occupied a yellow-brick block with a vaguely Chicago appearance just outside the dock gates, and manned their office round the clock, seven days of the week. All had passable, and some of them excellent, English; and at odd times of day, during their stints, they turned up and hailed us, as much from curiosity and friendliness as from a sense of duty.

Andrei and Boris arrived together. Both were in their late twenties. Boris, dark-haired, reticent and inclined to boils, was soon deep in consultation with Shay about shell-fishing in Kamchatka, the Soviet mainland's far east; matters of Japanese involvement, lack of towns, the constraints of climate (much like Britain) and the costs of getting out there. Andrei kept interrupting.

'Tcha!' he scoffed finally, fresh-faced and forward. 'Russia's expert on fishing! He wouldn't know a cod from a salmon, even if it jumped up and bit him.'

Boris declined to retort.

Andrei's appetites were voracious. He read whenever he wasn't talking and a paperback stuck out of his trouser pocket. Had we please a novel in English? Failing his preferred feeding of fish and Frederick Forsyth, he settled for Garrison Keillor with double Scotch and sandwiches. If he needed more, he said so, and he brought us his puzzlements too.

'I read about Vietnam,' he said, 'about the troops catching "crabs". What kind of crabs are those?'

It obviously wasn't shellfish, and a consultation among the resident panel produced a unanimous answer.

'Pubic lice,' we chorused.

On the word 'pogue', we passed (it's Irish for 'kiss', we discovered later) but, as a kindly quid pro quo, he brought us back to his base to sort out our own communications. He showed us the ranks of telex machines on which our first hopeful requests from Kerry had come through and then, with a patience belying his brisk demeanour, attempted for an hour or two to connect us to a newspaper journalist in Moscow, all the while standing in the sidelong light of a Sunday noontime under a wall map which, joltingly, but naturally enough, showed Russia at the centre of the world.

Intourist's only connection with the docks was via the Seamen's Club. This was miles away, in a former nobleman's house close to the city centre; even so, they solicited the crew of all the visiting freighters, and it was part of Natalie's duties to round them up, bus them in and out in the evenings and host the entertainments. It was no sinecure. On the Club's impressively ornate *piano nobile* were a bar and dance hall, and snooker, concert and reading rooms catering for various functions and exhibitions; but for Natalie to supervise and introduce them to hardened, world-girdling sailors, was a bit like setting a pullet to mind a den of foxes.

Her hair was tied very tightly back from bird-like features that were almost too slender and pale, and her ascetic fingers flicked and twisted incessantly, betraying a worrier and perfectionist. She protected herself with a bossy and brittle armour which, if we'd not first met her off-duty colleague, we might have misunderstood; beneath this lay a desire to please and a person all of us came to like; but a stronger contrast than that between her prematurely schoolmarmish manner, and the traditionally riotous, semi-inebriated and randy tendencies of the assorted Swedes, Finns, French, Filipinos, Germans and others would be very hard to contrive.

One evening later on, when our crew turned up in force, she'd had problems with all kinds of people. It was 'Greek night', and the Greeks had got out of hand, making hideously long speeches when they should have been quietly dispersing. Some Swedes, who were drinking, were supposed to be at a concert – a top-class classical programme by a professional chamber orchestra in full bow ties and tails – but sadly, there were almost more players than audience. The sea-horses had declined to be led there, or prised away from their pints of lager by Natalie's allure or cajoling. They tried to tease their 'mermaid' on to their laps instead.

'It's terrible!' she exclaimed to Susan, as they retreated together to the basement. 'They're so difficult; they behave so badly!' – but even below stairs there was no respite. There, she'd set up an exhibition for the 70th anniversary of the Revolution, and needed an opinion of its English text; and Shay and I had compounded her problems by arriving late from a hard day's filming and missing the entertainments entirely.

'Do you think they will come?' Natalie had asked every half-hour. Unknown to them we were spiralling in with a taxi-driver who was gamely struggling to make sense of our diagrams of stick-men on ships meeting skirts.

'Ah, ZEEMANZKLUB!' he exclaimed on arrival, delighted by his accidental success; but by then the damage was done. Natalie had instructed the downstairs babushka to look out for bearded men, and at least one hirsute candidate had been snatched off the pavement, propelled up the flights of marble and under the dramatic, oil-painted shipwreck, for Susan's inspection. 'Is this your husband?' the woman would ask, clutching the bemused man by the arm, as if to prevent his escape. Susan's high spirits knew no bounds.

But if Natalie really cares to know, our conventional pilgrimage to the Hermitage Museum, for me, was worth all her pains. As we fought to stay behind her through the single pair of entrance doors, skipping a queue of about ten thousand, she had been almost beside herself.

'We *must* stay together. All, please, now, this way!' Up white marble looping steps, dripping with nymphs and crystal and gold. Across literally acres of marquetried floors, inlaid in rare woods, unprotected from the trample of hordes.

'Relaid every three years,' she called out over her shoulder.

Long rooms, square rooms; rooms vivid with scarlet tapestries and flock; pillared halls; ranks of portraits, miniatures, Rembrandts, chandeliers. On and on Natalie leads us, clicking a little, making haste past the Rubens and Raphaels, accelerating through the Titians with impatient backward glances, across an internal bridge to the Little Hermitage, the New Hermitage, the Big Hermitage; out to the north side behind the enormous pillared flank overlooking the river, delivering us at last to be overcome by works of Italians and Englishmen – Leonardo's two exquisitely small, still, intense Madonnas, beautifully side-lit and accessible, and the huge gilt Peacock Clock perched inside its storey-height glass case in the fluted, fountained, mosaic'd and marbled and gilded and pillared Pavilion Room.

'Ah, at last,' called out the tubby man in a big rounded voice, bounding down into *Canna*'s cockpit. 'I'd given you up. I think you don't want me. Every day I wait for a call. Every day I ask Gennady – do they want to see me? He shakes his head "no sorry". I wonder. I think maybe the next day. Then when I don't hear today either – I throw my hat at it.'

He matched his action to the words, snatching off his linen cap and flinging it into a corner of the saloon, revealing a sweating, bald head, creased with humorous lines.

'I think you don't like me at all!' he boomed, beaming and passing around his card. 'TORGMORTRANS, SHIPCHANDLERS, LENINGRAD BRANCH OFFICE, BALTIC SHIPPING COMPANY.'

Ildus G. Minkhairov obviously meant more than half of what he said;

but Gennady's repeated invitations to the chandler, given our experiences with garbage and water, had merely conjured images of charts and shackles and anchors fit for a battleship, and only in the nick of time had we realized that they purveyed food and acted as factors too. Feeling deprived of fresh protein, Alan and Susan disappeared with Ildus to inspect his wares.

'Went off to get some meat and vegetables,' noted Corrigan, when about to leave from Kronstadt. 'Martin got 12 reindeer tongues (dried) for 4 roubles, some smoked salmon and lots of vegetables of all kinds. The best meat is only 4d a pound here!'

Things had changed in the city shops since. Susan had found some handsome pork, but at the stage of having it weighed and wrapped, had been frightened off by the price. Most other people were buying joints that looked mainly fat. Fresh vegetables were limited to racks and racks of football-sized cabbages and a few discouraged carrots. Fruit was almost unseen. 'Distribution to the city has been a problem for years,' we were told. 'The variety will improve as you go back west.'

But there was no shortage in Ildus's empire. At some distance from the Commercial Dock, Ildus presided over a warren of refrigerated brick vaults, guarded by a cadre of overalled women assistants, with jangles of oversized keys on their belts. For them the progress of our midget appetites through their white-tiled world became a spectator sport. No other ship seemed to be ordering just then. When they did, it seemed, they bought butter by the cubic metre. For *Canna*, a sliver had to be shaved off a block. The petite janitor of that particular cell hadn't the muscle to manage the wire and toggles, so she and Susan grappled the knee-high cube while Ildus used brute strength.

'Beef?' he asked, throwing wide his doors and arms to avenues of carcasses. 'Sausages?' There were mountains of them piled on fork-lift pallets.

Backing off, they had settled for two modest fowl and a sawn-off fragment of frozen fish, but what had looked right in those Romanesque surroundings seemed to double in size when delivered back to the boat. The poultry and plaice overflowed our plates for the next few days, but still there was surplus to be discarded: a shameful waste which, with the hard-currency shops where we gleaned salami at western prices, provoked pangs of conscience about sources of supply the man-in-the-street hadn't access to.

In fact the bustle of the ordinary grocers with their queues and clanging of crates and complications of payment gave us just as much shopping pleasure. 'Click. Click. *Click-clack*' went the dark and light beads on the abacuses, whipped to and fro at the speed of light. Sometimes we got it

wrong, coming out, startled, clutching two kilograms of marzipan choc-
olates in a cone-shaped bundle instead of 200 grams, and sometimes right,
especially in new-style, self-service bakeries; and once, a Seamen's Club trio
had sorted us out by invading a street-corner dairy. Our straggling
procession back to the bus had consisted of Susan and myself with
ice-creams in paper tubes, forcibly stuffed in our hands, Natalie and Lena
clinking the milk, and the driver strolling nonchantly in the rear with trays
of forty-odd eggs balanced at shoulder-height on his splayed-out fingers.
Thoughtless products of the waste-making age, we'd forgotten to bring
any bags. The eggs gleamed golden-pink and russet in rows, matching the
shaded colours of the long receding façades.

Staple foods were plentiful and cheap, being heavily subsidized, and
quality was superb. Almost too good – the milk so creamy and untampered
with that, in the 80°F heat that now kept us in shorts and sunglasses, it
lasted only a day; and the bread! – in varying shades and strengths of rye it
was half a symphony in itself, its succulence and wholesomeness lingering
wistfully on the palate weeks and months later. The Russian sweet tooth
added jizz. The shops were stuffed with Brobdingnagian sweetmeats;
hotels plied 'jubilini', speciality almond pastries that looked like small
brown hub-caps; and some of the rare and secret snack-bars indulged in
elaborate tarts and ice-cream extravaganzas. A firm believer in Coleridge's
dictum that 'A man cannot have a pure mind who refuses apple-
dumplings', it was reassuring to discover the Leningraders were as sound
on desserts as Lord Emsworth of Blandings Castle on pigs.

Conventional wisdom states that Russians are dour.

Most we met were quick off the mark (there were shrieks of delight
when we mentioned our family cat was called Pushkin), and some were
downright hilarious.

Shortly after his first visit at the Commercial Docks, Gennady had
returned with reinforcements, two roguish-looking characters both highly
amused at such an unlikely boat. They would attend to our weekend needs,
Gennady said, while he retreated to the country to recover from his recent
traumas.

Both Borises, for such they were, nodded brightly; and as Gennady
called over our bows from the edge of the floating pontoon, they propped
him closely on either side like book-ends, a sort of Boris-and-Gennady
sandwich.

'That's the overflow Passenger warehouse there,' he had shouted, indicating a building hidden by stacks of steel plate. 'You can use the toilets in
there . . .'

'. . . but they're closed until Monday,' chipped in spectacled Boris.

'Oh!' said Gennady.

'So you must keep your legs crossed,' hooted the other, beginning to sway in the middle.

'Or wait until you get home,' cannoned the first wit, slapping his knee in delight. Both slices of bread peeled away, completely doubled with laughter, leaving Gennady exposed like a stiff slice of cheese, anxieties and incipient grins chasing across his face. For a moment it seemed as if he might box all the Borises' ears.

'There's a toilet of some kind here, too,' he faltered, plucking open the thin planked door of a sentry box perched on the edge of the platform, an obvious adjunct to the caretaker's bunk-house. 'Perhaps it would do for emergency.'

Like the one in the Finnish forest, the basic earth-closet was more wholesome than most of the flushing ones. Russian loos seem to fall through a gaping hole in the system, as if through their own outlets. They seem to be nobody's baby.

In the Russian Museum, the ammoniacal waft around its basement columns was enough to twitch the nose of the purest Byzantine saint, or peel pure gold from an icon. Even in the almost-new Sea Terminal Hotel, the cubicles, slammed into a corner and forgotten, had all the appearance of a last-minute palm-to-the-forehead afterthought as the builders made their final getaway on a Friday afternoon. Polished stone and the twentieth century stopped at the doorway. The misshapen spaces within sprouted plumbing of mind-bending primevalism that snaked and lurched arbitrarily around the floors and walls like the trunks of hairy mammoths, all encrusted with gobbets of cement and undefinable rusty accretions from later epochs. The yawning ceilings flaunted clouds of efflorescence ringed with damp and leaks. For quality of workmanship, I reflected with perverse relief, the average Russian (if it was really his doing – many hotels were built by foreign contractors) could match the flamboyance of your standard Jerry-building jack or paddy any day of the week.

Ablutions were simpler – they couldn't be had. In the tiered rooms of the hotel, not one unoccupied shower could be found. The suggestions sent a frisson of shock through the bureaucratic procedures.

'Yes. No. I think perhaps. At least, a *theoretical* possibility,' an Intourist agent summed it up later. And 'theoretical' it stayed in our parlance, despite Shay's frantic mime of sponging his armpits and other junctions to the gangway guard at the Swedish ship, with whose crew we had shared the bus back from the Club on the evening of our third day. Radios had crackled, superiors were consulted, superiors arrived, but the rules for foreign ships couldn't be waived. Only later, much further down the coast, were we to discover the Russians' obvious and kindly solution. For the moment we suffered.

Even the *Ierne* in 1862 had managed a bit better, despite political problems. Many of the city's buildings were then still timber, and activists (students, or perhaps Poles, were suspected), finding them very ready to light, had started a rash of drastic fires. Hence the prohibition on smoking in the streets which Corrigan had referred to and, by the time Graves berthed his boat somewhere near the city centre, imprisonment was also a possible penalty for naked lights, which included their stove on board. Surreptitiously, they 'had it lit at 6 am for hot water and breakfast, and kept it very low for the rest of the day.'

Gennady was even more embarrassed. 'We find out what it is that yachts like yours need,' he said. 'Then the next time we do it better.'

I reassured him; we expected to be self-sufficient.

'But some of your crew, I think, are not happy,' he persisted.

This was true. Shay in particular was chafing at what he saw as lack of official recognition, and other personal irks.

'We're just not making the right contacts,' he said, 'and you're paying heavily for the berth, but what have we got?'

'Hold on,' I said, and Susan nodded, 'there's some misunderstanding. After all, we invited ourselves, and no one owes us red carpet. We're supposed to be delivering goodwill, if anything, not collecting it. But have we had anything but goodwill here, from anyone? They have all been trying to help. Presumably it's not their fault if certain things are difficult.'

But even as the Swedes had carried Shay off to their ship, on a premonition I'd resisted their encouragements and, with Susan, had hurried back. Beyond the dockside obstructions, *Canna*'s mast was out of position. We found her on the move, with Rupert slightly bemused on deck, and only a single mooring line to her bows as if to a toy in a pond. The white hair of a grizzled docker flared in the dusk alongside us.

'Any damage?' I called down sharply. A thermometer somewhere inside me was soaring.

'No Kapitan. No damage. Is all right,' the old man put in quickly and softly, bringing it back down again. I loved him for that.

The floating crane had taken a notion to leave and we had been in the way, Rupert told us. The young pontoon lad obliged once again, setting planks to help us remoor alongside him. But next morning, the pontoon itself had gone too. Before breakfast, a peremptory hoot told us we were under the bows of the tug that was coming to shift it. We ended up in a corner next to a scatter of ship's propellers.

Quite obviously, we shouldn't be there; and as much to make life easier for Inflot as for us, something had to be done. It was very good to be in the city, but not at the cost of causing disruption all round, and it was painful to see Gennady's kindness so strained. We ought to be at the sailing club. But were the authorities keeping us just a little at arm's length, like the Friendship Society? In four days, we reasoned, they had had time to judge that we were what we said, and weren't about to set the city on fire. In a very real way we now saw that the whole success of our venture depended on being able to meet and mix with our colleagues, the Leningrad yachtsmen. That evening, I promised we'd tackle the matter head-on.

CHAPTER 9

On the Little Neva

No one would have known I was the only passenger on the Inflot bus. Like all the other unlettered vans shuffling nameless people around, it was fully curtained like a camper, screening me, as if royalty, from the glances of the vulgar and curious. It was the evening of 19 July, our fourth day in Leningrad, and Alan and Shay, heading for a night on the town, had alighted from the carriage already, and so had Boris II, the agent.

'Have you been to the sailing club before?' he quizzed crisply. 'Is someone there expecting you?'

Thinking of the invitation, presumably still with Gennady, I hoped my reply carried sufficient conviction.

As we rattled out of the city through the dusty, low-lit evening, the driver leaned back to check our destination. 'Baltic Shipping Company Club,' he muttered, translating to Russian as I showed where it ought to be on the map; and bit by bit the buildings thinned and trees barged in more insistently until, finally, pure parkland swam by with kerbless avenues and grass and Japanese bridges with ducks beneath. A wood-scented waft of heady relief blew in through the windows.

The club is on the north side of the elongated Primorskie island, on the banks of the Nevka, the 'Middle Baby Neva', one of the delta meanders toward the north-west city limits. Its imposing three-storey concrete clubhouse, with cantilevered roof-top pergolas and sweeping ranks of plate-glass, sits among spaced-out birch, looking down on extensive workshops and forecourts.

The driver had set me down on the wide and empty road outside. At first, beyond the fence and gatehouse and the few boats on cradles being painted or tuned, I had bent instinctively to where a green-fringed finger of water pushed in and ten or twenty cruising yachts were moored to a duckboard under a wall; but, noticing a man springing up the entrance steps, I hailed, and caught him up in the doorway.

'We have come by yacht from Ireland,' I said, 'and we're hoping to visit your club.'

He stayed transfixed for all of half a second.

'That's marvellous;' he said. 'And welcome to here. But I've just sailed back from France myself, and I'm going in for a pee. Why don't you join me, and then we can talk?'

We couldn't have been more lucky – Viktor Gusev was one of the club's most senior sailors, who knew of the Terminal's berthing problems, as Russian yachts had to use it when leaving for other countries. In no time, he rounded up two colleagues, went into conference and, eventually, conducted me back to the gatehouse, to speak to the Commodore by 'phone.

It was an unlikely scene, as Viktor explained our case. We sat and stood each side of the watchman, a moustachioed statue with dark brown eyes and an ancient beret pushed back from his brow. A pre-Revolutionary archetype as solid as a bit of baked earth, who looked as though the building had grown up around him, he gazed through the glass and small speedboats outside as if they didn't exist, and the one-sided conversation broke round his ears unheeded.

Captain Pannin, too, sounded like someone from a more formal age, although a little less distant. He'd be delighted to welcome us all, he said, if Inflot would agree. But there was no way of checking that for another day at least; the Inflot agent on duty, in a rare revelation of hierarchy, admitted it was Gennady's affair; but Gennady had already fled to the country. For now, we would have to relax.

Viktor's yacht, *Flora*, 12 metres of beauty and gleaming mahogany, her teak-laid decks classically planked to the curve of her gunwales, lay at the end of the small marina. The crew were taking a winding-down drink – two young couples, exuding the first flush of love and one or two spare he-men, all presided over by Viktor's wife. The less reticent prised their schoolbook English into the open, to meet my clumsy efforts with dictionary and diagrams; and, under the glow of the skylights, the saloon table was soon thick with charts and exclamations, as we deciphered the routes of our cruises, and slipped easily into mutual problems.

Flora's Swedish engine was almost exactly the same as ours. Parts, we agreed, were far too expensive; sometimes, if theirs failed, Viktor didn't bother to fix it for months and simply sailed without it. It had nearly cost them their lives and his boat, though, one day near Kronstadt in a still fog, when they couldn't get out of the way of a ship. They'd been pushed aside by the bow-wave.

'My heart was somewhere here, above my head,' he demonstrated. 'But what about you? How do you manage for radio?'

He was vexed because, although they had the equipment, his call-sign hadn't been issued. I smiled wryly as I told him I'd had to make a special visit to Dublin to cure the very same problem.

The evening became more relaxed and exquisite. We talked on and on until the last shafts of sun lifted off the water, shifting up over the shoulders of trees, leaving them bare and bluish. The crew slipped away in ones and twos, and Lydia and Viktor finally tidied the boat. Could they bring me back to the city?

Absences, similarities, memories – one of my strongest is of that dusk as we walked back together, along a curving road, under the lazily twisting leaves, laden with midsummer fragrance and presaging autumn ever so slightly. It transported me to the bluebell woods and oaks and hedgerow elms of Warwickshire where I grew up, to the parklands of Kenilworth, Stratford and Warwick, and the long and timeless days that had shifted slowly into evenings like this. In the somnolent green and mauve quiet, time expanded in all directions in a way I'd almost forgotten.

'All this park was replanted at weekends by volunteers from the city,' Viktor said, 'to repair the damage. The design was a very big competition.'

We talked about our families, and the aftermath of the war and, in the bus, Lydia searched her bag for a photograph of their younger son.

'He's in the army, just now,' she explained with a wobble of anxiety. He looked uncannily like ours. From the jerking rectangle, strong and buoyant features looked back from under a shock of dark hair.

'Two more years – and he doesn't know what he wants to do yet.'

'Neither does ours,' I replied as, in the Nevsky, they lingered to see me catch the tram.

'I hear you're enquiring about going to the sailing club,' said Gennady, early next morning, crouched at head-level on the dock with his fingers clenched in his knees.

'Yes, but we hear it depends on you.'

'No,' he said. 'It depends on you. If you want to go' – he spread his hands wide – 'is all right.'

We hoped our relief didn't show too much; at the club we would be outside his range, and we had dreaded hurting his feelings.

Disaster very nearly struck at our furthest point from home. It was Monday 20 July, warm and bright, and as promised, Viktor arrived at noon. He had brought charts, as he scarcely knew the route, and it wasn't one to trifle with: there was weed and occasional pipelines, he said, and the mud-banks shifted around; and sometimes, when the water fell, big areas where birds promenaded. At first, all went smoothly – out through well-buoyed channels, where barges and minor cargo-boats plied, then an unmarked one with illegal stake-nets, overlooked by the Pribaltiskaya Hotel, rearing up to starboard like an outsized three-part mirror, and in again, pausing for a navy ship laying buoys for the summer regatta.

'That's the biggest and richest sailing club in the city,' said Viktor, making a friendly detour. The clubhouse, a truncated ziggurat of gleaming, zig-zag concrete, would have passed elsewhere for a Consulate.

'Trades' Union Club,' he said, heaving the tiller to turn to starboard.

'No,' Alan and I called out, lunging toward him in panic. '*No!*'

Our bows by now were bending toward the flank of a yacht, a white and shiny paragon moored at the edge of the river.

'Why . . . ?' stuttered Viktor, startled, as we swung her back with a foot to spare and circled the other way.

'Long keel,' I gasped. 'Turns slowly, and the self-steering too . . .'

Viktor watched in surprise as its fixed blade, right at the stern, arced a swirling swath in the water, making the slew even slower.

'My boat turns in its length,' he said.

We ought, of course, to have warned him; instead we burst into laughter and clapped him hard on the back. That I then proceeded to leave honours even by fumbling our mooring at Viktor's club and heaping unfair abuse on Alan scarcely seems to have dulled the main fright; for even now, after more than a year, the wandering id, visualizing our eight or nine tons driving a jagged hole through the pride of the Leningrad fleet, catches its breath and turns to ice.

After the weekend, official motors that had previously been only whirring and humming began to mesh and mince time finely. Minutes before we'd left the Commercial Dock, an Intourist girl had threaded her way between the recumbent ship's propellers and confirmed arrangements for our official reception.

The 'Executive Committee of the Council of Deputies of the People of Leningrad' occupied the grand classical bulk of yet another mansion, the Palace Marie, built for the Duchess Maria Nikolaievna, which faced across the Saharan expanses of St Isaac's Square to the gilded dome of the Cathedral. In the inevitable marbled and pillared hall, under the roof-top 'hammer and sickle', cracking and whipping in the sun, Ivan Shinkarenko received us, a trim and spare man in grey middle age. Announced by his card as 'Chef du Protocole, Soviet de Ville', he spoke excellent English, so that Tanya, our interpreter, elegant in a rose-coloured sheath of silk, was temporarily redundant. His well-holidayed face wrinkled with practised geniality, he absorbed our formal address for several minutes in silence, but eventually broke in on the slightly facetious account of Delap's services in preserving the life of Tsar Peter . . . 'which we like to think of as a very Irish contribution to the building of Leningrad.'

'. . . so if it were not for him, we wouldn't be here at all!' Shinkarenko laughingly protested. 'You know, we have had many other rulers, and later people involved in the making of the city . . .'

As we presented official letters of greeting, exchanged news of sailing in our respective countries, comments on the imbalance of sailors heading each way and examples of nineteenth-century yachtsmen, all the while Tanya's disturbing dark eyes, carefully watching our lips, swung to and fro between East and West like the pendula of twin clocks under the fixed and gilded stare of Lenin on the wall behind her. It was a moment to treasure; but a possible problem loomed outside. A crew from Leningrad TV, three men and two jeeps with drivers, patiently awaited a photo-call.

'They also want to bring you back to the club and take some film of you sailing,' said Tanya, interpreting for the man chewing gum, with greased-back hair and a bootlace tie. But would the club want them? We, after all, were only guests. Forewarned, but unable to check if the Commodore considered a media invasion appropriate, we 'phoned one of the skippers instead. The answer was crisp.

'But of course! It's necessary. TV has its job to do, and they must go where they want.'

We were no less relieved that the re-enactment went without major blunders, and its transmission as news to millions of viewers set the final seal for us on our arrival at the sailing club that Peter the Great had founded, and which is probably the oldest in the world.

'The bootmaker in Kronstadt told us the Russian soldiers were awful thieves, and that we should be careful of our pocket handkerchiefs – a nice character of his fellow countrymen,' Corrigan had noted; and, somewhere along the line, before we reached the club, a pilot handling one of our heavy stainless-steel yachtsmen's knives with studied curiosity, suddenly returned it, saying, 'Best out of sight, I think.'

Was it partly for that reason, we wondered, that the authorities advised one man on the boat at all times? It was an irksome precaution, if none of us felt sufficiently exhausted to volunteer; but the longer we stayed at the Terminal and the Dock, the less it seemed like a fear of potential theft and the more a matter of an ingrained prophylactic approach: a sort of combination of the Potemkin tradition of showing visitors only the very best, and a genuine fear that something might just go wrong. After a day or two at the club, we ended up with the feeling that, had we abandoned the boat and left the hatches open, nothing would have walked away except visitors looking to see if we were aboard and, far from taking, they gave to the point of inundation in gifts and hospitality.

Diesel was anonymously plonked on board. The boat was forcibly watered. Vodka, invitations to swim, boxes of matches with scribbled greetings, a precious copy of *Midshipman Easy*, with the difficult bits appended in Russian, were called or brought or handed over. A heavy-bellied, bare-chested man, trailing a small brown dog, brought us on to his cruiser, three or four berths away, the first of several such visits.

When club members called on us, the object of curiosity was often not so much our boat, which was quite like many of theirs, as her equipment: the self-steering gear, and particularly the Decca; but the traffic wasn't one-way. To a man, they were very politely scornful about the size of our compass. In vain we protested that actually ours was quite big; theirs, as they proudly demonstrated, were enormous brass-bound affairs, often set flush with the deck, that would not have disgraced a corvette. Small, they implied, is not beautiful. But what was our route, they wanted to know? And where had we started? How did it look? We soon discovered a very embarrassing oversight in our provision of photographs from home; the few we had vanished in all directions, like confetti in a high wind.

And who owns the boat? was usually the fourth or fifth question: a quietness normally greeted the answer, and perhaps a brightening nod when we explained it was used as a school. So what about yours? we would ask. Most were owned by the various clubs, whether scout or student, or navy, and therefore indirectly by the government, but there were some privately-owned ones too. As we'd arrived, Viktor had pointed out on the bank a group of variously patched and woebegone long-tailed cruisers, typical of a type that could be seen at any creek or staithe in England, bespeaking the painful effort of long-term restoration or a less than watertight dream; and in Leningrad and elsewhere, we were to come across the odd top-flight rated, glass-fibre racer or a carefully hand-sculpted hull, owned outright by a club professional coach. The individual effort was not obvious, but nonetheless highly prized.

'But where do the Russians sail to?' the Poles were to demand, weeks later. 'We build them any amount of yachts and never see them again.'

Flora gave one end of the answer. She was just such a one, built in Poland ten years before, and fitted with Polish equipment; but now she formed a far-ranging team with Viktor and his crew and often by-passed the Baltic coasts altogether. Before their just-completed tour to France, they had been to Britain in 1984, and in other years had voyaged to the Canaries, the Caribbean and Canada. Most of these outings, Viktor explained, were part of Russia's official representation at sail-training rallies, directed by the club, for which he received free food, some equipment and a modest amount of cash. It was a system he liked, although his programme was settled for him. At other times, he could sail elsewhere in his own vacations, and at his own expense.

In the middle ground were people like Bob Kallinin (the man with the dog and the hairy chest), or the pair we'd met in the Leningrad approaches, who vaguely limited their travels to Tallinn or Riga or Vyborg, occasionally visiting other socialist countries.

At the other extreme were the yachts which simply went inland. 'We have about sixty in the club,' someone told us, 'and most have gone there already.'

Between two and four am, the bridges over the Neva silently lift, splitting in the middle and hoisting the tram-way gantries with them.

Merchant ships pass through, along with yachts that can't drop their masts, heading up against the strong current toward the vast expanse of Lake Ladoga, more than 100 miles square, lurking unseen beyond the city. But most of the yachts, to avoid delays, have devised methods of de-masting: even as we watched, the varnished spars of two or three late-departers tilted and caught the sun as their white-hatted crews manoeuvred them down to their decks.

Alkor, on the face of it, was just one more of those who'd dealt with the chore a bit sooner. Her well-worn interior betrayed more age than some, but her mast was already neatly stowed across the pulpit and criss-cross crutches astern, sticking out purposefully fore and aft like an athlete's javelin. But the boat and crew were unique: she was the only other visitor, and had come from the other direction.

Moscow, as we were proudly reminded, is the City of Five Seas, the result of continuous expansion by the initially sea-less Rus: at first to the ice-bound White Sea in the north, then to the south-easterly Caspian. In Peter's time, the Azov Sea, which gave on to the Black and, finally, the Baltic Sea, had followed. *Alkor* was from Volgograd, 1,000 miles beyond Moscow, 300 from the Volga delta into the Caspian Sea. Her Ukrainian crew of seven or eight had barged her up through steppes and lakes, along canals and rivers, and later would sail her back. Among them was a boy of nine, a grizzled veteran of 50 or more, a scholarly engineer, and assorted tough-looking nuts with cropped hair or long, and beards that ran from black to blond. The skipper, a greying but comely psychiatrist, sang and guitared as well as she navigated (they said) and, far into the night, ballads in Russian and English mingled, as we swigged dark tea from enamelled mugs like craters, and spoonsful of even darker jam.

'Not in it – just with it!' they grinned, straightening a misconception.

The sailing club gave our morale a great fillip. It was good to be able to prowl the city, or bring back guests, or simply lie out under the trees without wondering when *Canna*'s next move might be. A tight crew at sea, we took advantage of the freedom on shore to split into ones and twos. The club was surrounded by acres of waterside parkland, and the banks in the warm afternoons were dotted with *grandes baigneuses* like Cezanne's. Scullers scooted and joggers jogged.

Shay sometimes just wandered around. Alan, who couldn't bear to waste time, disappeared with his camera, stopping whomever he met in the street, be it dogs or shoppers or a wedding party, or a heavily decorated war veteran with a very stern wife. They all obliged. He went for a haircut, and fell half in love with the stylist, insisted on taking her photograph too, and then stayed on for a shave. He rubbed his chin wistfully in the evenings, wondering how soon he could justify his next visit. The Intourist girls, seeming almost let down that most of us weren't religious, went out of their way to show him the Catholic church. After Mass, he snapped the priest too, an upright old man in a black biretta, complete with his crucifixes and candles; but the price of confession, he later confessed, had been one of his scarce rolls of film.

This lack of the predictable was one of our main delights. Why, for instance, had no one mentioned that *Pravda* was only three pages long and that it is pasted in showcases on the streets? That the men have nineteenth-century manners? That gypsies pass like chameleonic visions, but one doesn't see either rubbish or shops? (The shops don't have big windows and signs.) And then cars: the effect of the lack of them should have been obvious, but wasn't. When Viktor and Lydia had offered to bring me back to the city, I'd assumed that meant one of the modest limousines scattered outside the club, not Shanks's pony; and I still hadn't made the adjustment when, a day or two later, the Leningrad-based editors of *Katera y Yachty*, Russia's premier yachting magazine, came on board to interview us. Of course, I presumed, they'd arrive by car; but no, they walked from the tram, two unassuming men whose publication sells well over three million copies bi-monthly and has a readership probably greater than all other European sailing magazines put together. And why not? They'd arrived refreshed. No doubt, if they needed, they took a taxi; and the limited car-usership was why it was still possible to get around the city at reasonable speed, why the air wasn't totally fouled with fumes and horns and din, and why, perhaps, it felt more relaxed than London or New York.

In that case, where were the bicycles? In these flat wide-open streets (excusing tramlines and pot-holes), bicycles seemed obvious. But in Leningrad we saw barely half-a-dozen; most of those were racing models, and the other, on the deck of his cruise ship, belonged to Riho, the schoolboy from Tallin. In all the open countryside later, we saw scarcely another. Official statistics said they were made – but were they too expensive, or simply considered unnecessary? No one could give us an answer. But comparatively useless dogs there were in plenty. There were Afghans and brown Borzois, and spaniels that matched their owners' dresses. It smelt like a new phenomenon and perhaps a sign of the times. Viktor reinforced this idea as we watched a harassed girl, with high heels and fly-away hair, haul a diminutive scrap of pedigree through the closing doors of a bus at the very end of its scarlet lead, just in time to prevent it being bisected. 'That woman crazy, I think,' he had said, screwing a censorious finger into his head.

All the same, they felt for their pets. Once, Susan had been trapped on a pavement in a semi-circle of shoppers, three or four deep, surrounding a dog with a bleeding paw, their faces wrought with concern.

*　　*　　*

It was in the early hours of our first night at the club, and I was halfway into pyjamas, when someone knocked hard on the cabin top. A young official with epaulettes stood straightfaced in the dark alongside, silently flashing a torch.

He beckoned along the floating duckboard, and into another yacht. Two other serious youngsters in mufti were waiting in a small saloon, furnished and draped all in scarlet. The notion of interrogation switched to a kangaroo court. It changed again to a mugging as the three escorted me firmly away from the dock, out along the river-bank into a pot-holed and ditch-crossed wasteland shaded in black and purple. Where on earth . . . ? They marched me on for 200 yards, stumbling and groping around the back of tall, blind workshops, until a floating boathouse appeared, a mouldering pile of fancy timber that threw even darker shadows under its listing verandahs. They prodded me over the bendy gangplank and round to the other side – on to a modern cruiser and down to a dead-of-night supper of casseroled fish and red wine.

Just how three teenagers came to be in charge of an American-designed 30-foot yacht, I never quite figured out. Our language just wasn't up to it at that time of night. Instead, they showed me their instruments. Late back, apparently, from a day out on the Bay, and remembering us halfway through their feast, they had salvaged some and then waylaid me in force. It made their day when I explained their ringleader's gold-shouldered jacket had given me a start. It hadn't crossed my mind it might have been 'army surplus'.

Uniforms, I reflected, were like dogs and bikes, another presence and absence. Public transport employees didn't have them. People drove their trams or trolleys in baggy gansies and flannels or skirts as if at ease in their living-rooms. But the pavements were crawling with well-creased khaki, as though the army itself was in surplus. Shay, still slightly prickly, found it provoking; even though most wielded only briefcases, which were said to hold sandwiches rather than secrets. They drank *kvass*, fermented-bread beer sold from stalls at the side of the road, or aerated water at a kopeck a go from gadgets with a single glass that each customer rinsed out after him and, like everyone else, they gorged ice-cream and sat on the river steps in the sun.

There were plenty of them now, but 45 years ago, there had only just been enough, when German shells had come whistling down from the skies, killing, maiming and wrecking the streets and the city.

Viktor had seen it all as a boy.

He'd pointed out a four-square, bland, unpainted block, in the leafy suburb where his family had lived.

'But that's more recent,' he said. 'The old apartments have gone, and it's been rebuilt.'

'So how did you manage? How many houses and flats were destroyed?'

'Nearly half,' he answered. People had moved in with others to less damaged blocks.

But, even allowing for the half-million Leningraders who died of wounds or starvation during the 900 days of the siege, it spoke of terrible privation and crowding.

'Go and visit the city cemetery,' someone from home had advised us. 'I challenge you not to be moved.'

At least half of Leningrad's five millions seemed to be travelling as Shay and I made our way with tripods and cameras out to Piskariovskoe. They flooded into the metro tunnels in droves, jamming the gargantuan marble-lined halls of the stations. Women with flowers, students with rucksacks reading books, a very old man from the country with a shepherd's crook and an enormous basket of eggs, jostled on to the escalators and disappeared up into endless perspectives, or squeezed on to the labouring buses.

We *were* moved. We spent the afternoon there, filming. Like almost everything in the city, it is huge, simple, axial, grand. Twin white pavilions frame a courtyard, a central flame and a flight of steps descending. Between green banks, a canal of blood-red roses taper and rush to the feet of the Motherland, standing tall and dark at the focus, holding out a garland against sun-faded fields, and distant pylons and flats. She is flanked by inky cypresses and walls incised with names and desolate bas-reliefs. A man with snow-white hair and his wife sit as though carved, to one side. Sunlight moves across granite faces. The living circulate like cells or clusters around the gravelled arteries. A tiny girl with white-frilled knickers plays on the kerb of a shallow pool, throwing in a few kopecks. They wink and side-slip to lie with others on a watery green mosaic. A wedding group briefly pay their respects, gazing down from the upper level. A couple with a squeaky buggy; a trio of shy girls in trousers, a tourist group with a Russian guide dotted on one of the cross paths, and a solitary soldier, cap under arm, striding past clumps of pale peonies, carefully smoothing his hair. None are more than 40 or 50 years old. But out to the side, just visible over the ranks of long, steep-sided, grass-covered mounds, a pair of old men hunch on a bench. The mounds are identical, like soft concrete castings, or the upside-down products of oversized cake-tins. '1942' states a grey stone footnote, incised in black with a sickle and star. 1942. 1942. 1944. At least 10,000 in each grave we reckoned. 1944. The repetition is ghastly.

Beyond, where paths begin to meander, two heavy women and fluting bird-song wander through Orthodox graves under trees. Stiff iron railings enclose miniature benches for mourners, crosses set with shells or sepia photographs, scatters of fresh and plastic flowers. Beyond again are stands of birch, around the silver trunks of which, here and there, crimson headscarfs are tied. The scarlet wounds recede through the wood, their hanging corners stirring very gently, as if the sudden caws of unseen birds disturb a memory.

At first, the impact was one of shock. But after a while, a different perspective set in. People, it seemed, weren't simply brooding. Some were there just to savour the space and the peace. One lean man had come with his daughter, who was doing a project for school. And the greyish photographs of Leningrad during the siege, displayed in the cube-like pavilions, were mostly not about death at all – they showed women bandaged in bulky clothing, buttressing shaky buildings with timber or grappling with mountains of rubble, like willing slaves in the grip of a grand idea. And even now, I realized, as trams brought us back to the centre, despite the passage of centuries, despite modern equipment and revolutions, and traffic and buses and new-fangled boats, the city fabric still dwarfed its termites. It seemed to be built for giants. The roof-top Hermitage gods looked out as serenely as ever, ignoring the thronging midgets below. The streets were more empty than full, and once, pausing for a lemonade, I'd been startled to glance overhead and find myself under a triumphal arch, below which the kiosk dwindled to matchbox size. Piranesi would have been in his element, needing no exaggeration to point out the difference in scale; but, unlike Rome, here the ruins weren't ruins at all.

If anything, the roles were reversed; it was the lesser, newer buildings that suffered. Their slightly shabby air had at first been a surprise, like an animal caught in mid-moult. Bordering the outer canals, or the apartment courtyards with climbing-frames where toddlers played under trees and older tenants dozed or chatted, siennas and ochres of decades ago had faded and not been renewed, ledges grew moss, plastered reveals were cracked and chipped like old cups, and the down-pipes that had so appalled our friend David were indeed bashed and bruised at their bottoms, oversized to cope with snow-melt, and clumsily patched with tubes of tin.

But the monuments, the city's main display! – the Winter Palace, already gleaming, was being repainted and, if religious activities had fallen some-what from favour, incredible love was lavished on their buildings instead. The Saviour and Blood church, poking up pure-gold onions and turquoise lozenges and hundreds of coffered portraits of saints, had been suffocated in scaffold for as long as most could remember; and St Isaac's Cathedral, on whose foundations, in sucking bog, half a million roubles were lavished, and which became the subject of massive rebuilding later, when all of its monolithic 60-foot columns tilted in different directions, was once again labouring under the threat of collapse, the din of compressors, and hordes of ant-like builders clambering around its shoulders.

Any self-respecting expert with a clipboard would have long since told the city fathers to bulldoze the whole outrageous burden for once and for all, and to start the entire exercise again, on a more human scale, and in a more sensible place. Somehow it seemed unlikely that such modest people could indefinitely sustain the load, and almost inconceivable that they had done so thus far. A hundred years and more before, they had prised a 1,600-ton boulder out of a Finnish forest, and trundled it into the city as a base for a statue of Peter, an effort that encapsulated the city and its people. They seemed almost like an endless supply of uncomplaining rollers under a vast slab of granite, being inched carefully forward from one century into the next.

But at least the juggernaut was being preserved intact, free of advertisements and clutter, each building contributing in its own right, free of steel-framed glassy intrusions and skyscrapers with their heads in the clouds. Modern mammoths were built further out, as Susan and I discovered by accident on the morning of 22 July, the day appointed for our departure. We were making apologies for an appointment we'd cancelled, to make way for our mayoral reception, to an official of the city's Sports Committee.

'A pity,' he said, from a desk wedged between Corinthian columns. 'The President was here to meet you too. But maybe you can see him now, out at the Palace of Sport.'

He rounded up an interpreter and a car, and they whizzed us up the Moscow Road. The V. I. Lenin sports hall was proof, if any were needed, that the city still thinks big. Its enormous structure, like a columned birthday-cake with a sun-roof, is more than 200 yards across.

'And contains nearly a million cubic metres,' the training manager told us as we sat in a sloping field of plastic chairs. 'It can seat 25,000 people for meetings. We can take seats away and use it as a football pitch. Or, for hockey. Or ballet' – and western pop groups, although she didn't say so.

For a week or two now, it was ice. A chill breeze cooled the corridors and, under banks of lights and walkways more than 100 feet above, youngsters warmed up on their skates. The odd one casually skidded and fell. Miniature tractors watered and squeegeed the central pitch while, on a 1,000-foot outside track, speed-men snaked between the stragglers, with limbs jerking like heron's legs and tasselled scarves flying behind.

'Those are some of the best ones,' she said. 'And sometimes we train foreign teams too.' We were the only spectators. P. Tolstihin, the brisk and balding director, was also the talented yachtsman the deputy mayor had mentioned. Yes – they would like to have invitations to western sailing races. Their own Baltic Cup race was being held in three stages next year – perhaps our sailors could enter?

'And,' he had said as we'd parted, 'I can tell you definitely. Your yacht is the first in my time to come from your country to Leningrad.'

It was just the note to leave on – and leave we must, despite the thousand and one things undone. We were due away in the late afternoon, to clear the canal before dusk, but first we had to get *Canna* back to the Terminal, and we'd cut it rather too fine. Back at the club, the Commodore had arranged a pilot, and both were waiting to see us away. But where, for goodness sake, was the crew? All aboard, in the nick of time, except Rupert. He'd gone sailing solo dinghies in company, and no one had seen him since. Here was a fine fix! We either stayed and disrupted a dozen officials and others, or took a chance of finding him *en route*, somewhere out in the bay.

'I'll come with you,' offered a crewman from *Flora*. If we find him, I'll bring back his boat.'

We kept our fingers crossed. Captain Pannin waved us away. So did a small family cruiser, ghosting under spinnaker. So did a navy rowing-boat, full of cadets in traditional stripey singlets. A club launch followed, to watch we didn't get stuck in the mud. Our mainsail stayed in its cover, while the pilot kept us clear of the razor-sharp legs of hydrofoils and we anxiously scanned the horizon. By a lucky chance we found Rupert down-river and hauled him out of his dinghy; but at the Terminal the berthing problems were now spectacular. Our tucked-behind slot was effaced by a liner projecting way out beyond it, and where we had scanned for alternatives, the *Dar Młodziezy*, Poland's newest square-rigged sail-training ship, stretched her gleaming 100-yard length. Her triple masts towered 150 feet high, and she sported a vicious bowsprit. Gennady had organized a courtesy visit for us, but there was no chance of even getting ashore. As we doubtfully nosed to a corner, wash rolled us and threatened the rigging. Instead we plucked the reluctant officials on board (probably also a first for the port) and jilled around until they finished. There was a brief goodbye to Gennady. He apologized for a vest of mine included by mistake in the laundry. It had come back in frameable condition, as stiff as a board and small enough for a dwarf.

'Don't worry!' I called. 'There's been plenty of spirit to keep us warm!'

We took on our fifth and last pilot, and with him the first stirrings of regret. Six days had been a big mistake – we had needed at least sixteen. The Maritime Museum, Petrodvorets, Pushkin – there were a thousand things we hadn't done. Too late – it was time for Tallinn; with a brutal suddenness we hadn't at all prepared for we were away and gone, and facing a freshening breeze, and another long stretch of foreign shore.

As the city's domes darkened and slid away, we had little time to consult our feelings, to assess our reactions to the all-too-short sojourn, or appraise the fruits of our efforts so far.

Some crew were already in no state to do so. Shay and Rupert, although buoyant and smiling when leaving the dock, were exhausted by the frantic pace, and had immediately collapsed on their berths below. Alan, ministering to the pilot, and Susan, who was manfully stewing fish – the last of the chandler's outsized flounders – were far from free to ruminate.

For myself, the glimpses of the receding skyline, snatched while rooting out new charts, made me regretful but gratified.

So much had gone right. I had been hugely impressed not just by the city, by its timeless uncluttered solidity, and something of the same in the people themselves; but also by the surprising directness of personal reactions, by the ease of many relationships. I'd been pleased by our semi-private status which had allowed us to scatter and wander about, and to meet officials only when we needed – that had been a tremendous boon.

Other crew had thought otherwise, suggesting I discounted the drawbacks too much, but I couldn't agree with this. What truly is the point of travel if not to relish things as they are? Real disappointments had been very minor – a party on board for which guests failed to come – as against what we'd omitted ourselves, the gifts and greetings we couldn't match; and even Shay, I had lately noticed, had shown signs of breaking out of his mould. Leningrad had turned out for him to be yet another place in which to win friends and influence people . . .

But one particular shift of thought had by now affected us all. Geography and feelings were out of phase, and our goalposts had been decisively moved. That Leningrad was our furthest point east and the place from which we would make our return now seemed in this sense a mere accident: it was really the start of our main repast.

There was a lot more Soviet coastline to sail, which was bound to shed light on what we had seen, and we had no scope, yet, for sweeping judgements. The Baltic Republics were renowned for their warmth, and we hoped to explore them more contemplatively.

But just for a while, that wasn't to be. *Canna* suddenly reclaimed our attention, and for a while she needed it all.

CHAPTER 10

Estonia

'Why should you need a pilot out?' a skipper from the club had asked. We also wondered, and our present man, no better clad than the first, was probably sorry about it too.

The summer was firmly set in and the evening bright, but the wind, dead on the nose along the canal, built up a steep chop that combed the walls, and once again we were motoring. Earlier versions of our boat had had a continuous baulk round the cockpit, but on this one, for reasons unknown, it was missing towards the stern. As *Canna* bucked, gallons of Baltic picked up on her nose rushed aft, rebounded, and ended up in the well of the cockpit. By the time it got to knee height, the pilot, clutching the tiller, was dancing between the locker lids, still in his fancy shoes, as if a shark was chasing his ankles.

The stern got lower and lower, the exhaust was way under the water and there was nothing for it but to slow down; but at least the pilot, now looking even more like a Corsican bandit with boots and beret, moustache and dark glasses, was able to tell us a gentle night was due out at the pilot station. So it proved; and after passing even stranger traffic than on the way in – a floating chemicals cylinder dwarfing the tug it was tied to, and a latticed bridge gantry complete with approach ramps towed along on its side – we put him aboard his launch under a starry sky, half an hour before midnight. His gift of a painted spoon to Susan was our last connection with Russia, and on the stroke of 23 July, we once again hoisted sail.

After laying our course in Kerry, we'd heard that the right way to circuit the Baltic was a point of considerable argument. On balance it was thought best, by the Finns at least, to go widdershins, against the sun; the anticlockwise route, they said, made best use of German duty-free, and prevailing south-west winds. For now, they seemed to be right. The southerly zephyr slowly veered west and, as we crossed bearings from the Schepelevski and Ustinski lights, on the former Ingrian coast, *Canna*'s track was steadily bending away to the north, following the opposite shoreline round toward Vyborg and Finland. The shortest cut for the 200 miles to Tallinn would have lead through a maze of reefs to the south, inshore of Seskar and the other islands we'd skirted on arrival.

'OK in good weather,' a Russian skipper had told us. 'But if mist comes down, and you miss one buoy, what then?' He had rounded the hypothesis with the sound of ascending bubbles.

Although visibility was good enough, dawn found us many miles north of the hazards close to the island of Bol'shoy Berezovyy. Strategy was being decided for us; from here we could beat through the six-mile-wide gap between the Finnish border and the central shipping channels, and avoid the southern islands entirely.

By 13.30, *Canna* was into a fishing zone and seven miles short of Finnish waters. Half an hour more and we'd go about; but moments later, familiar brown and white tufts appeared, heralding patrol boat 12. Prickly and grey, she crossed acutely ahead and slowed. Concerned to get our flags just right, we charged straight past before noticing hers. Knots of uniformed heads at her rails swung open-mouthed to keep pace with our progress.

'What's his yellow and black?' called Alan, and the almanac had to be sent for. It's not so often these days we have to interpret dusters.

'Roger – good God – it's letter "L": "STOP YOUR VESSEL INSTANTLY!"'

'Heave to,' I yelled. No wonder their inflatable dinghy was halfway down to the water, and their crew had gaped incredulously, as if we'd just crashed through a road-block. But even as we examined each other from a distance of 50 yards, her alarming chequered flag came down and their dinghy dithered and then reversed with a mighty squealing of davits. Obviously we'd been found on a list and, for now, the risk of boarding was over.

'Right,' I said. 'We'll carry on,' and laid off on the same tack. I hate changing course before I'm ready, and it messes up the deck-log entries if you don't go about on the hour. Our friend disappeared for twenty minutes, and then came back to accompany us. Eureka! We saluted each other perfectly, dropping and hoisting ensigns with exquisite timing and mutual esteem; but by then it was 14.00 and time to go about. For a moment or two she was dead ahead and seemed taken aback as we drove toward her. She turned as if to keep out of our way and then swung quickly back alongside. We were still manoeuvring like dodgems when Shay, disturbed from sleep, came up to view the commotion, and the patrol boat commander, high above on his flying bridge, swung a huge bronzed arm as if to dispute our new course. By then we were heading south-west, slanting slightly away from the border.

'I wonder what he wants now?' I muttered. 'We'll just carry on for a while and see.'

'But Roger!' yelled Shay who hadn't quite got his eye in, 'we'll *have* to change. It'll send them completely mad!'

'We're bloody well not going back to Leningrad!' I retorted, vexed by such fifth-column advice; but my obstinacy was perhaps also fuelled by surprising comments we'd heard on the Navy.

'Far too much money, too little to do,' someone in Leningrad had said, in the casual way one might talk of a neighbour; and a Russian yachtsman had also complained – as Corrigan had – of a want of seamanship. Russian yachts were inspected, comparatively more often than shipping, he felt, and on one occasion, despite his warnings, a navy launch had damaged his gunwale. He'd given the man responsible a furious dressing-down on his foredeck. Problems with yachts were almost bound to occur, I soliloquized, to calm the crew. If the Navy weren't all trained in sailing, it would be hard for them to decipher yachting manoeuvres; besides, in our case, they weren't to know that we knew where we were, and perhaps they had merely been warning us away from sunken rocks that we were well aware of. But when, two hours later, our very next port tack was curtailed, there was no doubt left about their intent.

By then we were rounding blunt little Ostrov Sommers, but this time on the north side where, under the afternoon sun, the rusty bulk of a full-sized ship lay broken and ghastly across its reef. The patrol boats seemed to work in pairs and, for a few split seconds, when No. 125 idled right across us ahead, I didn't quite believe the blockage was meant for us. As Rupert quickly eased out sheets, I made to go under his squared-off stern. A touch of reverse, a swirl of water, and he soon put paid to that idea. We went about in a hurry, almost against his heavy grey hull. He blasted us with a big loud-hailer, we waved a telephone handset back; but for want of a common language both gadgets failed to communicate.

'Tallinn!' I yelled, pointing at the sail and slashing zigzags in the air; but again the flying-bridge Apollo, heavily muscled and bare to the waist, wielded long frustrated arms – now like a scimitars forming a cross.

Not 'skull and crossbones', Susan surmised, but simply 'border closed', and my mime of essential sailing tactics didn't impress him at all. He gestured straight forward repeatedly, until I gave in and gave him thumbs-up.

Boris, the Dublin consul, had asked if we were staying in Soviet waters during the course of our visit, and now at last we thought we knew why. The Russians, with their dread of avoidable trouble, kept boats at least three miles clear of the Finnish border, forming a sort of no man's land. It was charted that way on the Finnish side, but unfortunately not on the Russian. Now, the message was loud and clear, and we acquiesced with half-hour tacks that kept us further to the south, and away from the sensitive area.

For the rest of the day and the night, excitements were relatively mild. In the gentle evening, Gogland island swung inward from the horizon, reforming itself on the starboard bow, slope by slope and tree by tree. We could see the inviting anchorage far up on its eastern side, but it would have been tempting time and fate to nose in when we didn't need to. Instead we squeezed between a hazard and a hard place, between an overtaking ship and the southern point of the island, where a minaret-like lighthouse silently watched us pass, and a skein of birds skimmed low to the water. A single window was lit in the pastel-green keeper's house. *Canna* dipped briefly into the shadow of the land and out again, into very low sunlight glowing gold through her mainsail.

Long leg and short, starboard and port; as we crabbed south-westward during the night, the wind stayed mainly westerly giving us an uneven lope. It was a gait that was to stay with us for many hundreds of miles. South past Ostrov Virginy and Malyy Tyuters to port, mere scatters of rock and flat pancakes, then north-west to clear the shallow bank of Vaindlo. At dawn a patrol boat's searchlight momentarily glared, and the sun rose up like a blood-red ship, sliced into decks and funnels by cloud.

The Estonian coastline at last saluted with the tiny island of Mohni. We were glad of its reassurance, even though Decca was once again giving good fixes. The coast everywhere thereabouts was low, almost indistinguishable to the unpractised eye, and the coastal radio-beacons seemed to transmit very weakly.

Now we were into the stretches of shore that had entranced us during planning. Purikari Neem, Juminda Nina: the heads of probing peninsulas marched on by as we paralleled the land, motorsailing now that the wind was failing. Occlusions built up, and greasy patches of water; it rained a little, and cleared to sultry sun. We passed small fishing boats trawling.

Across the mouth of the Muuga Laht, where a deep-set new harbour was being built: the biggest Soviet port in the Baltic. Its pilot station was already charted, but a scatter of yellow buoys and markers which we cautiously wove through were not. On between the martello-like light of Keri, and the bald little island of Prangli Saar, sprouting masts like a few short hairs. At last, two days out from Leningrad, we made the final turning point: the coincidence of a prohibited zone and a spoil ground and a scatter of sunken reefs and wrecks, a mile north-west of the modest island of Aegna Saar. Rounding Aegna lighthouse, Tallinn Bay suddenly opened nine miles deep, and five or six wide, minutely dotted with sails.

'What do we expect here?' asked Shay, as a freshening breeze drove us in close-hauled, and the shores yielded only anonymous buildings set among patched and puckered woodland.

I was not sure of the answer. We were now already west of Helsinki, but still in Soviet waters; still within the Union, but entering a different country. Differences could already be sensed: there had been no time of arrival stated, and no response on the radio, although we had been trying for hours. A pilot boat had passed us by, and of the patrol boats that had momentarily accosted Bernard Hayman's yacht ten years before, there was no sign at all.

In complete contrast to our Leningrad approach, we suddenly seemed to be incognito. Tallinn, however, was quite unmistakable and closing quickly on our starboard bow. Its boldly Rhine-like castled profile, rearing up on a slanting hill, was echoed by fleets of ephemeral sails scooting under her pinnacles – and if the outlines of both seemed faintly familiar who, we wondered, was helming the one and who, in the past, had raised the other?

'DDR . . . SR.' The sail numbers of Olympic-class dinghies soon flashed back, as a few came close with crews dangling outboard from trapezes. 'East German . . . Soviet' – it was obviously a major regatta, with half a dozen navy launches anchored as committee boats.

And so who had built its fantastic backdrop? But to question the city's provenance seemed to have provoked a genie. The yacht-harbour had appeared three miles to the east and we made it only just in time. The afternoon tensed and turned suddenly twilit. A departing yacht was driven back by squalls. Gales of rain came down in spears. Black cloud boiled up from Tallinn's ramparts, and spilled across the sky like plague. Lightning flashed livid on conical towers, blanching them to pillars of salt, as the violent downpour redoubled its thunder, and the distant skyline seemed possessed.

'I never saw anything so mediaeval!' exclaimed Alan, while fighting to raise the sprayhood over the companionway.

Which exactly did he mean? Too wet to wonder; just time enough to get below. But he was right. The fireworks had branded the city's essence: it reeked of an older sense of time.

The original Estonians came from the east in times BC, even before the Egyptians had got going on their pyramids. One of the Finno-Ugric peoples migrating from the Urals of central Russia, nowadays their tribal descendants form an enormous arc, roughly centred on Moscow, like flames at the fringe of a bonfire. There are minor brands in the Volga basin, the Hungarians in the extreme south-west forming a separate tribe and enclave; the Estonians and their neighbours across the water, the Finns; the Livs of Latvia, whom we were later to meet; the Lapps of northern Norway; Karelians on the Finnish border with Russia; and a string of embers scattered through western Siberia and out along the Arctic coast.

Tallinn, of the defensible hill and sheltered bay, was an obvious magnet to all and sundry, and a continual east-west bone of contention. At first, the Estonians had absorbed arrivals of Slavs and Germans, and even adopted the German word 'Eastland' for themselves, but although Tallinn (according to a wandering Arab scholar) was already fortified in the twelfth century, Estonia as now defined didn't then exist. It took other invaders from the west to create it. Over the centuries, Danes shared it with Germans; Swedes and Finns tore it asunder, leaving Denmark only scraps in the west; then Sweden snatched it all, and for the first time Estonia was an entity. But not for long. Tsar Peter, inevitably, began to play grand-mother's footsteps, gobbling up coastal fortresses whenever the Vikings weren't looking, and soon, in 1721, Estonia and Latvia were confirmed as Russian possessions. The Russians ruled for two centuries, although the British, as elsewhere, continued to make a nuisance from time to time. In the 1850s their fleet had attacked here as well as in Finland, and the *Oriana*'s Russian host in 1859, a Colonel Krusenstern (surprisingly a naval title), who had lived through it as the commander of a large shore battery had com-mented to Corrigan on how tiresome it had made life for them, how the British gunboats 'used to come and pepper away at them . . .' and that they 'used to go where Russian boats never dreamed of going and knew the coast perfectly'.

The east-west tug of war had continued almost up to the present. For a few short months, in Bolshevik times, Estonia came under communist control, but then snatched at independence (or suffered bourgeois domination, depending on the textbook), along with Latvia, Lithuania and Finland, when Lenin offered autonomy. For 20 years she struggled, supported by Finland, Sweden, Denmark and Britain – Admiral Cowan's fleet was stationed in Tallinn, once again with the purpose of keeping the Russians at bay – until the Second World War finally knocked away her western props. 'And what then?' queried Rupert, raising an eyebrow. 'The national communist party took over,' I read. 'In 1940 she rejoined the Soviet Union. Her population of one and a half million is the smallest of any Union republic.' But they compensate (so the guidebooks say) by being some of the tallest people in Europe.

And what now? So far, the only very tall things we could see were flagpoles in the marina, from one of which the Soviet Estonian flag was flying (the same as the Russian, but crossed below with white scalloped stripes over a broad flood of blue, denoting the Baltic, making the rest of it look like a livid red sunset). The Russian flag was there too, and so, soon after, was ours to be, to our very considerable delight. Wheels were obviously grinding. At the onset of the gale we'd dashed to report to a look-out post, a multi-storeyed red and white cake-stand at the knuckle of the mole, where two militia, dressed like doughnuts, had mistaken us for Italians. A common error – but by the time the sun reappeared, raising columns of steam from the puddles, Soviet authority had arrived in force, and mopped up formalities in very short order.

Much of our four-day visit to Tallinn was antithesis to Leningrad. What looked like a pyramid with windows (in fact the gable of a ruined church) had led *Canna* straight toward Pirita: its Yachting Centre, a legacy of the 1980 Olympics, offered the best facilities anywhere on our voyage. Our berth at a cobbled and tideless dock lay under the buildings from which the

sailing events had been run. With the adjacent Olympic Hotel, they
stretched away in the town direction like a spruced-up armadillo, ribbed in
concrete and plated with steel. Here indeed was luxury. Somewhere in its
rambling depths, a babushka booked us into acres of empty sauna and
showers and, from the glass-walled restaurant, over breakfasts of prunes
and cheese, the view swept in across arcs of sandy shore to ranks of racing
yachts beneath and *Canna* idling among them.

Immersion in sailing was immediate and total. '"Socialist" Olympics are
in full swing,' the club officials told us, 'with entries from all over the eastern
bloc. Would you like to meet and film them in action? No problem!'

Shay spent two full days capturing 'Solings' and 'Stars' capsizing around
buoys, and catamarans precariously flying their windward hulls, against the
backdrop of the city, and ferries arriving from Finland: in the dock behind
the club were the cruising yachts. We shouldn't have been surprised.
Boating and sailing is in the Tallinner blood. Even in the 1920s, Ransome
reported the waterfront under the castle was littered with scores of ancient
hulls: 'the scrapings of the yacht club – being repaired by the cunning and
sold to the unwary.' Nor were distant foreigners new. For ages before then,
flat-bottomed Volga-built boats, sewn with leather, had been hauled there
upriver and overland, and sold at the end of each season by fishermen from
central Russia; and for centuries the sea link with Finland persisted
through almost everything. If the going got difficult in one place, people
had simply sailed to the other.

We too discovered connections. Lord Killanin's closing address at 'The
Games' was still very fondly remembered; and by a lucky chance we had on
board a new book of his on Ireland. It drew almost more attention from
Estonian TV than our crew lined up on the foredeck.

> In Revel we saw for the first time the Russian drosky. It is very small
> for 2 passengers and has nearly always 2 horses. The roads such as we
> saw don't deserve to be called roads. They are like the bed of a
> mountain torrent. Every cannon ball brought across country into
> Revel during the war cost 1 rouble = 3s 4d. for transport alone.

So much change in a century! The name for a start: 'Revel', the Danish
usage, lasted until the Revolution but, since then, turning the tables,
Tallinn ('the Danish town') has been preferred. Transport too: buses, still
with ample horses, are now a squash for a hundred; beneath them, the
broad dual carriageway runs in from Pirita as smooth as a bowling green,
skirting the curve of the bay, and the only cannonballs now to be seen are
embedded deep in the city walls.

Nor was the fabric of the city quite what Martin and Corrigan viewed.
Some of it, flattened during hostilities, had popped up again brand new;

the rest of it was glowing with pride after primping for the Olympics. Millions of roubles had blushed its walls. But as to its difference from Leningrad, the town itself hadn't changed: where Peter's city was flat, Tallinn was humped and steep; where its streets were broad and straight, Tallinn's were narrow and bent; and instead of ranks of congruent mansions, Tallinn boasted an amazing mish-mash of castellated town gates and squares, opulent angular burghers' houses, steep gables and elaborate windvanes and rainwater pipes in the shape of long leather boots, abrupt cliff faces and outdoor stairways jostling low-slung railway stations; even a renaissance palace confronting an Orthodox church, complete with garlicky domes.

And the names! All the towers and turrets boasted them: Tall Hermann, Fat Margarete; Pilsticker (the arrow-Sharpener); Stur-den-Kerl (Repulse the Enemy); and, best of all, Kiek-in-de-Kok (Peep into the kitchen). Streets too: Pikk Jalg and Luhike Jalg (Long Leg and Short Leg), an odd echo of *Canna's* mode of arrival, leading down to the Market Square, 'where everything moves', a nineteenth-century Estonian wrote. 'Peasants in squeaking shoes from the villages . . . rumbling carts with churns and sacks, grunting pigs and lowing calves; handicraft apprentices and masters . . . servants in grey skirts hurry along, and later, when the shops are open, the merchants' wives, holding the hems of their silk dresses high with ringed fingers; in thin high shoes they step demurely among the piles of hay, rubbish, cow and horse dung.'

It wasn't hard to imagine. Tallinn still ran its full historical gamut, making for contrasts of extraordinary piquancy; but now, if anything, they were even sharper. Through storey-height plate-glass could be seen wire baskets and check-outs; but it reflected eighteenth-century façades and old women's stalls with home-grown flowers and jam-jars full of raspberries.

'The town itself is a stall,' murmured Shay, and it obviously attracted a lot of takers – more than a million Soviets per year, and hundreds of thousands of others, mainly from Sweden and Finland. Droves of them jammed the streets, while scores of the more exotic varieties milled around the ramparts, wondering at the northern sea, silver between the spires and steeples, and the surprisingly wooded hinterland. Many, short and swarthy, were swathed in knitwear and raincoats: Georgians and Azerbaijanis, Irène said, people for whom this moist climate, for us quite comfortably warm, was their very first experience of how it felt to be cool in summer.

Irène was on secondment from Estonian TV – she'd volunteered to help us film and had organized a van which, if it lost us in the narrow streets, salvaged us by appointment elsewhere. She was alarmingly attractive, as generous in build as in nature, with strong blue eyes and startling platinum hair, but she seemed to echo a lot of our Leningrad notions, rolling half the people we'd met into one. Like the pilots (or the merchants' wives), she wasn't sartorially prepared: she too picked her way over cobbles and puddles in dangerously thin high heels; and huddled with us in empty candy-floss stalls to save her blue mascara from showers. But on professional matters she was sharp and crisp and quick to defend her corner. Should we, we asked, advise the manager before we filmed his shop?

'No!' she flared back like the yacht club skipper. 'You don't need permission. We go and film what we want to – and *you* do so too.'

And Irène had the same wistful bent as Nastasia, the Leningrad guide. The northern Soviets, it seemed, were fascinated by the southern republics, felt drawn by their strangeness and sun, but were half-afraid of them too. She had been thoughtful among the swarthy tourists and was soon due for a month's break in Georgia.

'It is very foreign, for us, down there,' she said. 'Very different, sometimes difficult; but yes, it is romantic as well.'

She also knew Tallinn from back to front. There seemed no detail she couldn't advise on: the literature, the history, which houses were Danish, which German. Had she been a professional guide, we wondered? But no – at last, unwittingly, I pushed her too far. Sooner or later we hoped to escape Tsar Peter's thundercloud ambit; but it wasn't to be just yet. In the lush depths of the Ekaterinental Gardens, named for Peter's first wife, the trees and ornamental lakes stood demure and dripping and silent; her palace, a miniature Hermitage, reflecting fountains in its white-framed rococo windows. But who, I wondered, had been in occupation when the *Oriana* gentlemen called?

Irène grimaced, and with the sweetness of Chinese sauce retorted: 'I am not your host, I am not your guide, I'm just ordinary girl.'

'Bring on more!' had been our reaction; and we weren't to be disappointed. Visitors came to us thick and fast.

Riho's pale, keen face was one of the first to pop up on board. Ever since coming home from Leningrad on the cruise ship, he'd been on the look-out for *Canna*. His dark hair flopped from a boyish crown, he was slight and had rabbity teeth; but a certain poise boosted his fifteen years. He turned up each day, learned the cameras, and appointed himself Shay's assistant. He soon became so much part of the family that Irène had assumed he was.

'But I thought you were Alan's son!' she had suddenly burst out, as we chewed fried sausage between photo-stops.

'Oh, Alan how awful! Congratulations! Half a family already, and almost no trouble at all.'

'No, *no!*' yelled Riho.

'You look so similar,' Irène explained, 'but I couldn't make out how Riho knew so much Russian.'

He and Alan gazed at each other, wondering too late if they ought to be flattered, then fell to trading embarrassed punches: nothing would suit Riho better than to have been sailing with us. He was desperately hoping to join one of Tallinn's maritime colleges to start him on his career. He pointed it out with pride one evening, a solid post-war building hugging a street corner in the centre of town; his eyes sparkling as he dreamed of his skipper's ticket.

The hankering for travel he seemed to have gleaned from his mother. A small, neat lady with a lace-trimmed blouse fringing a shark's-tooth necklace, there was something direct and forceful about her. Her hands were hot and her eyes rarely still. Their home was a modest two-bedroomed apartment, out in the middle suburbs, one of a low block of blue-tiled flats behind a bus-maintenance depot; but the entrance court-yard was quiet and green and, from their upper floor, the view spread wide to the south over the city race-course. A bedroom plastered with posters for Riho; and in the parqueted living-room, with Regency-striped blue paper and matching French-style cabinets, a table already laden with *baranki* biscuits and cognac and rose-hip syrup, and gifts of books secreted beneath the chairs.

'I've lived here for twenty-four years,' Krysta haltingly told us. 'From when the flats were new. The trees, we planted ourselves.'

We had an immediate problem with language. In the town, for official announcements, Russian and Estonian appeared everywhere side by side; but ethnic Estonians spoke their own language, for which we had no dictionary. Finnish was not quite close enough, and Estonian, although using a Roman alphabet, has few other western connections, and no Latin roots as clues. 'Eesti', as it is known to its speakers, would be a difficult enough language to get one's brain around for that reason alone; but it also has 14 cases, no gender, and three different meanings for the three different lengths of its vowels – *luup* (a sloop) was relatively simple, but what to make of *püüu* (a catcher or a fisherman)? Most words had double vowels somewhere.

'*Soome-ugri, Permisoome-ugri, Pohja-samajeedi,*' Krysta began, sketching in a spidery plan of the language variants of the various Estonian-related tribes, some of which are spoken by barely a handful.

'*Vadja* and *Vepsa* – those are some near Murmansk,' she said, squeezing them in at the edge of the page. 'Then there's *Kamassi, Nganas-saani* . . .'

Language was one of her delights, and she didn't let lack of it get in the way. She and Riho did a double act, levering out all kinds of onomatopoeic sounds or approximations to our languages until something finally clicked. But her real love was of travel. So far, it had been the Crimea, and Belgrade in Yugoslavia. She longed to go further, but it wasn't easy, and even internal travel needed to be carefully planned, she mentioned, as we made our way back to town. On impulse she dodged into the main station to check.

'At the moment, a week's delay for a main-line ticket,' she said.

But we wondered if Krysta had had other problems too. Her engineer husband was conspicuously absent. She showed us his photographs, but didn't mention his name, nor where he was working. It seemed a void that she skirted round with an almost palpable ache. Separation seemed the most likely answer. Two-person families are the norm in Estonia, and the divorce rate runs at 40 per cent. And Krysta was holding two jobs: by day she worked at a sub-aqua store, not far from us in Pirita; but by night she folded herself on to a couch in a small caboose as watchman for a teacher's college. Alan and I left her there, relieving a slightly grumpy colleague, as she arrived a few minutes late. The long, linoleum-covered floors of the Pedagogical Institute gleamed and reflected circular pillars and the plinths of Estonian poets, and smelt of layers of linseed oil. In a dull yellow glow, behind the glass of the reception office, Krysta started another shift. 'A remarkable woman,' Alan said.

Saturday 25 July, and our second night in Tallinn. The fact that the well-muscled doorman had been to Ireland did us no good at all. Every so often, unpredictably, he cracked open the door of the town's best restaurant, shaking his head at a dwindling queue, or admitting people past it. The fortunates were tourists with tickets; the less so were locals and those like us, hopeful of doing without them. In twos and threes, they all gave up and quietly departed, leaving ahead of us a single young man with a dark complexion and a strong hooked nose.

'No good!' he said, in an unknown accent, when the town hall clock had almost circled its dial – 'but I think we'll get in at one below.' He led us away to a rival restaurant, but the queue there was still not discouraged; and that left only the new hotel. We had hoped to avoid it. Hotels seemed to generate a friction that existed nowhere else. It took time to get used to the notion that one shouldn't breeze in and out. There were doormen at the foyer, and the restaurant door was locked. Stung by hunger, I pushed through the queue, knocked on the door and asked for a table. When it opened, we got it. Susan looked on with mixed disgrace and amazement as more than half the crowd stayed outside looking in, buzzing like a swarm of bees, while others filled the adjacent tables, downing four or five courses and continuous champagne, secure in their occupation and perfectly unhurried. Although more than welcome, the chicken was Kiev, the boeuf Stroganoff'd (named for the family who ran the salt mines), the dessert not quite what we ordered, and the waiter had to be leaned on to bring the local beer. ('Very bad,' he averred, which it wasn't.)

Apart from the shortage of restaurants, the problem was mainly of money. In Leningrad, around the hotels, one or two shifty characters had lurked, looking like black-market touts. Here in Tallinn, Rupert had already been mistaken for a clever lad on the make, to Susan's initial alarm, and our eventual high amusement. Turning up late for a rendezvous in the foyer, he'd eventually passed her at a distance in the charge of unknown men. They had disappeared for quite a while . . . so who on earth had got him in tow? But it was simply the doorman and management: he'd spent a half-hour behind the scenes bemusedly having his face compared with albums of mug-shots of wanted people, while sundry officials inspected him, and along the counter a woman patron was hotly complaining of a theft.

'But that's what your passport's for!' we told him.

'I know,' grinned Rupert, as cool as ever, 'and when they saw it, they apologized.' But he never properly explained why it took him so long to produce it. He was far too careful about his image.

Down below the castle, on a weed-grown siding and a Sunday afternoon, an ancient railway engine hissed and smouldered. Here were more of those startling contrasts: on the neighbouring tracks were ranks of Pullman coaches polished and liveried in purple and blue; there a gaggle of cleaners chatting; here, on the machine that was going nowhere, one very busy man.

'*Mazoute!*' shouted the greasy figure, carefully wiping his hands on a rag. 'Oil, oil-firing!' Dials danced and sizzed in the cab. He was one of an enthusiast group who kept the locomotive intact. Only just. The fire box was about to give out, he said, showing a rusted junction. But no matter, it would be fixed in time; and anyway, other things were important.

Rahu! Mir! shouted the slogans on its tender, in Estonian and Russian, ending for good measure with *Paix!* They seemed more vibrant with intent, roughly painted in three colours, than the premeditated decla-mations marching across the Communist Party headquarters nearby.

Mart Mikk went one better. The slogan down the front of his T-shirt read 'Peace' in Japanese. Of all the figures we were to meet, Mart was the most unlikely. He simply arrived in the cockpit one day, no one noticed from where. He was dressed entirely in black and white; black jeans, black velvet jacket, black spiky hair tucked away at the rear into a plaited pigtail that bobbed up and down on his collar. The whole of his restless body bounced around, as if he were conducting a pop-group.

That's exactly what he did do, he said. Well, not *just* that. He was lead trumpeter, but he also sang in a barber's shop quartet, and in opera too. He loved opera, he admitted wistfully. It was in his blood: his father had been an impresario, the first man in Soviet Russia to stage Mussorgsky's *Boris*

Godunov. But he wasn't sure if he wanted to go that way as there was a lot more money in what he was doing, and he was extremely keen to travel. That was obvious, he couldn't stay in one place for two seconds: 'Now can I take anyone anywhere?' and, to general disgust, the skipper decided he was the only man free on the instant. Mart's chariot was a white Russian Fiat he drove just as he talked, very fast and erratically, urging it on with great bursts of enthusiasm as he pointed its nose northwards along the coast, while explaining how his music group worked.

'It's under the protection of a drinks company – spirits and so on. They pay the costs; we play for them maybe five times a year. They like it a lot. No, they don't influence what we play. We have artistic independence. We perform what we want. What about you? What do you do? What is it you want to see?'

Modern architecture having been mentioned, without a word, he did a violent U-turn through the central reservation and screamed back toward the city.

'Two architect friends!' he explained. 'Live in Kadriorg Park.' But by the time they'd been prised from their dinner and a babysitter found, Mart had recalled a business deal depending urgently on crates of vodka, and vanished again with magical speed.

Tonis and Kadri were more sedate. Obligingly they picked up where Mart left off; Kadri, with permanently smiling eyes under a fringe of fawn curls, egging on her more serious husband. In a moment I passed the pyramid of Birgitta's fifteenth-century convent for the third time in half an hour.

'It was built by the city old men,' said Tonis, 'after a dream, a vision, to save the town from a Lithuanian blockade.'

It had obviously worked. Her spires had come into sight again through trees around the curve of the bay.

'And now,' turning off the main road, 'we shall go to see "the Merivälja Fisheries Co-op",' they sang out in half-satirical laughter. 'You know, it was held up to us – is right? – for years at school, as a good example' . . . 'until we almost got sick of it!' Kadri completed.

But the co-op was like nothing I'd seen. It stretched for miles across the landscape, a whole community to itself. Under the background of wooded slopes were strips of pasture and intensive cultivation. There were glass houses, farms, office blocks, housing and schools, spaced out around green undulations. The basis of its business was a long-distance fleet that combed not just the Baltic, but most of the Atlantic as well – some of the factory ships, I guessed, that often frequented our shores. Here, they did all their own canning, and even made their own cans. The emphasis on 'do-it-yourself' was part of the system, Tonis said. They designed and built all their own buildings, health centres and florists' shops and sports halls. They even had their own secondary school complete with a winter garden. We idled past it and came to a stop by the kindergarten. It looked like a child's toy itself, a small-scale construction in tile and brick with angular, child-sized windows painted in different colours.

'The workers here are very well paid,' said Kadri with a shade of envy. 'Most of them have their own private houses – but there are many here in Merivälja, even outside the co-op.'

The brown-bordered mono-pitches of the co-op houses gave way, around the perimeter, to types from the 1920s and 30s, with more steeply-pitched tiled roofs and stacks of neatly cut timber under their porches.

'It's more difficult now, to get plots of land,' they said. 'So people from the town are building further out,' and beyond again along the meandering, tree-hung lanes were scores of more recent examples, many still under construction. Tonis and Kadri, one an industrial architect, the other an interior designer, examined them all very critically – most were designed by architects they knew. Here was a two and a half storey affair, with a big car in the garage. It belonged to a champion weight-lifter, they said; but the style was restrained, they approved of that. Here were some with pitched roofs, there another with flat, and one with porthole windows. Finally we came to an affronted halt under a monstrous half-built Berber fortress, replete with slit windows and machicolations. It drew long guffaws of derision.

'Everyone wants to make their house more special,' they mocked. I knew exactly what they meant. There's a mountain valley near our home, I told them, entirely destroyed by one Spanish villa, built with pillars of concrete jelly, as if fossilized during an earthquake.

This emphasis on the private house seemed to be very important. Almost everyone mentioned it, or was working through the process. Irène had made time to show us some, near the park, surrounded by small plots of flowers, and had been markedly surprised and impressed when the driver suddenly stopped in a downpour, dashed to a front door and came back with his raincoat. Krysta had proudly shown drawings of one her husband was planning, sporting a diagonal entrance hall and circular rooms and turrets. Tonis had given us photographs of his personal masterpiece to hang on our office wall, and even tourist literature showed 'individual houses'.

But the most enchanting of them all was Tonis and Kadri's own. A little gate in a wicket fence gave entrance to a moderate-sized plot, completely shaded by parkland trees. In one corner was a miniature classical house of timber, complete with semi-circular fanlight, and a pair of fluted columns framing the panelled door. Japanese-style, shoes were kicked off before stepping inside on to the polished plank floor. The land, said Mart Mikk, had formed the garden of a larger house, which had not so long ago been burned down in suspicious circumstances.

And what indeed, are sailing cruisers, except houses that can be sailed? (with apologies for reversing Ransome). There was no shortage of personal initiative there either. The club professional's own boat, moored near ours, had unique twin doors leading down from the cockpit, each side of the central compass, a superbly practical arrangement which we'd never seen anywhere else, together with state-of-the-art rod-rigging, specially imported by ship from England, and fittings carved by local workshops from solid blocks of stainless steel. He explained how such things were managed and the whole ramified business of getting afloat.

'So, sailing is organized in two main ways – there are basically city sports committees, or else the shipping company clubs?'

'Yes,' he said, holding up an extra finger. 'And then there's the third type – what we do for ourselves.'

Our three or four Estonian days went swiftly by in a single stream, while we grasped what we could of all that flowed past us: invitations, impressions and proffered outings. Alan was more cheerful than ever, and Shay was now in his element; he mixed day and night with the racing sailors and muscled in on their various meets.

An effervescent tang filled the air. Even *Canna* began to be mildly neglected; but on the last night she hosted a party as friends from club and city collided. Home-made gateaux, strawberries, champagne, appeared on board like magician's rabbits, and vanished again with similar speed – Mart refused payment for vodka we'd asked for.

'I can earn that much in five minutes,' he said.

A Russian journalist (opinionated, the others opined) made points about easier travel. Talk went on to the following day. Tonis was the last to go. He was finally dragged away by Mart, who was clutching the old-fashioned silver post-horn he normally trumpeted from his car. From the dockside echoed a triumphal blast that split the night and echoed across the water.

Now, at a distance, memories of Tallinn are like its skyline – impressive and lasting, but spiked with pinnacles sharp enough to be painful . . .

It was still early the same morning when we tried to set sail. It wasn't easy. Shay, a minor celebrity at the club after showing a video of our cruise so far, was heavily hamstrung by female admirers. Ago Papp, the club manager, rushed up to us with extra gifts.

It was about then I discovered a vexing error. In fact, I'd made several: the effort of trying to organize ourselves better, to get around and meet more people, had backfired on us embarrassingly. Our personal contacts had blossomed, I'd found, at the expense of official ones. We had contrived to arrive at the Seamen's Club, where the manager, like Ildus, had enquired for us, on the very day of the week it was closed; and due to a simple misunderstanding I had failed to locate the city's House of Friendship, the only one to reply to our letters and offer us hospitality, until we walked right past it while filming, and Irène providentially made us backtrack. Now, and most frustrating of all, I discovered I'd just missed by two or three minutes a senior Russian sailing official, to whom we'd written in the early stages, and who had apparently been visiting the boat next to ours.

'But I've met him for the last couple of days!' said Shay, freer and more gregarious . . . 'how could I know that you'd wanted to see him?'

If the situation seemed Kafka-esque, I had only my own brittleness to blame. Bad management, not bad luck, was at fault, and it was too late now to make amends – even Inflot were slightly brusque, as we were overdue at the customs quay.

Already Riho and other friends were hugging our crew and waving us off, and not least because of the welcome we'd had, I was particularly galled that in the one port where we'd most wanted to keep the goodwill record straight, we had done so much less well than we should.

It was the morning of 28 July. What more could the month still have in store?

CHAPTER 11

To Latvia through the Irbenskiy Strait

The variable south Baltic coast was a fascination, and so far we had seen only a small fraction of it. We had looked forward to squeezing into all of its major cleavages; but as we threaded our way between the tireless dinghies toward the outer edge of Tallinn Bay, and around the wood-and-sand fringed island of Naissaar (where in 1855 French and English forces landed for picnics and cricket, and cries of 'Howzat' had amazed the few resident peasants), and then turned once more to the west, the idea took shape that we might miss out Riga entirely.

This defeatist notion was neither justified by the weather, which continued gently south-west and sultry, occasionally dropping to calms, nor entirely insinuated by the notion of staying at sea for a rest, away from the exhausting engagements onshore. It was provoked by another Tallinn setback, our failure with the Muhu Vain.

'You must read *Racundra's First Cruise*,' friends at home had chorused on every hand on hearing of our intentions. 'Have you read . . . ?' but it had been as elusive as the Holy Grail. Just as well, or our present disappointments would have been even sharper. Only later did we discover that Ransome, of *Swallows and Amazons* fame, had spent years in Russia in the course of his journalistic career, played chess with Lenin, fallen in love with Trotsky's secretary and had lured her away to sea. He'd spent time in Tallinn, and ended, more or less, by building his 30-foot yacht *Racundra* in Riga, and sailing her to Helsinki (with his Russian mistress and an old man – 'the Ancient') out through the Muhu Vain and back.

Much of his book hinges on this hazardous passage between the main offshore islands of north-west Estonia, Hiiumaa and Saaremaa, the much smaller Muhu itself, and Vormsi. Then known as Dago and Oesel, the two largest had since reverted to their Estonian names, but the channel itself, which Ransome reported as being littered with sudden twists and rocks, and with wrecked ships that had unwisely tried to cut corners, had not been in the least improved, as we could see at a glance from the Russian charts shown to us in Tallinn. Although it ran for barely 40 miles, it twisted and turned like a hooked fish, often through shallow water, heading first for this beacon, then for that, and cutting through gaps that would make eels think twice. When Ransome's company first passed through, there had been a Russian battleship stuck on a shoal, and a British freighter had only just been towed off after being stranded for all of three years. Lack of tide is sometimes a major hazard. He and his crew had their hearts in their mouths, despite clear air and a following wind; no wonder our charts stated firmly and flatly, 'Channel closed to foreign shipping'. All the same, we did try. So did the coastguard officer at the Tallinn marina, with the first display of official temperament we'd seen, slapping and banging the arms of his chair in frustration as he hollered down the 'phone to superiors.

'You know, of course, even Soviet yachts, yachts from here or Riga must get written permission to pass through,' he apologized, filling a pause in the proceedings; then, during the final vollies, his face began to fall.

'I'm very sorry,' he said finally. 'I really am very sorry indeed, but the answer still is "no".'

Despite our offer to take a Tallinn yachtsman with us, the Muhu Vain stayed closed. We hadn't expected otherwise but, once the hope was raised, the refusal failed to lop 100 miles and a full day off our journey.

The distance to Riga by the outside route, via the Irbenskiy Strait, was at least 300 miles, probably three days' sailing; but bit by bit the light breeze and familiar motion as we moved easily through the rippled blue sea lulled us out of our slough, and gently, by tacit agreement, we fell back into our plan. Yes, we would go to Riga.

Over the next long days and nights, as Shay stretched himself in the saloon filling out photography logs, I scribbled urgently in my journals, which had a knack of falling behind. Alan took up the navigation. He was practising for a yachtmaster's course, and took fixes with a hand-held compass on everything that failed to move. Rupert played endless solo patience, and Susan sang stirring hymns on watch 'to keep herself safe and wide awake'. She went about this helpful chore with due religiosity and in alphabetical order, beginning at 'Abide with me', 'All things bright and beautiful' ('if only they would!', some mortal muttered), then exhausting all twenty-six letters in turn.

Along this lonely sector lay an extensive prohibited area, pecked in purple on the chart. It closed off access to Paldiski: the 'Baltic Port' and winter harbour for Tallinn beloved of Ransome and Adlard Coles, the mariner and publisher who eventually bought the *Racundra*, and sailed her back to England in the period between the Wars. The zone kept us five miles off the headlands that pushed out faintly and tentatively – and here, for the first and last time in the voyage, we encountered Soviet submarines.

As the first evening drew in, they came slanting from astern in ones and spaced-out twos of different types, heading almost south, keeping clear by three or four cables, then bending more to the west, all making perhaps for a point onshore, or the channel we had hoped to travel. There can be few more ominous sights at sea. Sullen and blind, the conning-tower looms first like the end of a cake of grey soap, with not a porthole to indicate human involvement; then suddenly, beneath, the full awesome length is revealed by waves rushing over its ends. It's hardly better by night. In home waters marked as 'submarine exercise areas', the thought always lurks that a single red light might not be what it seems, that it could be the extremity of something barely half-surfaced; and, in the Irish Sea, submarines had failed to notice both trawlers and yachts had dragged them around by their nets, or sunk them. That night off the Estonian coast was dotted with single lights that followed no known pattern and, between sudden downpours and patches of mist, the dramatic flares of xenon lamps signalling 'A' or 'D'. Momentarily, they flashed on our sails, but whether they were meant for us we had no way of making out. We had watched the long dark forms intently until they melted into the land, or simply became imagination.

By dawn, *Canna* had cleared the 20-mile mouth of the Vain, and the occulting light and huge white pillar of Tahkuna Nina lighthouse on the northern tip of Hiiumaa stood bold against piled-up, blue-black skies. We altered course for Ristna, the most north-westerly headland, which we made by ten am.

These isolated landmarks took on new significance. The shallow water round their points was marked by slender cardinal beacons, mere wands of black and yellow; and some, as the charts had warned, were missing, forcing a check on safe distances with compass and sextant instead, by a measurement of angles from the lighthouse towers.

They were symbols of our progress too, swinging towards us as blue silhouettes in an agonizing crawl, watching for hours as we sidled by, and retreating as slowly over our shoulders. In between, the land disappeared entirely. Estonia's coastline runs for 2,500 miles, much of it due to her islands. We could believe it. It felt as if we were digesting half of it in rounding the massive curve to the south, rather than barely one-tenth. Worse, *Canna* was once again motor-sailing, plunging steeply against a head wind, and watches would start with weary and incredulous glances forward.

'What? Hasn't that headland got any closer?' Alan or Rupert or Shay would complain.

In the late afternoon of the second day, when Susan, on her third or fourth watch, had worked through 'Y' and was grappling for 'Zion' or 'Zebediah', we finally made Kiipsaare Nukk, the furthest finger of Saaremaa, the largest of all the Soviet Union's 1,500 Baltic islands, which flings out its limbs with a dancer's abandon; and once around it things happened quickly.

Canna began to sail again. The bliss of killing the engine! – better even than extinguishing a particularly hated soap on TV. In the silver silence that followed, we momentarily ran down-wind, topping up the diesel from cans and then, close-hauled, laid off east of south in a freshening south-westerly breeze, heading at last for the mouth of the Irbenskiy Strait.

Sometimes, in the quiet of home, we have looked with retrospective wonder on various memorable situations, considering if we had properly lived them, whether at the time we'd sucked their marrow.

About the next night there are no such doubts. A strong whiff of danger saw to that. The Strait, 16 miles wide and 30 long, is bounded by the Latvian coast, lying now across our bows, that sweeps east in a single, clean curve like a gigantic saw-tooth to the point of Kolkasrags at its inner end. But first we had to negotiate a final, crucial obstacle, the evil fangs of the Sorve Riff, a seven-mile reef and shoal stretching down from the southernmost arm of Saaremaa. This last angry gesture from Estonia toward her southern neighbour reduced the width of the channel by half and deserved a very great deal of respect. To avoid it completely we'd have to beat out to starboard and go many miles out of our way; if we cut it too fine, we'd rip the bottom out of the boat. The depth was less than our draught in places. It was twilight already; away to starboard a few fishery vessels loomed dully, but the channel lightvessel was missing. Latvian lighthouses showed up shyly ahead; and then it was time to make our move. We went for a middle course, skirting the blue water on the chart, the ten-metre line of soundings. As we bent more and more to the east, the speed picked up. Five knots, six: spray flew. Six and a half knots. Alan stood by the echo-sounder, calling continuously, 'Nine and a half – nine – ten.' Seven and a half knots. We eased out the boom as we curved to port and she bolted away like a horse. Foam swirled past with ferocious speed as we hurtled on through the dark, rolling and dipping down the fronts of the waves. Shore lights that had stuck on our nose for hours now beat a hasty retreat. The speed, the fleetness, the exhilaration! It was like sprinting over hard, smooth ground after being stuck in a bog.

'Still ten metres,' shouted Alan.

'We'll crash on!' I called to Rupert in triumph. 'We'll ignore the main channel to starboard. If we keep this course, we'll clear the whole strait in one . . .'

A sudden searchlight lit the sail, flashing 'T' – but far too steady and bright for a trawler, too continuous for a submarine. It had to be a patrol boat. Reluctantly, we bent toward the shipping channel, slanting across it, still racing headlong. The light tracked us, shut off, then picked us up later, each time a mile further on.

'It must be stationary,' we agreed; but just as we made to run east again, another light came in from starboard. They seemed to be trying to funnel us between two buoys on the chart. Some were supposed to be lit; but the Pilot had mentioned big moorings that weren't. To hit one at this speed would sink us in seconds. Rupert went to the bows to look out, away from the cockpit lights. It was four am, still just dark, and almost as soon as he got there the fag-end of a flaming white flare whistled down near our stern.

'Now who's messing around?' I mused, drunk with the sounds of sea and wind. 'Sails are inflammable. Whoever it is, they might be a bit more careful.'

We didn't connect it with the patrol boat behind, and another half-mile flitted under our keel in a series of swoops and surges; but when a soaring red glare clove the sky and turned our canvas to carmine, we suddenly got the message. Reaction at first was automatic.

'*All hands on deck.*' I yelled down, then quietly, 'Oh, *hell*. This is it. We'll be boarded. Caught speeding at the very least.' Rupert fought to control the sheets as with an enormous heeling swoop we wrenched around and hove-to. The patrol was already very close – or its searchlight was. It drove toward us, disembodied, like an interminable flash of lightning. Shay and Susan, stumbling up half-clad, instantly were pallid ghosts, their solid shadows plastered across the decks. From 20 yards away, behind the blaze and glare, was a slab of extra darkness, a hint of steel and the guttural grind of engines. All of us were mesmerized. The mainsail shrieked and slapped in frenzy. Then abruptly, the light went out, leaving us totally blinded, and shocked. The only thing we could detect was the sound of a prop-wash moving away.

By dawn we had rounded the tip of the saw-tooth at Kolka, passing at last into the Gulf of Riga under the empty eyes of a square stone castle on the blade-flat mainland, and a modern off-lying lighthouse. The sky lightened. It was a turning point of many kinds. Now at last, we had left behind the unpredictable broken coastline and the rocks and reefs of the Gulf of Finland. Close to starboard lay even stretches of low sand dune that ran for hundreds of miles in both directions. We'd arrived in the southern Baltic. Gone too, for the moment, was the steep chop of the open sea: here we were doubly insulated from the oceans, gliding along in a cotton-wool world, a lake within a lake. The land quickly closed around us, leaving no obvious entrance. The water was flat, and the wind disappointingly aimless – but it was strong enough to waft away the night's dramas. Now there were no more misconceptions. We had finally learned that in Soviet waters a yacht is a ship, no matter what. We should have aimed for buoys 10 and 11 in the first place, the checkpoint for all traffic. It said so in the Admiralty List of Signals, when I got around to reading it.

Although in terms of inducing fright patrol boats didn't compete with storms, in truth we'd become a little blasé. Since our first encounter after leaving Finland, I'd been secure in the knowledge that our papers were good, and that we'd every right to be where we were. Wasn't someone on shore keeping tabs on us? If so, the navy boats' periodic eruptions became matters mainly of curiosity. Susan also concurred with this view, confiding that she'd been much more alarmed by the bulk of their horribly hard-looking hulls than by doubts about their general intents . . . 'and besides' – referring back to the night – 'you know how difficult I find getting to sleep, without being woken when I've succeeded. As skipper you should plan it better.' Susan was ratty when not rested. On all fronts I needed to watch my step.

In its sense of enclosure, the Gulf of Riga is not unlike Vänern; it's larger, at 90 by 70 miles, but shallower too, almost everywhere less than 50 metres. It also has islands. Tiny Ruhnu Saar sits far out, 20 miles east of Kolka. As the southerly breeze pushed us slightly off course, Rupert made out the long flashing light, two every nine seconds, and the delicate blush of its pastures. Had we read *Racundra* by then, we'd have been sorely tempted to put in. In 1922, although it was already Estonian, the inhabitants still spoke Swedish. They *were* Swedish, Ransome swore, even down to the pigs. If he didn't speak their language they bit him. The 300-odd islanders lived mainly by sealing, operating a form of perfect (but strictly Protestant) communism before any such thing had been invented elsewhere. Their homespun tweeds and sealskin slippers were very much, it sounded, like those still worn on the Aran Islands in the west of Ireland 50 years later. It was on this unlikely outpost, this anachronism, that Ransome had suddenly found himself pitchforked into politics, when the lighthouse-keeper had asked him, out of the blue: 'Well Mister, and how is it with Ireland?'

'The Irish,' he'd riposted, disgruntled, 'are settling their affairs in the Irish way'; but if Ransome couldn't avoid such conundrums on his cruise, no more could we. The same question had already several times been gently prodded in our direction (it came about tenth in an ordinary conversation) and was no whit easier to answer for the passage of another 65 years.

Nor did it seem a suitable quid pro quo to enquire deeply of Estonia's nationalist problems; of the minor troubles and demonstrations that had flared before we arrived, nor the ambiguities of loyalty that sometimes scented the air. Instead we had watched and listened, but the most that had been volunteered by one or two was disquiet at Estonia's dwindling proportions of natives – once well over 60 per cent, they are now down to nearer half – and for us it was to make Estonia's subsequent tumultuous self-assertion all the more remarkable.

Rather than divert, we had made on south-east; and Ruhnu Saar had long since died astern, sinking slowly behind 50 miles of quiet water as we finally made land on the evening of 30 July. Striped chimneys first appeared, marking the southern fringe of the Gulf, then cooling-towers with nineteenth-century waists and parasols of steam, and finally their foundations, a whalebone-thin strip of land laced with trees.

Alan picked out the Daugavgriva light – a black and white banded affair like a candy-stick marking the river mouth – just as port control came through.

'Please attend by the buoys for a pilot.'

The pause on Riga's front doorstep was pleasant: a decorous interlude, like yanking the doorbell of a large country house and then waiting for the maid to arrive. Although we didn't yet know it, it was to set the tone for our visit.

Idling in the gathering calm a mile or so offshore, we watched two ships, almost the first we'd seen in the Gulf, nose out like important personages. A factory-ship and a freighter, they caught the slanting sun in full brilliance on their creamy top-hats, while pilot boats fussed round their feet like poodles. A large yacht tiptoed out toward us, an elegant lady under full sail, crammed to the gunwales with people waving – a hostess or a reception committee? No, she was simply taking the air; but by now, the doorman, a grey police launch, was hovering quietly at our elbow, and its officers, encrusted with golden braid, motioned again to the radio. Now it was, '*Canna*, proceed without pilot.' Someone had obviously changed his mind.

There can be few finer harbour approaches than Riga's. It runs for seven or eight miles in gentle, sway-back bends along the Daugava river. The banks are dotted with docks here and there – heaps of coal or grain and blocks of containers or timber – but mainly they're fringed with green and lines of parading trees. Foliage smothers the small latticed beacons lighting the curves of the channel, shelters the mould-green fishermen decently spaced out beneath and, between and beyond, lush meadows stalk into the distance.

It had not been always so quiet. In Ransome's time, Latvia was in her first flush of independence, having routed a land-hungry German army three years before. Somewhere here, in 1919, the Letts had surprised them, crossing the river under cover of auxiliary fire from British and French warships anchored there for the purpose. The ambitions of the German commander, Von der Goltz, to re-establish a monarchy on the Baltic were frustrated; his forces were flushed out of Riga itself and jubilantly pursued south-west through Lithuania by the victorious Letts who then, for a while, attempted to master their own affairs.

Slowly the hump of the city drew closer. The police launch now behaved less like a footman and more like a sheep-dog, anxiously veering from heel to heel to show us the best part of the channel, and once running right up alongside to warn us off from the shore.

'I think it might be better if Rupert came down from the boom,' said Shay. We were passing a submarine dock just then and he was idly panning their slithery forms with binoculars.

A huge bridge reared, arcing in a single trajectory clear across the river, hung by scores of slanting cables in the form of a gable-end from a pillar several hundred feet high. To port was a squarish basin, bounded on one side by ships and trees. A club-house glowed deep gold in the sunset, a shaded line of yachts end-on beneath it. On them, as we circled, a small crowd of helpers eagerly beckoned. There was just time before it darkened for an impression of handshakes, a simple brick dock, a clubhouse stuffed with horse-hair sofas, and trophies, and a very low, rotund, and almost spherical man, cheerily hoisting our flag. Latvia looked as though it might be different again. We'd arrived in our seventh country, and were already glad to have come.

We spent the night with our neighbours to port, savouring a nice irony. Their yacht, as long as ours, but willow-leaf slim, flew an unfamiliar ensign – black, red and gold with a crest in the centre – East German! 'From Stralsund,' they told us.

For all their efforts, the Berlin authorities hadn't kept us apart, and Heinz and Wolfgang, Wolfahrt and Jung were the most riotous crew we were to meet on our voyage. Momentarily, faces purpled and blackened when we told them of our refusal.

'*Of course* there are places for yachts in Stralsund!' they thundered, smacking their fists in their hands, their eyebrows knitting together. 'But then, they don't trust us either. We can't go to Sweden, for instance, you know – and it's hard enough to come here. There's a lot of papers to deal with, and visits are rationed between the clubs. It's ten years since we last came.'

But aggravation passed like a cloud, giving way to goonery, whisky and schnapps.

'Rat-holes!' pealed Wolfahrt, sticking his fingers through the incredibly delicate wickerwork of the cabin-doors that reminded me of parlour chairs and Protestant Sundays.

'No rats,' contradicted the skipper, a toothless wonder called Heinz, 'and no engine either. We simply sail and get wet. Fast, but very wet boat,' he confided.

They had no instruments at all, apart from a compass and log, and their voyage had taken a week. They too had threaded the Strait by night – they too had encountered patrol boats, searchlights and things like that.

'But how many flares did *you* get?' they queried.

'Two,' Shay sheepishly admitted.

'Aha! – we got *three*, a white and two reds!' They gurgled and slapped their knees in delight, hilariously reliving the gauntlet of the furious rockets raining down.

'But what about coming up river?' Alan could hardly believe that they'd sailed. But yes, they confirmed; they'd had to beat all the way.

'And the police launch – did that zig-zag behind you?'

'Oh yes!' Wolfgang hooted, trailing twin loopy routes with his fingers, 'and it took us nearly five hours!'

What about us? Jung wanted to know. How did we finance the cruise?

'We don't know,' I replied in like vein. 'Maybe we sell the house, or maybe the boat.'

'Or maybe his wife,' put in Susan. 'I think perhaps he'd prefer it.'

As their violent paroxysms began to look dangerous to health, Susan and I abandoned them all to the serious work of the night. Stars came out to the pop of corks, and the slapping of imaginary lederhosen.

'Hey-di-*ho*-li! Hey-di-*hi*-li!'

Between times, snatches of vulgar yodelling kept us briefly from sleep.

CHAPTER 12

Riga

Having thus disposed of the wine, Riga became the city of song, and of women.

Nina, the Inflot agent, was the first. She'd arrived like an opera singer dressed all in black, and her tight skirt made it difficult to get her on board at all. The usual queries about tugs disposed of, events took a serious turn.

'So you really have no de-ratification certificate?' she quizzed, pursing and frowning. We didn't have rat-guard plates on our mooring warps either. Very quick thinking was called for.

'Here it is!' called Alan, pointing out a long-tailed stuffed brown rodent, the 'Ruski stoor', a mascot donated in Tallinn and strung up by the neck in the galley. 'That's the thing – the very last rat on board!' (Tristan Jones had had one which grew to two feet in length in his bilge).

Nina had accepted defeat with a smile. Good humour seemed general. At the clubhouse flagpole next morning, the very squat man squeezed all our hands again, in between hoisting the Irish ensign (it was brand new – where had he got it?); the clown who had almost gone overboard when we arrived, and turned out to be an actual drunk, the first encountered since Helsinki, waylaid me into the club watchman's hut to present a hair of his favourite dog. As we sipped from doubtful glasses and cracked mugs, he told the usual seaman's story.

The whole club, in fact, belonging to the Latvian Shipping Company, had a deceptively casual feel. Mooring arrangements were very *ad hoc* – one tied up to a water pipe – but on the city side of us were a rank of identical small cruisers, suitably giddy for the lightly-breezed Gulf; on the other, beyond the Germans, a disparate collection of sloops and hefty steel ketches, and further again, approached by spindly gang-planks from the crumbling banks of clay, one or two wing-mast catamarans of the very newest type, almost as big as basketball courts.

It was to one of these huge craft that a bearded young skipper brought me, in the course of our enquiries for gas, trampling airily across the vast safety net between the widely-spaced hulls and down into each half in turn. Still more casualness. In fact, the boat was in a shambles. There were piles of gear, and two girlfriends (presumably one for each hull) muzzily straightening out blankets. They nodded and smiled at me shyly. But it had its impressive side too. Perhaps the chaos was due to her speed. She made 15 or 20 knots, Ivan said, and soon the three of them would take a spin to Leningrad and back; she could gobble the route of our six days' hard labour in two – and there were half a dozen more of the same type at the navy club further down river.

Casualness and seriousness seemed to be Riga's keynote, and an easy-going self-confidence that still held strange astonishments. Every so often, beyond the sailing-club's hedge and gate, a vast locomotive hauling trucks graunched to a halt in an incongruous siding, grinding slivers of steel from the rails and sandwiching would-be pedestrians.

When the view had cleared, there were wide grass verges, a wider road, brownstone façades and trees. But mainly trees. On the route to the centre, trams curved and burrowed through vaulting green tunnels like miniature trains at a funfair. Trees stalked the smaller avenues singly and two by two, marched down the main street in a dozen parallel ranks and sheltered its outdoor cafés, swirling and meandering into a park that formed the true hub of the city, surrounding its lakes and shading its paths and benches. The town looked in from the fringes. It was as though the trees had got there first, and then obligingly shuffled around to give the buildings some foot-room. To one side lay the newer quarters, dating from the later tsars, their decorous, eyebrowed, arched and ochred façades all of an even height and quietly ebullient temper. Opposite, beyond an old boomerang branch of the river, was the older city, as beautiful and intense as Tallinn. Restoration was making it more so. Polish craftsmen were labouring on ranges of old brick bulwarks, gutting the trussed timbers of long, slated roofs, and encasing domes in copper. Tourists squeezed through the narrow gaps to stand back and view the 'Three Brothers', a trio of ancient houses standing shoulder to shoulder with their hands in each other's pockets. But even there, some green persisted. Within the castle walls, a sculpture garden spread among oaks and wizened walnuts; and from the spire of the oldest church, St Peter's, one could gaze out to the distant turquoise countryside across the spread of the winding river, and down to the crystalline city. Its scale was just right, neither as twisted and secret as Tallinn nor, like Leningrad, outrageously grand.

'A place I could live in,' Susan pronounced.

The Hotel Latvija was a rare disruption, a vile, upended slab of glass that cocked two fingers at all around it. Riga people loathed it (even more than the Party building which, although of a sensitive design, had usurped their site for a concert hall). It had its uses, for money exchange. We were still declaring all our currencies as we entered and left each Soviet country, and were not supposed to carry roubles between them.

Most importantly, it was there we met Valda, one of a line of enquiry clerks, who, unwittingly, started a chain of encounters. She had long mousy hair and looked tired; but her soft, pale-grey eyes sparkled into sudden disbelief when we showed her the route of our cruise. All the while, as she advised on hire cars and internal travel, her glance wandered wonderingly over us as though something startling had happened, and she stood silently watching as we departed, clutching a guide-book she and her colleagues had pressed on us as a gift.

Touched, I'd returned next day with a token.

'I'm so very glad you've come!' she burst out. 'I've been talking to all my family about you, and about your wife and your crew. They think it's wonderful, quite marvellous. They cannot even imagine how it could possibly be done. My father too – he says you meet people like that only once in a hundred years.'

'I hope not,' I murmured, very gratified.

I didn't know what else to say; worse, the small parcel in my hand became suddenly inadequate.

'And have you been to the outdoor museum – the one I told you about? No? Good! Because I have something here for you too.'

The book she passed over was fit for a king. A superb illustration of Latvia's past, it's been a source of delight ever since. I left the hotel extremely pink, with only one place to go.

Latvians are not the same as Estonians. There are nearly twice as many and they come from a different root: they are Balts, one of the Slavic group, with strong links back through the river trade routes to ethnic lands near the Black Sea. The language is quite different too: Lettish, now called Latvian, shares only the Roman alphabet with Estonian and is distantly related to Russian. Latvian and Lithuanian are the only two Baltic languages left.

Religion divides down different lines. While Lithuanians are Catholic almost to a man, Latvians, like Estonians, are mainly Protestant; and a Lutheran church of timber set among pines is almost the first of the preserved buildings to greet one in the Ethnographic Museum, spread out among acres of lakeside parkland beyond the fringe of the city. Its low planked ceiling, oddly curved like the hull of an upturned boat, awash with musical angels and clouds and not the somehow expected seaweed, re-sounded with sacred echoes. A wizened old woman, guarding the portal in its transom, grasped me briefly by the wrist – wouldn't I find some prettier and younger one to photograph? Where was my wife? But, as she asked, she touched her white skirt and scarf into place, and adjusted her embroidered emerald-green belt.

Camouflaged between trees were courts and ranges of old farm build-ings, houses big and houses small, verandahed summer pasture-huts with carved timber posts and doorways one had to duck through, their hefty logs, roughly or neatly trimmed at the corners, mostly perched on boulder foundations and staggering under gargantuan hoods of thatch. The rooms were boarded and whitewashed or bare; and in them was the still, sad quietness of old worn implements long since unused, planked beds no longer creaking and strange strung instruments left untuned. Incongruously leisured visitors drifted through the stock-yards and doorways and, towards the lake, knots of children hesitantly tracked between drifts of purple loosestrife and red-berried bushes and barns.

I found it mildly embarrassing. I kept bumping into the same people. Every time a honeymoon couple walked through a cottage, I was there on the other side. In a private moment, when he posed her in front of a windmill, set up a tripod and galloped back to be in the picture, I was there to see him go sprawling over a tree-root. I moved away. But then, almost everywhere else, there was a girl in a bright blue jacket who figured in most of my photographs. She knew she did too, and eventually we agreed we had to stop meeting like that. Nana had jet black hair and umber eyes, was very dark, and Armenian. She was not alone; there was Helen hanging on her arm, and their older friends, who were Russian Rigans – Sergei, a huge redhead with hands like spades, his pale and heavily pregnant wife, Natasha, and a boy with a plaster covering half of his forehead.

The introductions had brought us back out to the road. With a sudden flurry, Sergei hailed two yellow taxis and the girls bundled me into one of them.

'What's this?' I demanded, as the cabs gunned back down the carriageway, overtaking and tail-gating wildly at 70 miles an hour.

'How can you two be cousins? You're dark brown, but Helen here is nearly white.'

'Oh, she's half-and-half,' said Nana. 'Her father married a Russian!'

Helen merely winked a mischievous eye.

'So how do you manage this trip', as we cut sharply in on a tram, 'from the other end of the country?' I asked, and then heard myself repeating the standard official question, 'Are you part of a group?'

They weren't: they had come by air, were staying in a small hotel, and had organized it themselves.

Back in *Canna*'s cramped saloon, as Sergei and Natasha stared around them in disbelief, we got a bit more of the story; and the rest came out in the Russians' flat in the suburbs next day, over a miniature banquet, at which Susan and I were guests of honour. Nana was a research secretary in the Armenian capital, Yerevan, she told us, between carrot salad and hot sliced avocados; Helen, her bosom pal for years, was now a secondary teacher. And our hosts? The youngsters interpreted for them – they spoke no English, and Sergei, it transpired, no Latvian.

'Natasha is "economist" with a bread factory, just now on two years' maternity leave.' Sergei nodded.

Unlike the voluble southerners, they had a steady and measured life. Sergei could organize his shifts as a graphic artist in a packing plant to give himself five days off in a row, which he spent at their *dacha*, a timber cabin in the country. At home he played percussion . . . With a grin he showed the drums he had made, with felt on the sticks so as not to bother the neighbours.

But Nana did most of the talking. She had an opinion on everything, and particularly on Armenia: the tragedy of its terrible history, the battles with the Turks and others, the sadness of Armenians being scattered around the globe. She found it very hard to believe we hadn't met one before.

'But you must come and see what is left,' she insisted. 'In Armenia, I myself think . . .' and every other sentence started, 'I myself', until it became her nickname. Helen simply twitched her lips and rolled her eyes to heaven.

There were less attractive parts of Riga, as we began to see in the course of our travels: tight suburbs with less of green and heavily shadowed pavements, looser ones further out, with flats aligned like playing cards; but still with incongruities. What was a trotting carriage doing circling a suburban roundabout? And beyond the railway underpasses lay the enormous market, part closed and part outdoor, where stalls stretched out for 100 yards, spread with small farmers' produce.

Riga itself lived off high tech, by producing TVs and radios, and it boasted, too, a highly developed artistic sense with very long standing links to Europe.

The crew had succumbed to another siren. Birgitte from the Friendship Society lured them all away in our absence. When Alan, Shay and Rupert disappeared for a second full day, we guessed she was something special. She was. A gentle Boadicea with her hair in a bun, she suddenly invaded one day with an army of females ranging from the minute to mature (correction: a single male, far too tall for a beanpole, had to fold himself double to get down into the cabin), and in minutes we were entrained in their crocodile, wriggling its way back to the city centre through the burrows of foliage.

It was highly confusing. Tiny Hirta, in a bright blue dress, an Ethiopian orphan, clung tight to Susan's fingers. She'd been adopted by a girl of barely eighteen, but which? It wasn't Fanny of the curly hair, nor Irène, both of them younger. The only other older woman was the mother of someone else; and it wasn't helped when Birgitte nodded toward a group of children cleaning out fountains with barrows and rakes.

'These are my childrens, too,' she said, sounding like Latvia's Earth-mother in person.

But Birgitte was simply an artist. She made and directed films for TV, in one of the city's main studios; in summer, she gathered the young of her area under the banner of PEGASUS ('poetic inspiration, you know?') and showed them what they could do – and what things! They painted in oils, and held exhibitions in back street apartment courtyards; they played folk tunes on an accordion, and Bach on an old piano. They mimed and sang: love-songs in Lettish and Russian, and 'Down in the Valley' in English. They were starting to learn Japanese. They ran an animation unit, and turned out Walt-Disney-type films. Birgitte had shown Alan the artwork, with 'casts' of hundreds of characters: 'which they must play out first on the stage.' She told them how to do that too, complete with whys and wherefores.

'I suppose if my children will be great mens, and important persons,' she told Alan with a blend of vehemence and humour, 'if, for example, George [the beanpole] will be President; if he will be good actor, he will be good President, because from what I see, bad actor is *not* good President. And I suppose, if he good actor, he will be good teacher, good captain, good architect . . . many architects are jazz players too [her father, apparently had been such]. Many *médecins* is jazz players – why? Because they have good emotions.'

There was no doubt of Riga's commitment to music. In full force, Pegasus propelled us that evening towards the city cathedral, on into the uneven old square under the huge brick bulk of the Dome. There were thousands of people milling, like Oxford Street in the sales. Recitals on her famous organ are Riga's biggest event, especially when, as that night, the organist was famous ('One of our Armenians', 'I myself' had proudly informed us). On every hand, unfortunates pleaded for tickets. We found we had extra, Birgitte's girls declined them from pity for foreign visitors, and a virtual riot broke out. We were mobbed, and made a forced escape as money was stuffed in our pockets. Inside, under the vaulting, purple space, yet more thousands packed every available seat and inch. Heinz, the East German skipper, was squashed up against a pillar. The occasion was quite electric; but perhaps for that reason, the music was a slight anti-climax. The maestro, after a brief appearance as *deus ex machina*, ducked below his balcony brow, rarely to be seen again, and the programme, for all its trills and aweful reverberations, seemed academic and dry. We left comment, in the Gothic exit, to the first English accents we'd heard for two months.

'Well, that was a terrific performance,' she said.

'Abso*lutely*,' came the reply.

So perhaps it was me. Perhaps, I suggested wryly to Susan, I wasn't a good enough architect. Unlike Birgitte, I didn't swing Gershwin on the piano, or croon, nor had my fiddle seen daylight for years. More probably my emotions were simply not quite in order.

No matter. There were smaller queues with more decorum nearby and other feasts to savour; in a plain, long, cream-painted room, with dark carved mirrors and woven hangings, our reservation tickets caused no problem; and parts of the menu, handwritten in Latvian and at first a fine conundrum, eventually resolved themselves into marinated anchovies, sour cream and trout – *forel* in fennel, in fact – exquisite! '*Put Veine!*, Blow wind!' opined Mr Fodor, 'is perhaps the best restaurant in the Soviet Union.' Probably. But not a breeze stirred the sign above its reticent door, and over fresh strawberry juice whipped with cream, the ceiling fan turned slower and slower until all sense of time disappeared. No wonder the high leather chairs were all full, and people waited in vain outside.

It was the 1st of August, the third of our evenings in Riga. The summer was passing, but we barely noticed, except that dusk came a little sooner. Nothing yet was calling us back. But the whole of our diet, people included, was in danger of becoming too rich. It was a relief that evening to stroll the river embankment, to touch the soothing strands of air, and watch the sun sink behind the harp-strings of the bridge, like a pale pink cameo on grey brocade. A single small boat went slowly down. Just Susan and Rupert were with me. We wandered out on to the span, trembling under a trickle of traffic, and idly peered far down at the flood. For what millennia had it flowed this way, and how many millions before us had watched it? To the left, slender spires staked out the old city.

The city had pushed out growth rings for 800 years, ever since the native Livs had been tricked by migrant traders. Proudly, they at first refused land for the ship-borne foreigners to settle, but finally, scornfully, during a feast, conceded a plot as big as an ox-hide. Before their hosts had come round from their cups, the traders had razored the hide into strips, joined them and marked out their settlement.

Others had come and gone: Swedes on the left bank, Livonia, Courland Poles on the right. Then Germans, too, in mediaeval times, and later during both Wars. The Daugava for centuries had been an important divide. The city, once a free Hansa port, often besieged and invested, had been a moveable pivot, swaying with one side, then with the other; but now, it was different. Bonds were patently stronger. Both banks were linked by the bridge on which we were standing, by the tulip-stem of the TV tower (the fourth-or-so highest in the world) sprouting up from a distant eyot, by Latvia's distinctions from the bigger republics. It formed, now, a single country, and the Letts were still there, half a million among the capital's million alone, and the spirit that sustained them for centuries was apparently still as strong as ever. As we wandered back via the Sea Passenger

Terminal nearby, a young Latvian bride in white took time out from a boisterous reception to flop in the public foyer. Head fallen against her silent groom, heels in the air, white shoes askew, she lay like a plastic doll across the rank of vermilion chairs, all pretence of style abandoned as she drew breath before procreation.

Somehow that evening, as when approaching Norway, the feeling returned of the overwhelming hugeness of our surroundings and the strangeness of such a minuscule voyage, as if of a beetle exploring a carpet. The country stretched inwards indefinitely. So far we were barely on the fringe, just inside the mouth of one river, and with only the faintest notion of what lay upstream.

Next day, we had just enough time to probe it. It's a far cry from Viking longboats: nowadays, for destinations, the railway station displays an idiot-proof chart, 43 metres wide, with tickets dispensed mostly from machines; about 60 kopecks for 100 miles. The open platforms were clumped with travellers visiting home, or heading inland for a break. Women, almost invisible behind huge offerings of flowers, a rare pair with touring bikes, men and boys carrying metal buckets with lids or muslin for bringing back berries or fungi. The heavy diesel ground slowly out of the city, past the occasional smart-skirted woman using the railway-track as a footpath, stepping from sleeper to sleeper. Stations soon became fewer and farther, and pines began to push in. There were no huge ranges of pasture, merely patches between the forests; and yet more forest, rearing up on humps and embankments. Platforms were lower and smaller at stops and then merely halts, with sandy tracks leading away. The rails began to climb and weave, swerving around incipient valleys.

At Segulda, fifty miles on, we stepped gingerly across the tracks and into a different world. There were even more trees than in Riga, and only the lightest sprinkling of plaster and tiles between them. Health clinics in converted castles; shops and houses with geese in the gardens; a flower market in full swing; and, down below them, in a deeply-upholstered green velvet ravine, the sienna Gauja, Latvia's other main river. A bridge and a silent cableway spanned it, a distance of almost a mile. Wooden ladders led down its flanks, frequented by frogs and fishermen in matching green fatigues. Even on the upper levels, the heavy midsummer foliage extends out almost unbroken. Planted houses are splodged with huge patches of shadow, trunks thicken in receding rings and shaded people filter endlessly through, as if between the wings of a stage. Here a man up steps, his head enclosed in an apple-tree, and there a whole platoon of soldiers in a public sculpture garden, inspecting, as part of a cultural exercise, collections of fanciful cocks and horses erupting in bright ceramic from lawns. But the sunlight bursting down on them is untypical and almost indecent. To the Latvian, leaves are a strategic defence, as important to him as a city man's brolly; which is understandable, considering that for centuries timber heavily sustained the country and, unlike others such as Ireland, she had sustained it in turn. At one time, half Europe's navies, including Britain's, depended on Latvian forests for masts, the logs being floated down as rafts with little cabins on board for their crews. Before tarred roads and railway, the rivers were quite vital. It was not surprising that the Russians could hardly secure them fast enough; as Ivan the Terrible had commented of the Daugava, no doubt with a greedy glint in his eye: 'Its banks are silver and its bed is gold.'

Susan was suffering. Grey, exhausted, and belatedly aching from efforts at sea, she confided that the rest of that day went by in flashes, as if under street lights seen from a car.

Back in the city, while I delayed at a four-storey mural, a depiction of historic Riga with modern windows here and there opening through its castles and moats, Susan trailed to the boat. Her bunk was black with Birgitte's children. She retreated to a park, where even smaller tots were screaming and pedalling hired cars, and from another corner came chanting. 'Hare Krishna! Hare Krishna!' it burbled through tambourines. What . . . ? But yes, the genuine thing, a swaying group of fervent mystics although, instead of conventional beads and earrings, some were wearing smartly-pressed suits. A crowd of onlookers heckled politely, and a few uniformed men sat around and watched.

By now, finding her missing, I had half diagnosed a suicide, and looked nervously out at the river. But the bizarre did her good. She was ready for Sergei when he sent a taxi to bring us away for a party; Rupert, one minute late, missed the boat.

Our own jamboree got under way later. It was becoming a habit. People came from all over the place. There was Alexander, a keen young sailor first met in Sweden; Yuri, the engineer from the Leningrad ship that had now caught us up, suave in a striped pink shirt; a namesake, a raunchy professional yacht-skipper, weatherbeaten and sideburn'd – and Yelena. Oh, Yelena! What a girl! (Susan was not yet back.) Her velvet black trousers were slender and long, and her dark hair fell to meet them. Her flimsy blouse was ruched down the front, her smile wide and alluring. Quite beautiful. Alan fell in the first few seconds. Luckily for us she was Alex's girlfriend, or else Alan would have defected. He couldn't get over how she said '*Da*', and made her lisp it again and again (where 'yes' might get him, we couldn't make out). A musician with hands like a Raphael madonna, she was training for yacht-racing too, as a member of Riga's all-girl crew; but Shay (at last discovering a match for his Göteborg friends) was aghast.

'What happens if your fingers are caught in a winch?'

'I won't do just one thing,' she shrugged. 'I could be concert pianist – but I prefer to teach, and do what else I enjoy.'

It was nearly dark when Valda, who'd presented the books, arrived. I'd left word, but had doubted if she would come. Straight from her 12-hour shift she looked more slight and vulnerable than ever, and almost completely worn out.

'We're going away to west Latvia tomorrow, and my husband has driven to fetch his father. But, you see, I come. All my colleagues said: "If a man brings you a note of invitation at one o'clock in the morning, then it's certain you have to go".'

She came on board without hesitation, faltered in the companionway, and sat in the saloon as though lost. She ate or drank nothing, and looked shocked by Yuri the skipper. Not only had she never been on a yacht, she probably also didn't encounter outsized, outdoor people like him, using his voice like a foghorn and siphoning whisky like water. He was so well influenced when he left, that he made to take with him a gift of bottled smoked fruit he had brought. Alex chaffed him, and even Valda smiled wanly.

Around midnight, I walked her back to the tram; over the railway track, under the trees. A distant streetlight threw her face in deep shadow.

'I hope you all get back safely,' she said.

'We will. I only hope we can do some good.' I talked of our hopes for the cruise and the future.

'It's up to us all, I know,' she said as we waited. 'We're all supposed to try. But we're so little. My job, for instance, is hardly important at all.'

We argued the point to and fro, forming a very strong bond. I caught the glint of her wedding ring in the light of the oncoming tram, and I didn't kiss her goodbye. We simply squeezed hands, and I didn't expect to meet her again.

By now, we'd got sense. We went for a noon departure. Birgitte brought us to a 'hello' and 'goodbye' reception with her Society President, Edvins Pumpurs.

'All countries live in a cage they have made. They lock the door,' he gestured, 'then throw the key away through the bars.'

She detoured to show us a magnificent street of houses designed by Sergei Eisenstein's father. Shay lagged further and further behind as he frantically captured their stunning plaster-cast swags and swages, the nudes and busts and humanesque corbels, their spiral stairs and exquisite frescoes. The link with the Finns was suddenly concrete. 'All wired up for blasting when the Germans retreated,' Birgitte mentioned. 'Small boys went in and undid the wires.'

She stood at our bows on the dock as we left. So did 'Da', Yelena, apparently close to tears. The khakied guard, posted since Inflot had

Canna *at the furthest point of her voyage - alongside the pontoons of the Baltic Shipping Company Club on the Little Neva in Leningrad.*

Susan Foxall. (RF)

LEFT: *Rupert.*

BELOW: *What an amazing co-incidence! Yanka Bielak pops up from the yacht we moor to in Norrköping. 'Come and meet my friend the Russian skipper.'*

OPPOSITE ABOVE: *The minute bu* *idyllic harbour of Haapasaari cuts the island almost in two. The black and cream marker poles are typical of the cardinal beacons in Finnish and Russian waters.*

OPPOSITE BELOW: *'Where on earth can we tie up?' The massive fenders fronting the dock at the Leningrad Sea Passenger Terminal. Between the Russian cruise liner and the new Polish sail-training ship, on a courtesy visit, stands the hotel beneath which* Canna *found a berth on her arrival.*

ABOVE: *At the Baltic Shipping Company Club in Leningrad, the only other visitor was a remarkable yacht from Volgograd. Alan, second from right, joins in a late-night party aboard her.*

LEFT: *The club professional coach takes an early morning shave in the cabin of his high-tech racing yacht.*

OPPOSITE ABOVE: *In Poland, sailing comes second only to football in popularity. Sailing clubs ring Gdynia harbour.*

OPPOSITE BELOW: *Near Jurmala, Riga. The Latvian and south Baltic beaches, backed by dune and forests, run for many hundreds of miles.*

ABOVE: *Alongside the Seamen's Club in Ventspils, Latvia, the 'Lenin' signboards listing high achievers seem to be temporarily disused. (RF)*

OPPOSITE ABOVE : *The small fishing and naval port of Ustka. Beyond* Canna *is the hefty steel lifeboat,* Huragan, *whose skipper, Andrej, befriended us.*

RIGHT: *From inland, and adjoining countries, holidaymakers swarm to the Polish beaches like lemmings. It's normally warmer in summer than in Britain.*

BELOW: *Private initiative in Ventspils...a new house being built from railway sleepers by its owner.*

LEFT: *All the crew assembled for the reception given by Edward Rataj, at the Mayor's office in Gdańsk.*

BELOW: *Rupert and Susan with Krysta-Elle in her Tallinn flat. Her son, Riho, hugging Alan, was sometimes mistaken for his son. (RF)*

cleared us, stuck his thumbs in his shoulder straps and discreetly looked away. Alan was extraordinarily busy with warps at the stern of the boat. 'All clear!' was as much as he trusted himself to call.

Deviating only to avoid a floating crane under power and to round up and hoist the sails, once out of the basin we steered a straight course down-current; but the police launch behind us seemed completely non-plussed. As if willing us to give it something to do, or practising ma-noeuvres the East Germans had recently taught it, Rover, or whoever it was, zig-zagged wildly behind us all the way out to the Gulf.

CHAPTER 13

Ventspils

'*Put, veine!* Blow, wind! Speed my boat to Kurzeme!' So begins the haunting folk-song that is now almost a Latvian anthem, a hymn to the country's traditions.

It did blow; it came fresh and strong over the port quarter, rushing us out of the river-mouth at six knots, heading north-north-west. It faltered slightly over a most untraditional, mile-long oil slick, laid by a ship that had gone before, in which a few fish kicked and gasped; then wafted in again more gently from the south-west, soft, warm, free, and faintly scented with pine. And it was winging us on toward Kurzeme.

The westernmost of Latvia's four historic divisions prods northwards like a very fat rhino's horn, forming the western wall of the Gulf of Riga and its buttress against the Baltic. On the way in, a southerly wind had kept us limping unevenly and nudged us away from its coastline; now we were able to close it. Sternwards, there was nothing to be seen, not even the last hazy waverings of the needle-top TV tower, but to port, ten or twelve miles off, the Kurzeme littoral unravelled like a wandering thread of blue wool, and the by-now familiar fascination with unknown distant land came back in full force. Just once, the bulge of a headland pushed closer, with the merest suspicion of sand beneath, and a vivid dragonfly, four or five inches long, hitched a lift on our dan buoy.

We were quiet, and peaceful. The sun glowed occasionally through banks of grey cloud, and we seemed loth to disturb their reflections by talking. Riga had been an enormous success. Only Alan was less than euphoric – not all his hopes had been realized. He'd complained of mild brush-offs once or twice, but I suspected it was really affairs of the heart that this time had made him the odd man out. For the rest of us, our stay had gone with a swing. Like the change of coastline from rock to sand, our time had seemed smoother and more relaxed. But if the cruise was at last really coming together, to remember that we'd come close to skipping Riga entirely brought on mild pangs of shame. By the same token, nothing obliged us to call to Ventspils, but the unspoken consensus ruled that, from here on, we'd miss out nothing. We had merely to follow the blue line for another 100 miles, around the tip of the horn, and back through the Irbenskiy Strait.

The afternoon slid into evening, a red light slid by to port. By midnight the moon had risen, and so had the Gipka light near Kolka, flashing once in six seconds. The sense of isolation in this inner lake was still strong. We were well beyond range of our normal broadcasts: Swedish was faint, and the usually clear East German forecasts from Rügen, for unknown reasons, couldn't be found. English programmes had long since faded, and world news for now was a thing of the past. For want of the proper almanacs (a major omission on my part), radio links with the Soviet shore were haphazard, to say the least. Since telephoning Moscow from near the Finnish border, we'd had no contact with the wider world at all.

But, '*Yate, yate.*' Something crackled on the VHF. Had we imagined it? Was it really intended for us?

Again it was barely dawn. Again we were into turbulent water, and sailing fast through the Strait. Once again there were searchlights.

'Di-dah, *di-dah, di-dah* . . .'

Not for the first time, we called back into the twilight.

'Patrol, patrol. This is yacht *Canna*, yacht *Canna* . . .'

'Please, repeat please . . .' came back thickly. At last! Connection, comprehension!

'*Yate Canna*, I spell, Charlie, Alpha . . . *yate Irlandski* . . . over.'

In the very long pause that followed, we reflected on our good luck. Our wind had held. Had it gone to the west as expected, we'd have been in for a very uncomfortable time. The Irbenskiy is one place where current is strong, and with wind and stream against us, we would have been forced to zig-zag through shipping and surveillance. But now, we were just able to lay a straight course, making it slow for pounding freighters to overtake us and, not least, we were keeping the patrol boats happy. They sounded not merely pleased that we'd been finally cuffed into shape, but delighted, too, that we'd come.

'*Canna*, thank you. Thank you very much,' had been the eventual reply from the first and, later, as we made a triumphant break-out back to the Baltic, a few miles north of Ovisi head, a second grey shadow came close to look us over.

'What country are you?' she called.

By then *Canna* was heeling so heavily we had to scale the gunwale to see her and then clamber below to yell the answer. Another big gap.

'Well! . . . well!' came back, in deep tones of utter astonishment which, with the pregnant pause between, sent us all into fits of laughter; but just then a heavy lurch threw all the porridge out of our bowls and the slurp as it landed somewhere downhill drowned out their flabbergasted 'Goodbye.'

Goodbye to breakfast, but not to the Soviet Union. We still had one more port to come; the one we knew least about. After a slow creep south against a coastal current, Ventspils showed up on the afternoon of 4 August; a solitary chimney, then ships at anchor, and two low lights on the ends of two short moles. Ventspils was a mystery town. It figured nowhere in tourist pamphlets, and was listed in no gazetteers. Even Riga natives could tell us nothing, apart from the fact that it was a commercial port. We had selected it only as a place for a break, or a handy refuge in case of storm and, almost as though sensing our passing interest, Inflot had simply cabled back 'no objection'. A smaller place than any we'd so far called at, it was hard to imagine it could offer us much.

Events soon proved us wrong. From the start, the place was idiosyncratic – no pilot and no radio. The north-west facing harbour entrance was short and simple, and *Canna* swanned straight in. It immediately opened to ranks of tankers and jetties; and, to starboard, a small shipyard carving up rusty wrecks, and an inlet sheltering trawlers. Obviously that wasn't the rumoured basin: a guard had waved us away. Next came the old fishing harbour, hardly as big as a dog basket and with barely room to turn round. It was dotted with ageing drifters, floating and human; and, as we made to tie up to the one, the others shifted us further. 'Squashed flat, if you stay there!' they signed with a grin, squeezing their palms together, but even that wasn't right; under a sudden black cloud that spouted like a watering can, a second guard galloped up, his khaki splattering to the colour of rich manure. Commandeering a work-boat, he showed us further up-river. Ranks of patrol boats, crews eyes-forward, reddish pinnacled silos to port; a few straggly trees and blue domes, the odd watch-tower, scrubland and fences. Across a bend in the widening Venta river, a high concrete wall drifted sideways toward us. A vast white shadow hovered over our bows: the stern, perhaps, of a liner. A black ship brought up the rear. *Canna* was like a mayfly between a duck and a swan.

Then people. The guard awaiting us vanished behind a thicket of donkey jackets and elbows, and work-roughened hands reaching down for our lines. The dockers clustered around the edge, grabbing at the chart of our route, pushing back helmets and whistling at the distance from Ireland. But it was the seamen's club visitation that startled us most, by whisking us straight back where we'd come from. There was Danis, the manager, and sad-looking Sergei, and shy Galeva in a white blouse, flaunting a porcelain delicacy. In the comfort of *Canna*'s saloon their talk was mostly of literature – they knew Casey and Yeats, but not Shaw, had read most of Joyce and could list every last one of his works.

'All in Russian translation,' said Danis, 'except *Ulysses* and *Finnegans Wake*. Those we find a bit difficult.'

A bit! Was this real? Were these really Latvians talking? Later, it transpired that Joyce's terrible twins are something of a touchstone for Soviet literati – in Tbilisi they boast that *Ulysses* is available in Georgian – the language of their southern republic – but, at the time, our visitors' voyages through literature seemed no less extensive than our own overseas.

Taken with their measured English, it felt strangely as if we hadn't left Ireland, as if we were still chatting with friends under some Dublin quay; and with more than a touch of disorientation we ventured no further that night than their club outside the dock gates.

It was as well, Alan and I reflected, as we went prospecting next day, that we hadn't cruised the Baltic anti-clockwise and called to Ventspils first. The river wasn't intended for yachts, and they almost never called.

'One Polish, and perhaps one East German,' Vitaly, Inflot's agent said. 'You are the first western yacht as far as we know. Ventspils is only a trading port.'

So we found. The import-export quay curved round for a third of a mile. Rows of railway lines ran along it, some being dug up and relaid by gangs of sweating navvies; others, under hoppers and cranes, carrying an endless succession of trains shunting to and from ships. Brown timber wagons and long grey closed ones ran so close to the edge of the dock, the engine-drivers could have spat on to our decks. The enormous cranes came even closer; when they travelled, which they did very often, warning bells rang continuously and their waist-high wheels ground by within two feet of the brink. Between their legs and all over the dock, the detritus of previous cargoes lay, and drifts of darkening pig-iron dust. The huge black fenders shed granules of rubber, which got ground into *Canna*'s decks. Passing tugs lurched her, to make matters worse, and the hawsers of neighbouring ships cut in closely from front and rear, twice as thick as her mast. It would have given a really boat-proud man an apoplectic fit. But we had been forewarned, we weren't being charged and, in any case, wouldn't stay long – a day or two at the most. By now, we were almost inured.

The huge white swan ahead of us wasn't a liner at all, but a freight ship. She was also a male professor. Whether *Akademik N. Vavilov* had specially distinguished himself by converting milk into roubles wasn't immediately obvious; but there she was, with his title blazoned across her transom, unloading EEC butter. At long last, we could see and touch a part of that mythical butter mountain; and what a mountain it was! Two cranes dug deep in her bowels day and night, plucking out brown cardboard cartons. Hundreds, thousands of tons came out. But the Professor's unloading had only just started; and for as long as we stayed in the dock, her waterline barely inched up more than a foot and a half.

Alan, as usual, was feeling puckish. 'Maybe, Roger, that butter we bought in Leningrad came from the top of your road!' he grinned. The same thought had struck us both. Perhaps it had started as our neighbour's grass and ended in Intervention; but, if so, it got us nowhere. Having yesterday been drowned by a shower when we didn't need it, it seemed cussedly difficult to find one when we did. At the head of the gangway, a neatly bearded officer in white cap and full gilt regalia greeted our enquiry most courteously.

'. . . but most unfortunately this is a very modern ship. We have only individual cabins, and therefore no communal showers.'

So much for EEC munificence! It was a nice irony: the Common Market was the one thing we'd never been asked about, since the Soviets, so far, hadn't officially recognized it.

We had no more luck with the East German ship under her bows, loading little grey gherkins of pig-iron with a vast electro-magnet shaped like a hamburger bun. Like all foreign ships, she was under continuous guard, and the two young soldiers turned us away. Only one more chance – the black Russian tub behind us, also thundering castings into her holds.

'Yes, of course!' the moustachioed third mate said. 'Please, it may take some minutes . . .' and left us in his cabin while he went to make the arrangements. There was a single bunk to one side, a typewriter on a glass-topped table, a few postcards stuck to the wardrobe doors; and, when in borrowed slippers we returned, half-naked from somewhere down by the engine-room and quite the best shower for two months, he had laid out breakfast for three.

Over rolls and salami and coffee, Alan and I glanced at each other, delighted. We came to know Sasha quite well. At first he explained his duties on board – showing us the elaborate coloured ship's plans he used to supervise loading. If he got his calculations wrong, and loaded the hull unevenly, the boat could break up in bad weather.

In turn, we asked about something that often worried us – how far a yacht's lights could be seen from the bridge? Even masthead lights would often be lower than the bows of a really big freighter. He confirmed that ship's watch officers usually preferred them to be down almost at sea-level, where they'd expect them, rather than gyrating aloft apparently unrelated to the yacht's hull.

'But normally it is no problem. We just keep out of the way.' We were mighty relieved to hear it. Russian merchant ships had a good reputation among yachtsmen and Sasha confirmed there were usually plenty of crew; although that, he said, with a shadow of doubt, in the future might have to change, as many things were beginning to.

From there our conversation led off deeper and wider. Sasha was a thinking man. His oval, Ukrainian face looked more artistic than practical. Then and later, in the club, he ranged over many topics and feelings, and connections through Russian history. Light allusions to Stalin's era, the 20 million dead in the War; he'd lost his father and grandfather, and one or two uncles too. Every family lost someone. But he passionately believed in his country. He was proud of it, and agreed with the Revolution. He was very deeply upset by indiscriminate condemnation of the USSR from abroad; most of the accusations just didn't match what he knew of himself and his friends.

'Such criticism is nonsense,' he said. But he wasn't blind to the nation's problems. Interference elsewhere was one. 'To get into Afghanistan was wrong. It's all their own business – why are we there, getting our young men killed? For why, for what? That is all nonsense too.'

Chauvinism was another thing. All countries, we had to agree, east and west, were smitten to some degree. 'And it happens between the Republics of the Union, too. All right, we all speak Russian, all of us learn it at school, but still we are different countries. Russian does not make us one. One Republic thinks it knows the best way to live, and that most of the others are rubbish.'

Prejudice did exist. One of his friends had a Korean wife; with her Asian features and half-caste children, she sometimes suffered difficulties. There were problems at work, problems of party, promotion, old-fashioned rules. But they were still peripheral to his thrust.

'There is much I feel, here inside, which I want to speak but cannot,' (because of language, he meant). 'What I really want is for other countries to see us through their own eyes and hearts, and not just through their Governments.'

The echoes went deep. It was the start of another departure. Over the next few hours and days, we were to meet many new faces from the ships and the club and, suddenly, new perspectives opened. There was a curious sense of double-take, as though someone, somewhere, were casually uncovering the second layer of a chocolate-box.

Perhaps it was because Inflot and the Seamen's Club, in twin buildings, side by side, co-operated so closely; perhaps because of the outpost atmosphere, people talked a little more widely. Perhaps it was just us, properly adjusted at last. Whatever it was, it filled in a fourth dimension.

Glasnost came to be part of it. Nobody much had mentioned it so far. True, Ildus, the chandler in Leningrad, had bounced in with typical verve: 'Here, you know, we just begin a new life!' he had exclaimed; but perhaps his forwardness was due to his being not Russian, but Tatar, and Tatars are renowned as extravagant. In Riga, some people had praised the new leader, but his new ideas weren't on everyone's lips.

One evening, heading into the club, I was arrested by Mikhail Gorbachev going full blast in the foyer. He was declaiming at length and with perspiration from a TV on the reception desk manned by a large lady knitting. She took not the least bit of notice. I got help from a trainee dentist with prominent teeth and a fringe. The programme, she said, was meant to end with the news, but had been extended to cover his speech to a trades' union congress. The setting, indeed, was low-key – a table, a glass of water, no big posters behind him – but without doubt, he had the bit in his teeth. Points were repeatedly nailed with his fist, and *perestroika* and *glasnost* came out in a single breath.

'He's telling of the need for democracy in industry – among managers and union members. He's persuading people to voice their opinions.'

'So what are yours? What has been the reaction?'

'Not much for the first two years, before he became Secretary. Then it was all talk. Now, for the last year and a half, people are waiting to see if there is action. Yes, they see he means what he says, and yes, they agree with him. But will it work, will it come to pass? For many, there's a suspension of belief – and perhaps they don't want to believe, in case it's risky, or lest they be disappointed.'

But, yes, even if all failed, she felt, there would be some permanent change – things wouldn't entirely revert. Further she would not go. She seemed to be sitting very gingerly astride her personal fence. So did most others. One crossed his arms, just as the patrol-boat skipper had done, to indicate how reform might end: 'road closed'.

It was obviously a hugely momentous junction, at which, from aboard their runaway juggernaut, the right road had to be picked; at the same time, it was a 'landslide of hopes' as a Canadian journalist termed it, looking for the right time to happen; and while waiting for it to get started, people's moods swung violently between depression and elation, between seriousness and humour.

Humour, in Ventspils, won out. Problems were shouldered aside by a flood of political jokes. Between bouts of table-tennis or dance, or a film on the life of reinstated folk song hero Vladimir Vissotsky, shown in a church-like hush, our new friends savoured their collection hugely. 'Have you heard the one about . . . ?' they would ask. 'You not . . . ?' The classic Russian train, for instance, crossing an empty steppe with all the post-revolutionary leaders aboard had been brought right up to date. Now when it stops inexplicably in the middle of nowhere, and the track – oh, no! – is found to have petered out, Lenin still urges the track-layers to work even harder, Stalin still shoots the driver and fireman, Khrushchev still bangs his shoe and shouts. Brezhnev lazily takes up rail from behind and lays it again in front; but nowadays, comrade Mikhail makes his contribution too. He leans far out of the carriage – our raconteur cupped his hands to his mouth – and yells to the world, 'No rails! No rails!' Riots and torrents of laughter.

These new imponderables were laid down on personal uncertainties, and this was another thing we came to like Ventspils for. Elsewhere, everyone had seemed mainly successful, but here, there were engaging human failures.

There was the club host, Sergei, for instance, kindly but extremely serious and sad. His marriage had broken down heavily, and his face got longer each day. Perhaps, he wondered, even the only child wasn't his. He was keen to move away for promotion, and had organized interviews for a tourism posting in the Crimea. So far, he hadn't heard, he said, and now, with the new restructuring, his prospective employers might not take on new staff.

Then there was Timor, the Georgian docker, who turned up with gifts of chocolate (always dark and expensive). He'd arrived in Ventspils almost by accident, one of a group of four mates. After college they'd followed up advertisements, moved down together from Leningrad and shared one flat in the town. Before his studies he'd lived in Moscow.

'And which do you prefer?' Susan asked provocatively.

'Why, the city of course. More cinemas, much more to do.'

'Was Ventspils a bit of a mistake then?'

His eyes widened. 'A big mistake,' he snorted, then grinned. It had apparently all snowballed from there; he now had a wife and a baby, had lost touch with his mates and was awaiting a three-room flat.

Ventspils, through it all, began to round itself out. It wasn't at all a tourist resort, but a backwater where, over a period, various peoples had churned and melded. Not just Letts and Russians, either, but Livs and gypsies too. The Livs were a Finnish-related tribe of fishermen-farmers, who in times past inhabited the two wings of the Gulf of Riga – north of us in the horn of Kurzeme, and the land to the east of the Gulf that used to carry their name, Livonia, and that, confusingly, for a long time, became synonymous with Latvia itself. Their characteristic dug-out canoes, hacked from a single log and used well into the twentieth century (Ransome reported one with an outboard engine) could still be seen in the woods. Nearby were the quaint remains of the narrow-gauge train that had strung their villages together, the boxy carriages boasting shiny brass port-holes and its cast-steel sleepers snaking between the trees.

'There are very few Livs left now,' Sergei dolefully intoned, as we crossed the only bridge to the town, quite distinct on the opposite bank. There were barely a dozen true-bloods in Ventspils, many more perhaps hybrid-ized – a case of Liv and Lett live together – and several thousand in the coastal villages northwards. But their language still just survived with the help of a revival attempt, and poetry and news-sheets in Liv; and so did their quarter. In the narrow roads around Liv's Street, *Liv's Iela*, sloping up from the fisherman's co-op, the Livs and half-Livs dwelt on in clustered old low wooden houses, their carved and painted doors and shutters hiding under chestnut trees. The restless wind-blown light and shade shifting across planks and sandy pavements could have come straight from Maxim Gorky; children pointed curiously and shambling, ponderous women with push-chairs shielded themselves from our evil eye as if warding off a taboo.

Gypsies lived among them, too, swarthy, small and mercurial, and others of race unstated.

'Nothing much happens here,' we'd been told with apologies and deprecations. The provincial town had seemed half-unloved, its features revealed almost grudgingly, so that its hidden depths were sharply surprising.

'Valda!' – I could hardly believe it when our friend from Riga arrived the next day with her family. They had driven up from Liepāj, a town two pot-holed hours to the south, scoured Ventspils in search of *Canna*, and finally collided with us as we left the club for a bus-trip. 'How marvellous! Meet Susan and Shay . . .'

But it was such a completely unexpected thrill, and the warmth of their friendship so palpable, that our time together was painfully short.

For a while, they came with us. Janis's love was photography. The camera slung around his neck was an enormous, two-portholed affair, built like a diver's helmet. Janis himself was equally solid: he said little, but watched all around him, viewing the lush green land stretching beyond the river bridge, the bleak blocks of flats, the straight-laced Lutheran church in a dusty main square, for all the world like a Western town, and chatted briefly to a scatter of men in naval trousers hacking a ball on a patch of grass under a waterside castle.

'He had a one-man show in Riga, once,' said Valda proudly, hugging seven-year-old Ia, as we inspected a granite monument to fishermen lost at sea; but when she gently nudged a return to the club, we were once again at a disadvantage. We diverted the bus to show off *Canna*, from the other side of the river (they wouldn't be allowed in the docks). What more could we do? Nothing, it seemed: ordering coffee in the club buffet had straight-away started an argument. Janis wouldn't hear of me paying.

'But I am a seaman, this is my club,' I said, determinedly blocking the counter.

'And this is my country,' he shot back, equally stubborn.

'Roger, *please*,' pleaded Valda, touching my arm.

They dug yet more goodies out of their car. There were fresh peas and fruit from their garden and platoons of home-made pastries. We could only thank them. Janis pulled the wing-mirror out of his pocket, refitted it, and they drove away.

'Can we extend our visas?' we wanted to know from Inflot. We too were soon due to leave, but by now we didn't want to, and three days more would cover the gap where Klaipeda ought to have been. We weren't due in Poland until the 11th.

'Yes,' they said. 'We'll arrange it.' And were all set to do so, but in the capital, Riga. I cursed myself for overlooking such an elementary point, nor having done it while we were there. Now, with our visas valid for only one more day, we'd all have to travel to Riga by train (not possible, as one had to stay on the boat) or kick our heels in the docks for a day while Inflot took the passports and did it for us; and then the enquiries of the young volunteer official as to whether some of us could accompany him for the purpose met an unexpected refusal by 'phone.

'But why, what is the problem?'

'Perhaps it's to do with restricted areas,' he offered uncertainly.

'But we're just not interested in things like that.'

'I know; but sometimes it is hard to explain to other people.'

From there on we waltzed each other deeper and deeper into a morass of embarrassment. Seeing we were momentarily startled by being unable to go as we pleased, Vitaly, sympathetic and desperate to help, cast around for gaps in the palings.

'Well, perhaps we could arrange for one or two of you to come,' he thought out loud eventually, making complicated suggestions about travel by train and bus. 'But you just can't *believe* how unofficial it is.'

The boot was now on the other foot. It wasn't fair, we decided, to put friends or officials in parlous positions, by bending rules if it wasn't essential. In any case, it could rebound on us, so backing down with considerable regret, we told the now crestfallen Vitaly that we wouldn't be staying on.

With just one more day in the Soviet Union, we began to look round us more acutely. By night, as the lights of beacons and the distant town glanced across still water, and starlings infested the walkways of cranes like mites on a stick insect's legs, the docks looked almost romantic. By day, they altered entirely: in the draughty guard-house, the women in duffles and fingerless mitts who checked our papers between perpetually slamming doors, or waved us through with bored expressions, definitely didn't look ravishing; and the intentions of the docker with a yellow helmet and scarlet lipstick seemed a little uncertain. She offered a cuddle of her furry stray kitten (I think) in three successive languages – I tried three more, but not one matched.

By then, she had other things to think of. Butter was still being unloaded, a pallet or two at a time. The ship was still edging higher. Fork-lift trucks whizzed it into a warehouse where gangs of her colleagues labelled and checked, and out again into the wagons. When full, an official scaled their doors, and awkwardly wired and sealed them shut.

There seemed a lack of equipment: the Russian ship could only load iron if it was too wet to discharge the butter. The East German freighter had been replaced by another loading synthetic rubber, and room-sized bales of silk and cotton hauled to the cranes by a string of lorries, lurching through piles of coal.

Now *Canna* too had to load stores, which brought us to the business of oil. We'd assumed that the three or four tankers in the outer harbour were bringing the refined stuff in. Nonsense – they were taking it out. A pipeline runs down from Siberia, and the oil goes all over the world. Even back in 1974, the Union had exported well over 100 million tons, and much of that seemed to flow through Ventspils, not just in pipes but in wagons. It was always a bit of a puzzle to get out of the dock at all. Every time we attempted it, goods trains on their several tracks had shifted and altered the maze; we were forced to detour around the end of one, backtrack along another, or duck under a coupling when desperate. But it was as nothing to the occasional problem of crossing the track outside the dock gates. It was wise to bring a picnic stool and a copy of *War and Peace*. Once, we'd waited for 25 minutes for an oil train to pass: scores upon scores of gargantuan silver cylinders shaking the earth and squealing from one vanishing point to the other.

So what chance 30 litres of diesel? That, we found, took lots of patience and seven people. It also provided endless amusement. The expedition began with just three: myself, an agent, and a driver with an estate car who carefully propped our containers away from his fishing rods. In the compound, a mile up-river, were small brick sheds and a scatter of drums. I presumed we'd get a few gallons from those, but Yuri disappeared for an unduly long time. When he came back, he looked doubtful.

'They've got a slight problem,' he said, leading me to a dock round the corner, and on to an unnoticed bunkering ship. Black with pipes, she was three hundred feet long, and full to the brim with fuel. Three men in overalls stood doubtfully on her catwalks; one levered up an enormous oval deck hatch, changed his mind and tried another. A metal ladder led down and down, and disappeared through a blue reflection. We leaned in and looked at our ring of black faces, then all stood back and scratched our heads. Yes, they would gladly spare us six gallons, but how on earth could they get it out? There was talk of sending a man down with a bucket. The sooner the better. Like doll's teapots, our containers took off in a puff of breeze, and I chased them over acres of deck. In the nick of time, they remembered a disused hand pump.

The paperwork took no less effort. The office cabin was in the after-quarters, its curved and portholed walls studded with rivets and shiny with paint. The elderly ship and her bunkering boss oozed oil from every pore; he, with his sleeves rolled over his elbows, faced up to the Inflot agent, crisp and cool in a pin-striped suit, while above, on a curled and relict poster, a red-starred soldier was just as busy, bloodily triumphing over the Nazis.

Soon there were sharp exchanges, in Russian, and quintuple sheaves of dockets to sign.

'You'd think it was the Crown Jewels!' we laughed, but no! Due seriousness broke in. They'd missed one – six were needed! More careful scribe-work, more signing.

I've treasured our customer's copy since. It cost us all of four roubles. The diesel's vital statistics: quantity, cost, viscosity (35 seconds) are carefully entered, even down to the sulphur content. This last is not just academic. The low sulphur of Siberian oil makes for less pollution and fumes, so we could belch out smoke with an easier conscience; it was also why rail and bus companies bought it. Unawares, we'd already been travelling around for years by courtesy of Ventspils oil.

Fuel for the boat, fuel for the body. A quiet suburban supermarket, with overalled assistants in white. We kept a close eye on the prices. If diesel cost 13 kopecks per litre, milk cost 24 to 50, depending on quality. Cream was ladled by the litre from a galvanized churn on the floor. Butter, at 3.50 roubles per kilogram was rather more than we'd pay at home, at the official exchange rate (1 rouble = £1), but very much more expensive for someone on earnings of 150 roubles per month. Cheese was a little bit cheaper. Bread cost only 12 kopecks for a substantial half rye loaf. But fruit and vegetables had gone through the roof: 'Because of the cold, late spring,' the Inflot secretaries told us, 'there are shortages all round, and sellers can ask what they like.' For anything other than potatoes, rhubarb and cabbage, we had to go to the market, where small bunches of small onions were selling for 80 kopecks, and carrots for 1 rouble. 'But most people have access to a garden somewhere. Many people used to grow their own and now they do it again.'

So it seemed. Struggling back laden, a man with a collie and a mane like a tinker dropped his bag of redcurrants on to our shopping, and slapped our hands as if clinching a deal at a horse-fair.

Food for the mind too. *Pravda* at 4 kopecks, about 1p per sheet. We could have bought the Soviet Constitution at a small bookshop nearby.

Fragments for the memory. A veteran soldier displaying his stripes, a single black figure between sunlit walls. Two men with leather hats, goggles and ear-flaps flying a motorbike-sidecar. A café that served *tvorog*, curds with cream and lemon-juice with pips in and, under the eaves of a wide thatched house, a skeletal old man swinging a vicious scythe.

And finally, food for the soul. Out beyond the streets altogether, beyond the trees and all restraint, and out to the Baltic beaches. They ran for miles, tapering off into silvered wet sand and high blue dunes and forest. A few changing shelters with legs beneath, a few dark figures swimming or walking, then nothing to be seen or felt or heard except sand in the toes, the sun beating down between humped white clouds and the whine through the marram grasses.

We put to sea next morning. We didn't get very far. The departure had felt unusual. Inflot pushed the time from midnight to 9 am, the customs search was thorough, and we'd been able to get no forecast. No matter. The weather looked perfect – sparkling, bright, the wind a brisk north-west – or was it? It freshened more as we went down river, raising sail at the moles was a struggle, and once outside them it really piped up. We were reefing down, the horizon looked dirty, and the wind began to back west; and as the harbour sank astern, below a nasty cross-sea, a providential message came through. It was the *Alpine Rose*, a British cargo ship lying off that we had briefly radioed before. From a mile away, we could see her beginning to heave at her anchor.

'*Canna*, we have a storm warning. Westerly, and three-metre waves.'

There was nothing at all to argue about. We turned around and went in. Some crew were relieved, some neutral. Alan worried for his pre-booked passage out of Poland. Other parties were downright puzzled.

'Yes, *Canna*, I hear you!' said port control. 'You come in again, but why?'

The 'why', it seemed, was that Latvia, like Ireland, wouldn't let go: we hadn't yet seen her extremes.

Charging in past manoeuvring tugs, straining to keep her in hand, we slipped, or rather slammed, back into berth number six. The river-bend by now was catching the first of the gale and waves were already spurting up between the big rubber fenders. We took the precaution of pointing *Canna* up-wind.

So what happened now? The rigging shrieked, and the first spits of rain went by as though on an errand. It didn't take long to find out. A thicket of uniforms clicked to a halt and changed us from tourists to seamen. Our visas having by now expired, for the first and only time on the voyage *Canna* was graced with a permanent guard. It was highly impressive – first a solitary figure in khaki, then two, and a snazzy green desk. They set it up on the edge of the dock, as if for a liner in Leningrad, then guarded it for two days. All that night, as we got up a fug in the cabin, above us the storm built to a crescendo, driving spray and rain sideways in drifts; and in watches of eight or twelve hours, the teenagers stood there like trees.

For a time, they found a meagre lee by the leg of a travelling crane, but when even that had trundled away to huddle behind a ship, they had nothing left but their greatcoats.

'You should have no trouble taking your travel snaps,' ran the footnote to a map of Russia, 'as long as you never train your camera on military installations (these include soldiers).' Instead, we waved the coffee-pot, repeatedly, until it seemed pure cruelty; but always the 'installations' refused.

'What character training!' Susan marvelled. 'So long as it doesn't sour them for foreigners.' Apparently not; traditional manners obviously insisted our lady be handed up and down, and they conducted affairs with exactitude. Passports were exchanged for seamen's passes, even for a stroll on the dock. The crew, at least, had to co-operate, and be back on board by midnight, for fear of being a pumpkin. But the skipper was a privileged person. He got an extra glance of respect, and his passport handed back. What other entitlements went with it, I didn't think to enquire – I hadn't felt so exalted since the pilot had called me 'Kapitan' – but the exemption wasn't *carte blanche*. There were limits. Sometimes I brought back reading material from the club and once, my copy of *Moscow News*, an English language weekly (and a 'stormtrooper of *glasnost*', as I discovered later), was carefully queried on their walkie-talkie. But the youngster was making doubly sure, and I swear I caught him smiling.

That night had been one to remember. *Canna* lurched ever more heavily against the dock, and the Baltic itself was never so rough. We set three-hour watches to tend the fenders.

Next day the sky showed signs of spring-cleaning; and it was at about that stage, after a bothersome winter, Ratty had thrown down his whitewash brush and rushed out. Most of us felt much the same. We just had to get clear, get away; somewhere, anywhere, to soak up a full day's rest.

Susan and Rupert and I fled the docks with not a thing in our hands. We just walked – out past colleges, flats, suburban surgeries behind tall hedges, a water tower and a heating plant. We walked until we cleared the town. A distant factory intercom finally faded to nothing. At the road-sign cancelling Ventspils, the last side-road led off, enormously long and straight, with a single distant figure against the glare of the dust. Resinous forest moved in to greet us, and kerbstones gave up the ghost. There was a smell of hot tarmac under the sun. The unfenced verges were bright with flowers. The road swung off ahead in mile-long tapering reaches, and the very odd whine of a car or a bus, taking ages to swell and pass, only deepened the silence. After a while we turned off under the trees. They stood not in rows but spaced out very unevenly, with a blanket of shaded low green beneath, a natural, native forest. On a sandy track a man and a woman picked small fungi with penknives. A ranger went by in his jeep. Electric-blue dragonflies, inches long, flitted between the clearings. But deeper in there was no one and nothing, only the smell of dead needles under one's back, shafts of sun streaming down, the tall trunks towering and fragments of racing sky between.

Oh, the peace! For months we had been rushing and striving; and everywhere something had contrived to keep us apart from the common-or-garden countryside. Haste, or windscreens, or simply appointments; a film of something transparent. Even in Segulda, although the forest had beckoned us out of the train, we'd not quite come into contact. Now we had; so had Alan, unknown to us, in another part of the wood. For just a few hours, there was a sense of absolute content, of acute and rewarding happiness.

We got back to the boat with fingers stained purple from picking blueberries, and clutching a milk-bottle full of cream. For a while, I was vexed we'd taken no camera; but not now, not later. Slowly another memory drifts in to join this most vivid of all from the voyage, from another tract of anonymous forest, 20 years earlier in Yellowstone Park – the same feeling of being completely in tune. That too was much sharper for not having been entrusted to film.

By the 9th the wind had died down. Now we could leave for real. When we'd first departed, the white-helmeted dock manager had wished us well. Dockers had waved and cheered. The driver of a distant shunting engine had blown a victory blast on his hooter. This time there was only a pilot launch, overtaking down-river, but their crew nonetheless gave a clenched salute, like the sailors of the yachts in Leningrad Bay we'd met when we'd first arrived.

Soon we were out in a gentle, south-westerly wind, once again almost exactly against us. It toyed with us for most of a day, as we slanted through glassy ripples on the skeletons of a dying swell, skirting the long, deserted shore; the 'amber coast' that runs on down to Lithuania, where the resin of 30-million-year-old pines is cast up in storms on the sand.

We left Ventspils at ten in the morning; at noon had passed the round, white light at Uzava, sprouting from a bright red house; but by midnight had made only 40 miles to the low blunt headland of Akmenrags. For a while the north-setting current held us zigzagging helplessly, making almost no ground at all.

We had a little time in hand, and felt no need to hurry. It was almost as though we were filtering all our Soviet impressions slowly, deliberately, like sand through our fingers, letting them go only little by little. They settled, among other things, to a sense of solidity, of warmth, and of permanence so far barely disturbed.

This palpable framework of social cohesion became clearer as we left it behind; and the realization suddenly dawned that, whereas when approaching through other countries we had heard a very great deal about Russia, once there, perspectives had changed completely. There had been a stillness at the centre, and a very different sense of scale. The Soviets' attentions seemed mainly focused on their own affairs, or trained on their rivals across the Atlantic. There had been no signposts to guide us to Poland.

Part III
POLAND
AND THE
RETURN

Notes: (1) In 1987, £1 sterling = approximately 500 zlotys

(2) A brief gloss on Polish phonetics: ą = aw
                                          c = ts
                                          ę = un
                                          j = y
                                          ł = w
                                          ó = u
                                          w = v
                                          y = i

CHAPTER 14

Gdynia and Gdańsk

When our memories of Russia and the Baltic Republics had settled into little heaps, and the sharp sadness of leaving her shores had finally begun to soften, the weather made up its mind to take us firmly in hand.

At first, it was the merest breath from the north-west in the quiet of early morning. It tiptoed unseen to the east of north and breathed from there instead; it veered even more to east-northeast; and then the wind-gods really began in earnest, wafting, puffing, then finally, unmistakably blowing, pushing up white wave-crests on the grey-green sea.

It was unusual for the time of year, and a great stroke of luck. The wind that had been entirely wrong for us up the west coast of Ireland was now pushing us helter-skelter, poled-out and goose-winged to Poland. The seas heaped up, jacking the stern with an imperious hydraulic movement, tilting and sliding her down their fronts. Rain began to spit, the northern horizon got darker and darker. This part of the Baltic was extremely empty: no birds flew and no aeroplanes. No ships stalked the horizon, and we were entirely on our own. We almost missed the patrol boats. Rupert navigated by dead-reckoning as the Decca once again sulked. Alan came down dripping and made a curry on the heaving stove. I shirked the decks, peered out at the darkening sea and wondered. Should we reef? Should we in fact have reefed already? Accepted wisdom says, if you think of it twice, you've left it too late. *Canna* was making her maximum speed, and if we had to manoeuvre, say to avoid a ship, we'd find ourselves over-canvassed. Getting down a spinnaker-boom in half a gale wasn't a safe or an easy job. And at the back of my mind was the warning of *Oriana*.

Just three weeks earlier, in 1859, they too had put in to 'Dantzic', and had anchored off. They ought not to stay in the open roadstead, the Head Pilot had told them, 'as the weather was very changeable, and if it blew strong out of N or NE they would be in a very bad way.' The Gulf of Gdańsk was entirely open to those empty quarters we were crossing, with a fetch of 400 miles from Finland, forming a potential death-trap in storm. And *Oriana* nearly did pay the full price. The wind and sea rose so viciously that night as to finally burst her anchor chain and, with time to hoist only a bare scrap of sail before being driven ashore, she made Danzig harbour with inches and seconds to spare. 'I'm not easily frightened, but I thought then that sixpence would be a dear price for our lives,' Corrigan had confided.

Then, as now, the barometer had given no sign. Ours was steady at 1013 and was even beginning to rise – a strangely disquieting phenomenon, as the northern sky by now was near-black. Time and again, we made to shorten sail. Time and again, the strengthening blow seemed to fade. We still had a full day's sea-room to land, I reasoned, and we were heading for Gdynia, not Gdańsk; the newer port fifteen miles further north was tucked in tighter under the lee of the long Hel peninsula, for the tip of which we were aiming. Besides, on the unseen Lithuanian coast, speeding by 40 miles away, there was still Klaipėda as a possible port of emergency: 'They wouldn't turn you away,' a Russian skipper had told us. Gritting our teeth, we pressed on, savouring a dangerous exhilaration.

I am not clear now, after more than a year, why my impression of Poland is grey. All rational thought says it's an unfair label, but something still hovers in the emotional part of the mind. Perhaps it was the memory of those empty, somewhat anxious wastes, as we made our approach with no company except two old-fashioned propeller planes and two boats, or of the muted foggy days we encountered along the coast; perhaps it exuded from the grey uniforms of the *milicja* when we arrived; or perhaps it was our own mood, an unwarranted sense of anti-climax in the return from our furthest point, in the incipient dwindling of an adventure, or the waxing of long-term exhaustion. Maybe, with hindsight, it was the mood of the country itself, composed of the raw, plundered feel of its towns, and layers of current despairs, but somehow it's still there, a prejudice to be conscientiously fought.

Poland, in fact, reared up, in another classic but accidental dawn approach, not grey but blue: first the densely-piled carpet of forest, behind the isophase light of Hel, flashing equally every ten seconds; then blue turquoise flecked with white as we made to Gdynia proper. In the bay the wind eased, and we lay to it hard, close-hauled, leaving the odd patrol boat and occasional shipping in complicated deep channels to port. A final approach, almost nosing up to a swan-lined beach between the harbour moles and a detachment of the Polish navy, brought us to the marina.

It was a sharp surprise and a delight, after 1,000 miles of almost uniformly low coastline, to once again lie beneath cliffs and a rise of ground. At home, we have lived on and under mountains for 20 years, and I suddenly realized how much we had missed them. Not that these were mountains, but it was at least an impressive swelling of ground, pushing out to the water's edge like the knuckles of a huge fist, half-clenched and fuzzed with green in the creases. On the gentler slopes were the odd thin spire, an Italianate row of poplars, or a flash of white and terracotta peeping out here and there. The scent of eucalyptus drifted across with the first bright rays of the sun. Beyond the immigration berth, in the generous harbour basin, a few sails turned slowly from gold to white as they glided between the catwalks. Many more lined the low timbered quaysides, and soon we were among them.

Gdynia's history was unusual, and also extremely short; if Gdańsk was to be our oldest city, Gdynia was the youngest of all. A dozing village in the 1920s, by the start of the Second World War it was the most trafficked port in the Baltic, with 13,000 ships annually. The transformation had been a necessity. Gdańsk, at the mouth of the Wisła river, the traditional outlet for the country's flood of produce, had been excised from the newly con-structed Poland and placed in charge of the League of Nations. It tended towards Germany. Poland, squeezed between a western neighbour that now occupied nearly all the south Baltic coast, and East Prussia on the eastern flank, was left almost coastless and entirely portless. She had had to do something fast.

The town bore the marks of its hurried birth. *Ad hoc* tracks crossed unkempt grass toward haphazard sheds and a bar; and the main street seemed curiously lop-sided. On one flank, along its steady rise, ranks of stone and brick façades, of a typically austere and strait-laced type, looked across to Wendy-houses with steep red roofs, and low, cabin-like, temporary-looking shops, as if someone had mislaid some drawings or the money had simply run out. The more mature streets, and a brand-new Catholic church, almost blending with a slab-like hotel ('Why does God need such a tall house?' a young Pole had enquired) were tucked incongruously behind, and made no contribution.

'A very curious place!' murmured Alan, for whom it represented the end of his voyage. Even allowing for our sea-dulled senses, there was no perceptible style. Built and human seemed oddly at odds and formless, with no discernible pattern and a very Irish casualness.

But Gdynia is deceptive. The visitor from seaward is at a disadvantage – only when he goes about-face does the place reveal its *raison d'être*, and why its shop windows are thick with maritime books. Few towns can have such a forceful connection with the sea. Looking back, the main street sweeps down like the shaft of an arrow, splits briefly around a futuristic fountain, welds itself beyond into one finger of the docks, between the grey bulk of the maritime college with its feet almost in the water, and its ship, the famous square-rigger, *Dar Pomorza*, opposite and even taller; and, at the end, it collides with twin monuments bursting up into the sky, against the glittering horizon. Not twins, in fact: one, a triple spire of silver steel surmounted by crosses, symbolizing her three sail training ships to date (*Lwów* was the first) and beneath, a broody chunk of stone, with the moustachioed figure of Conrad Korzeniowski, Joseph Conrad, materializ-ing from a granite prow.

Conrad had also lent his name to the ubiquitous class of timber ketches encountered all over Poland and Russia that are built in the Lenin Shipyard in Gdańsk, and his obsession with the sea was quite obviously far from unique.

The quays were open to all and sundry, and by now crowds and coach-loads of all ages, crunching pop-corn and lollies, milled along the walls and gangplanks, queueing at the museum-ships, inspecting heavy, black-hulled gaffers from outlying ports, wandering along past *Canna's* bows, fingering rigging and fittings and peering curiously at our ensign. The whole marina was a tourist attraction.

'You must know,' said Zbigniew Szpetulski, a small tornado with grizzled face and hair, 'that sailing in Poland is very, very important. Almost a fever – it's second only to football.'

The director of 'Akademiki Club Morski' and our host, Zbigniew enlarged on the phenomenon as his wife bustled round with tots of Polish brandy, *winiak*, in the cabin of a nearby yacht.

'We don't have much money – come with me, I'll show you our primitive club – but what we don't have or can't buy, we make.'

There was just one small office-cum-common room; but also a chart room stacked to the ceiling with charts from around the world, a workshop thick with engine parts, and well-muscled athletes marking out sails on the floor of a gymnasium.

The club was one of six or seven. Unlike Leningrad, here they were grouped all together – the discreet and plush-looking Navy, the Para-military, the more workaday Shipyard and Trades' Union, the modest Scouts and the Academy. One and all were abuzz. Boats on cradles were being prepared; the *Konstanty Maciejewicz*, timber but long-hulled like *Canna*, was being craned into the water. In one corner, a flotilla of dinghies like prams with handkerchiefs were being raced by toddlers; in another, a mean-looking ketch of orange steel was being feverishly prepared for the centenary in Australia. This last was making Zbigniew frantic.

'She should have been gone two weeks ago,' he agonized. Six others had already left. She had a voyage of 12,000 miles to face, and was already laden with three and a half tons of food, intended to last her all the way there and back.

The Poles sailed amazing distances. With Swedish and Danish coasts normally out of bounds, and many others difficult, they ranged north to Spitsbergen, Greenland and the Arctic Circle, (some we met had come to grief there, and had been fished from the icy White Sea by Russians); others ventured west to the States; and the famous Krystyna Choynowska-Liskiewicz they reckon to have been the first woman to have circled the globe single-handed.

Nor was the interest in sailing confined to sailors on the Polish coast. That evening found us aboard a well-worn ketch, crewed by mountainy men from Zakopane, a town in the southernmost tongue of the country,

600 miles away, tucked in under the 8,000-foot summits of the Tatra mountains along the Czech border.

'They're big and strong and make the best crew of all,' said their skipper, Mirek.

It sounded like it. The panelling of the cabin reverberated like the innards of a drum as they pounded out the songs of the *górale*, the natives of their high and difficult land.

Sailing was one of the easiest ways for a Pole to travel abroad, hence much of its attraction, and their quite different reaction to our visit from that in the Soviet Union. The length and physical details of our cruise were a matter of no great surprise, but there was an immediate, almost professional concern with our route and visas and the possibilities of a two-way exchange, and we could sense the network of co-operation, which we were assured ran like scutch grass through the length and breadth of the country, gearing itself up to help us.

'But you set me an examination in English!' an immigration official had complained.

Now, where I was supposedly the expert, I sorely felt a lack of Polish. Most officials had less English than their Russian counterparts, and the matter of visas was becoming more important. Our permit listed the eight or so ports we had selected, but allowed us to visit just four; and each port was a separate arrival, as if a separate country, with customs and currency checks in and out. We needed to ensure that the list approved in London would appear on all the documents we were to carry from port to port, and early on our second day I set about it.

The police at the main station were cavalier and off-hand, even slightly alarming. Nervousness seemed to hang in the air. But around the corner a maritime agency official gave endless time to ensuring our papers were as watertight as possible.

'It is difficult to tell the customs what they should do,' he said, providing a carefully worded letter.

He also arranged meetings with the Mayors of Gdynia and Gdańsk. 'About Gdańsk, ring me tomorrow,' he had said. 'Gdynia, today – would noon be all right?'

Noon! It was well past 11 already.

'Oh, and by the way, he doesn't speak English . . .'

Back at the boat I rounded up crew, then like the host of the wedding feast of Cana went out into the highways and byways in search of an interpreter. I took the first man I met. Jacek was just coming out of the club. Actually he was almost crawling out of it, making the average-height doorway look like the flap of a hen-coop. He must have been seven foot two at least, with arms and eyebrows to suit.

'Will you come, and follow me?' I urged, with yet more Biblical overtones but, unlike the Apostles, his wife came too. Ewa was exquisite, immaculate in cerise and navy and exactly matching cosmetics; but the taxi-driver declined more than four, so while Susan succeeded, Rupert was abandoned in a cloud of dust. The taxi-driver was not the only person a little short on goodwill.

At first all went well. Mr Kukietka, the Deputy Mayor, was interested and percipient – he had been a visitor at the Norrköping Tall Ships Rally, as Gdynia would host one five years hence – but, in the most serious part of our exposition, as Jacek struggled manfully to convert English vowels into strings of musical consonants, a medium-sized woman exploded in through the door, clutching a small girl by the arm, and dragging the deputy's secretary behind on elastic strings of vituperation. The girl seemed the butt of the argument. Whatever the official's faults had been, they had certainly reaped results. As livid as a ripe tomato, the citizen was fit to disintegrate and flatly refused to leave. The best that could be managed was to get her to stand behind whilst our minor affairs were completed. The deputy stuck well to his post. Taking the cue, we played it cool too; so cool we forgot the seething volcano at our backs, forgot to ask Jacek afterwards what the problem had been.

Nonetheless, we were learning fast. Here in Poland, things were not cut and dried. There was room for interpretation and fudging; some things were not what they should be, and some people let their fuses burn right down to the powder.

'Yes, we have some troubles still!'

The *Wiceprezydent* of the *Miasta Gdańska* (don't go looking for actual mayors in midsummer), a genial and vigorous man by the name of Edward Rataj, admitted it straight off, cards face-up on the carved black table. Around its circle, our crew, for once, was complete.

'. . . he knows,' relayed his nervous interpreter, when he didn't switch into French, our only common language, 'that last year, Poland, our country, was the biggest subject in the press in your country and other countries all over the world. Some of these papers were good for Poland, and some unfortunately not so good.'

'Et nous disons que c'est meilleur que les étrangers . . .'

'. . . it's better for the foreigners to come to visit us.' (About three million a year manage to get to Gdańsk alone.)

'Poland has its problems,' he admitted, 'but you must feel as you feel at home. We are open and show our life as it is, and we try to get the condition of travel *without* visas. We have signed with Austria already, and with other countries, we talk . . .'

Mr Rataj had good reason to wish for easier travel: his background was extremely mixed. His father was born in France, his mother in Germany, his wife in the USSR, and only his daughter, it seemed, in Poland. Gdańsk, for him the most beautiful city in the country, did what it could. It was twinned with Bremen, Shanghai, a town in France and another in Algeria.

'It had a history of a thousand years,' he reminded us, 'and had been one of the richest towns. The most sad part was in the last war. It was damaged about 70 per cent, the old town about 80 per cent. There was no building left, no bridge. And we were rebuilding it for years. After, there was hunger – and problems. But at last we decided to rebuild it because it is our history and culture.'

'And is it yet completed?'

'No, not yet,' he answered, taking off his glasses to smooth his brow, as if wearied by the thought.

Some of the damage is still to be seen. In the brickwork of the *Rathaus*, the Town Hall, are vicious pockmarks, rayed like meteorite strikes. The famous Crimson Room within survived, its ceiling ornately decorated with startling *trompe-l'oeil* panels of triumphal arches and avenues; so too did its tower, soaring up as straight as a pikestaff from the main pedestrian street, the Ulice Druga.

'But only just,' said Dirka, a physical education student seconded by the Major of Gdynia (as good as his word despite his more pressing problems).

As he led us up the square spiral of steps within its walls, he pointed out the massive corset of concrete and steel that had been inserted to prevent a total collapse. From the bell near the summit, a centuries-old folk-tune is rung on the hour; and, from the dizzying ledge above it, around the rim of its steeple, one could look down on the curved and decorated gables, the studio windows and steep tiled roofs, the frescoed frontages and profuse window-boxes of the townspeople's and merchants' houses and mansions. Right under us, the tablecloth check of the paving ran clear from one end of the street to the other, from under the Golden Gate at the western end, past the bronze fantasy of Neptune's Fountain, wielding a jetting trident, out through the multiple arches of the Green Gate at the other and through to the banks of the Motława canal. The whole scene was thick with the erratic wanderings of ants. Out beyond the ruddy ramparts of the old town, and the bulk of the mediaeval hoist and warehouse hanging over the wharfs, the newer city stretched out on three sides: apartments, offices, colleges, highways, scatters of smoky factories circling beyond the old canals; beyond again, green level land stretching far away to the east, and south and westward gentle folds in the bedclothes of the land, shadowed with tousled woodland. To the north, though, lay a thin blue line, and the reason for Gdańsk's existence – a mediator between the farmer and seafarer. Gdańsk, like Riga, had been a Hansa town, and an extremely formidable one too. For centuries she had been a city-state, making fortunes from shipping grain abroad in the short and sturdy timber 'cogs' that featured on the city seal, and contributing her own taxes as she saw fit to the Polish crown. She was one of only two cities in the country strong enough to keep the sixteenth-century deluge of Swedes outside her walls. And between our precarious eyrie and the sea lay a jumble of symbols from past and present that make up the usual modern perception of Gdańsk, and of Poland: churches, cranes and communist slogans.

We were not at the highest point of the city; even higher reared the vast, smoke-darkened, twin towers of St Mary's Church, which was already complete when the invaders arrived in their longships and is still, now, the biggest brick church in the world. Between the lance-like spires of its transepts, the cranes of the Lenin Shipyard reared up; and here and there, on the walls of old brick warehouses, or blazed across the head of a solitary skyscraper were exhortations in the red and white national colours. 'BYLIŚMY – JESTEŚMY – BĘDZIEMY', read one, with Roman overtones. 'WE WERE – WE ARE – WE SHALL BE.'

As I jotted it down, with the whole city ranged beneath under a purposefully sliding sky, a Polak asked me what I was doing. He sounded aggrieved, until he noted my accent.

There were hints and depths of meaning there we couldn't yet fathom, but the shipyards themselves, Shay and I found, were surprisingly accessible. They form the left bank of the river, a winding pageant for the tourist launches that ply to Gdynia, and to Sopot, the long-piered resort in between. Huge hulks of new ships, sheds like monstrous aircraft-hangars, the cavernous boom and clang of curved steel, the alarming blue crackle of welding. Smaller and prettier vessels too: two new sail-training ships being built for the Soviet Union; further on down, a Russian tanker unloading; and on the right round a humped-up bend, the peninsula of Westerplatte.

Dirka had pointed this out, too, from aloft; the dead-end east bank at the outlet of the Wisła that played a pivotal role in European affairs. It was here, on 1 September 1939, that World War II broke out, when Hitler's forces shelled a Polish position from seaward, with an ancient battleship, the *Schleswig-Holstein*. A blocky monument now marks the rise, sliding fitfully through the gaps between tugs and cranes. The Pope had made it part of his pilgrimage; but the badly-organized last boat of the day left us no time to do likewise. Instead, for a few short minutes, we traced puddled tracks across a scrubby neck of land between the river and the open sea. To seaward lay the moles of yet another new port with a few ships anchored off; and, out on the horizon, the barely discernible strip of the Hel peninsula, the first Polish land we had seen, and the very last piece to fall to the Nazis, where a garrison bitterly held out for more than a month behind the occupied lines.

It was perhaps not surprising that this quadrant of the city had occupied most of the news. It was certainly the most spectacular; but the Mayor's exasperations by degrees became clearer. Even from home, the coverage of events had seemed too simplistic, too one-sided, as if the city were nothing but shipyards and strikes and barred gates. There had been no mention of the miracle that the city existed at all, of its amazingly plucky rebirth from a heap of smouldering ruins, nor of the foresight that carried it out slowly and beautifully; no mention of tourists, in ordinary times, from Sweden, Yugoslavia, Greece, meandering between museums, galleries, pavement artists and earringed jewellery hawkers, and the displays of antique glass bottles on terraces between elaborate gargoyles and carved balustrades; and no mention that in the evening, after a spell of quiet as the town relaxes and begins to fall into shade, the city-dwellers take over themselves, drifting in through the streets in small knots, like a Sunday evening in a north Italian town, until the whole extended plaza is filled with long-legged shadows, strips of slanting sunlight, decorative friezes ever more deeply incised between vivid fronds of laburnum, and the echoes of pigeon-coo and clatter and uninhibited laughter as youngsters loaf and cross from café to cinema (*Pozbgnanie z Afryka, Out of Africa,* was showing and something a great deal more raunchy later).

There had also seemed to be very scant reference to the other three-quarters of Polish life: the countryside, the 'field' from which the very word Polen derives, and the extraordinary complications of her history.

Yes, of course there were problems, Dirka had said, as the van brought us back the 15 miles to Gdynia along a concrete highway. Problems with money. It was no wonder that the cars around us were small. It didn't take much to maintain them, but to get hold of one in the first place cost an arm, a leg and a wait, and at least a million zlotys. Problems with prices. Inflation was high. Problems with jobs. It had improved a bit in the last year or two, with new independent non-state workshops and service industries starting. There, the pay was much better. But it was difficult to get started in one: everyone wanted a job like that. Overall, the prospect was bleak. There wasn't much optimism around and people feared for the future but, all the same . . . He tailed off, meaning, 'At least we are still here.'

'Problems . . . but' was bit by bit to become a theme song. That the two women from Tarnów, whose young sons Shay had met on the beach, certainly also had problems, was obvious when we visited them one evening at a students' hostel, with a roof like a ski-jump, perched, appropriately enough, halfway up the cliff. One was a teacher, the other worked in a post office. One at least was divorced, and both were very short of money; and the 'but' for them consisted of this one week's break in the year by the sea. The room was bare of anything except basic furniture, and an odd steel wardrobe or two. A teenaged daughter sat on a bed behind us as they proffered a spread of Hungarian wine and pastries.

Ewa and Jacek seemed to have had better luck. So did we, to have met them.

East of Gdańsk, the 'field' spreads flat for 30 miles. It even dips slightly downwards: large stretches, as in Holland, lie below sea level. There are long expanses of pasture and tillage, lower than the road, with lines of willows receding into the distance, mirrored in long open ditches. Assorted barns and farmsteads, of plaster and tile, of brick and timber and stone, punctuate the levels between the deeply-scored grooves like cloves stuck into a ham. There are no roadside signs, and almost no cables: the land is dotted only with tethered cows, flocks of geese, scatters of hens ranging dung-heaps and, further off, solitary storks carefully stilting. They nest in twiggy pancakes on occasional leaning poles and, beneath and beyond, uncluttered open fields with no fences stretch taut to the far-off horizon. After a while, the main road sweeps up and over a bridge, over the Wisła river – wide and rippled like braided hair. Between the reedy banks it's empty now, except for a few small buoys leading far in toward Warsaw. On again to the further bank of the flood-plain where the land rises once more. Beyond the town of Nowy Dworgo, it swells up, dome-like, with another larger town at its feet.

'Come and see us in Elbląg,' our friends had said, emphasizing the *awng* with a laugh, one of the most characteristic dipthongs in Polish; but here we were already into what had been Prussia, or rather part of it; East Prussia, Royal Prussia, a country with strong Germanic connections. Elbląg, Elbing in earlier times, had been founded by the Teutonic Knights (a monastic order modelling themselves on the Templars) as the main trading town of their state. Rivalling Gdańsk for a while, and supporting a large colony of English and Scots, it had wandered in and out of Polish hands for many centuries since, had fared no better than elsewhere in 1945, and now a town of 100,000, living mainly on industry, it featured just occasionally as one of the centres of discontent.

Jacek welcomed us to his parents' flat in the suburbs. The block was small, the flat light and bright, with views across sloping ground and trees; the walls lined with cabinets and books; no garden, but a garage and a Polski Fiat.

Jacek and Ewa mentioned no problems, although both were still students; and as their baby crawled around our knees, Jacek showed photographs of his cruise on the *Dar Młodziezy*. Jacek in Lisbon, Port Said, Djibouti; covered with suds when crossing the line; Jacek in Columbia, Penang, Osaka; with garlanded girls in the Philippines.

'I was very sick in the English Channel,' he said.

Now, he was at maritime college, and Ewa, once an Olympic sprinter, was studying economics. They were an attractive couple, and we took to them warmly.

Eagerly, they drove us on further north-east, edging around the coast road, which followed a narrow-gauge railway. The landscape had changed dramatically. Here the road twisted and turned, lined with hefty, dark-trunked trees right at the edge of the tarmac. Rounded slopes and small ravines were clad in deciduous woodland, filtering green light down to the traffic tunnelling through; rumpled acres of corduroy fruit trees, patches of grain and pine, then finally more open stretches with parallel strips of cultivation bespeaking family ownership. We stopped momentarily to kiss the earth at a stud-farm in a quiet village, where in its dark interior, thick with the tang of straw and horse-dung and creosote, the thoroughbreds thudded and snuffled and steamed, and outside, in the corners of somnolent fields, herds of them stamped and twitched.

But Jacek and Ewa hadn't finished. They still had something in mind they were quite determined to show us.

'*Jest daleko?*' I queried anxiously, as yet more country sped by. 'Is it far?' We had appointments that evening.

The something was Frombork, a sudden apparition on the flank of an inland sea. A huge reddish wall rises up, topped by a steep church roof. In through the portcullised gates, a jewelled microcosm opens – a fortified monastery. Around the grassed courtyard are ranged the delicate fourteenth-century church, defensive platforms and castellations, a classical house with a sundial over its door, a solitary tree and a solitary dog beneath it, another turreted gate. In a corner is Copernicus's observatory, a tall converted Bastille.

The man who set the world in motion, and made the sun stand still (although it's still hard to visualize, as we track it with the sextant) lived here for 30-odd years, watching the unpolluted heavens and writing his revolutionary thesis that later, indirectly, sent Galileo to death. Copernicus himself died a few hours after its publication. On its steps, a group of schoolgirls sit struggling with theses of their own; inside its remodelled brick silo, stairs spiral up like an apple-peeling, circling dizzily around a Foucault pendulum.

Beneath, the coastline winds away in naïve, defective perspective, just like the painted background of Botticelli's *Venus* or a mediaeval saint. It's not the sea, but the Wisła Zaliv. The shallow lake, famous for ice-yachting in the winter, is screened from the Baltic by fifty miles of forested dunes, the incredible Wisła (Vistula) Bar. The broad stretch of water and the dark antenna of land melt away together through an invisible distance up to Russia's back door: the lake floods up to Kaliningrad, the capital of the Kalingradskiy Oblast, a strategic outpost of the RFSFR, the Republic that forms the 'mainland' of Russia; the Bar sweeps on past and almost links with the coastline of Lithuania, which for so many centuries had formed an uneasy sparring partner for Poland.

Here one is only ten miles from the border, which now slants in an arbitrary line east-west, across the Zaliv and out to sea. Beyond and parallel to the boundary, where it bends and stretches, away to the south, is the long curved strip of territory, previously Polish, lost when she took the 'two steps to the left' agreed by Churchill and Stalin. Some maps show only a few main roads crossing it; others minor ones abruptly curtailed. What was the two countries' relationship now?

It's a sensitive question and one, we found, that few people dwell on too long. We refrained from asking Jacek and Ewa, as we returned by a different route. We kept safely to comparisons of countrysides and of languages: to the number of hares we each might accidentally run down, and then have to roast, in a year; or to points such as whereas the Polish for bee is the seemingly impossible *pszczoła*, a bee-hive is simply an *ul*. But the topic was one that had begun to drift to the surface. It had cropped up in the marina. On the eastern mole, by themselves, were five Russian yachts, two at least from the Leningrad club where we'd survived our near disaster, and one of those, the *Maalba*, was quite the most magnificent yacht we had so far seen. Built in Warnemünde in 1938 to a Rasmüssen design, and taken as part of war reparations, her perfect lines left everybody else's boat looking dowdy and frumpish. But the Russians' yachts were rare birds, unseen for the previous five years, 'because Poland suddenly became for them a dangerous place.' At least one well-placed Polish sailor was unaware of their rearrival until we pointed them out.

As before, we had been virtually kidnapped and force-fed – there were plankfuls of marinated fish, potatoes and vodka, slung by ropes from the roofs of their saloons – but other visitors to them seemed few, and when one of their skippers had called on *Canna*, things hadn't gone so well.

'*Nie rozumiem*' had been the reply to his queries from the Poles who had also been aboard, 'We don't understand'. They shrugged, shook their heads and looked blank. In the end, discouraged, Ramon had left.

Sadly, Alan too had now to leave us. By stretching his furlough to the limit, he'd cut things fine for starting his new hospital posting, and needed time at home to prepare. In Gydnia, he cut things even finer. Getting back from Elbląg in time to see him off to his train, we found the saloon in total uproar. Clothes and film were strewn everywhere. At our farewell feast in a restaurant, he abandoned his trout (pstrawng) in mid-fillet; outside in the dark, all the taxis were full. Three of us raced down the street, waving and grabbing as if they were straws in the wind. The *milicja* leaned from a car and whistled. Alan and Shay at last lassoed one and we heard the rest of the story later. He made the train with seconds to spare, which then stayed where it was for an hour. His reserved seat was already shared by two women. He stood for most of the night to Szczecin, was savaged by a termagant for falling on to her daughter. Finally he caught his ship, from Świnoujście to southern Sweden, and connected with a flight to Dublin.

For comfort, he'd have been much better off staying with *Canna*. The weather held calm until we left Gydnia on 17 August – but fortunately he was well buoyed up. The trip for him had been pure magic. Already exhilarated when he'd joined us in Finland, by the time he left he was over the moon. 'I was on such a high,' he marvelled later, 'I just couldn't stop talking. It carried me all the way to the States.' We were bound to miss his company.

In retrospect, we too should perhaps have stayed on longer, hired a car and toured the countryside, which proved impossible to organize later – but by now I was keen to move west. The two days more we gave ourselves mainly revolved around food. We ate like swallows stoking for an autumn migration. It wasn't difficult, although meals were more square than rounded. We stood at shingled stands by a watermill in Gdańsk, while the river streamed through sluices each side, and grease trickled down to our elbows; the speciality was *golonkę*, pig's knuckles with very hot mustard, and *kiełbasę na gorąco*, sausages as big as bedrolls, washed down with beer that looked, smelt and tasted weak, but promptly weakened our legs – and those of many around us.

Next day, more refined, we sampled the restaurant 'Cherry' (or so it sounded). It looked and tasted it too: the tablecloths were a shade of cerise, and they seemed to serve nothing else. Cherries must ripen early in Poland. There was cherry and macaroni soup, cherries to garnish the ubiquitous *kotlet schabowy* (pork chop), cherries in cherry syrup to follow, and – surely not? – tall glasses of cherry cordial too. I, for one, won't need another *czereśnie* until I've circled the globe. But for all our careful preoccupations we attempted to victual the boat on a Sunday. The faithful, naturally, were all at Mass, not out on the street selling food to heathens. The all-glass Hotel Gdynia, home of gorgeous Hungarian gateaux, was a port of last resort.

'Could we have bread, and butter, and eggs?' we enquired at the marbled bar, where guests in sunglasses rotated on gilded stools. The waiter's eyes gleamed with a killing.

'*Tak, tak! Słucham pana*, yes, certainly sir, the eggs hot?' and by the time we'd thought up the Polish for 'cold' he'd vanished into the kitchen. We carried the 40 red-hot mistakes back to the boat in a paper bag, at the cost of a great many zlotys. Point taken – don't ask the Ritz for a take-away.

The other lesson we learned much later, at home. Piotr was the mate of a shapely sloop from Wrocław, one of the super-enthusiastic inland breed who barge their big yachts along the rivers for hundreds of miles at the beginning and end of each season. We'd arranged a photo-rendezvous outside the harbour when we'd both cleared customs. Our clearance took longer, but we joined them as planned, idling through a limpid sea heading north-eastward for Hel.

'Can you put me on board?' asked Shay, but on a scruple I turned him down.

'We haven't arranged it beforehand, and if damage is caused, then it's all our fault.'

We simply came close, and rolled film; as the wind backed we left them heading in for Jastarnia village, while we made out to sea. But our two blips had joined on a radar screen onshore and, even as we cleared the outer headland, four or five miles away, the *Ballada* was being searched.

We had already begun to wonder, if Russia had been a coconut – tough outer skin, but milk within – was Poland the pomegranate, perhaps: more porous, although rather more seedy inside?

CHAPTER 15

The Polish Coast

Poland, so far, was a puzzle, a maze of unrelated impressions: unstinting help and friendliness, a variable official courtesy, undercurrents of tension. Of all the countries we were to visit, it was the hardest to get to grips with. Who are the Poles in any case? I mused, watching the scarlet self-steering vane wag lazily against the shoreline, which was slowly unwinding like a typewriter ribbon beyond it. The breeze was light and off the land. Heading north-west, bordering the finger of Hel, we had simply to follow the clear sandy forearm for a hundred miles to Ustka, in depths of about 20 metres. The merest murmur came from the bows.

'What do you mean "who are the Poles?",' countered Shay, with mild exasperation, stretched half-asleep on the cockpit seats. 'They're the people living in Poland.'

In a way, the simple answer is best . . . but what in that case is Poland? What she is now is not what she was. Other countries have been relatively predictable. Denmark, Norway, Finland have stayed in much the same place. Sweden spread vastly, and then retreated. Russia simply kept spreading, bulging outward from Kiev and Moscow and Leningrad in huge concentric rings: 'leaning on its neighbour's walls', as Ustinov so tenderly puts it, 'until these collapse under their own weight, and then helping to rebuild them a little further away.' The result was a sprawling but always definable edifice.

But Poland has defied all prediction. Over the centuries she has swelled and shrunk and distorted like an amoeba, and occasionally, as if a pricked bubble, has vanished altogether, without apparent rhyme or sequence.

In the fifteenth century she was the biggest kingdom in Europe, stretching almost 1,000 miles from the Baltic to the Black Sea, engulfing Lithuania, huge tracts of Russia almost to Moscow, all the Ukraine, Moldavia, Hungary, and Bohemia centred on Prague nearly as far west as Berlin.

Her armies had invaded Russia and argued the toss for her crown; twice won it, and once burned Moscow; and although the first Polish tsar came to a sticky and high-flown end (he was deposed, dismembered, roasted, stuffed in a cannon and shot back west 'whence he came'), it didn't cramp their style elsewhere. Her dreaded cavalry, the Husaria, decked with hoops of eagle-feathers, cloaked in leopard-skins and encrusted with jewels,

swooped south and laid waste the Turks. She accumulated enormous
wealth. Her diplomats paid visits abroad with 1,000 or more retainers, their
mounts loose-shod with solid gold shoes to scatter as largesse in the streets;
her merchants travelled with huge trains of wagons, and camels to carry
their libraries.

Then, at the other end of the scale, three times in the nineteenth and
twentieth centuries, Poland as a place had ceased to exist at all. Bite by bite
her neighbours had gobbled her up and, finally, wiped her right off the
map, a form of consumption politely titled, 'Partitions'. All that was left
were subject people in Germany, Austria or Russia, and intellectual
expatriates in Paris, say, or in London. Like Jewry, 'Poland' then was
simply an idea.

In many ways, it still is. It has always been used to comprising different
peoples. At its greatest extent, the Slavic 'Polonae' were in a minority;
others included Germans, Armenians, Jews, Italians and Tatars; and there
were six official languages. Now, although back to borders encompassing
mainly the 'original Poles', with minorities much diminished, the distinction between nationality and citizenship persists, as we could easily see
from the passports of our Gdynia friends: nationality might be German or
Jew, but citizenship would be Polish; and it's the Polish tradition that
counts. It's a tradition studded with unsuspected grandeurs. We had
already passed through the portals of some: even now the town halls,
cathedrals and churches of Polish Commonwealth times dominate their
surroundings on a positively awesome scale. Redolent of morale and
confidence, they still loom up, the biggest constructions in sight, like
dreams persisting into the light of day. But what was the thread, what the
idea they transmit? Only historians give the answer, a story of precocious
enlightenment. While other European nations painfully dragged themselves from the starting block of mediaeval fragmentation toward a national
consensus, Poland had already sprinted ahead. The Seym, her parliament,
was second only to Iceland's. The duties of her elected kings were early
defined in law; as was religious tolerance, to a quite extraordinary degree.
(Zamoyski relates an incident, for instance, in 1580, when a wayward Polish
Calvinist snatched a host from a priest, spat on it, trampled it, and then fed
it to a passing mongrel – for which he suffered merely a reprimand from the
King and was told not to do it again.) Political beheadings were thin on the
ground, and foreign observers at electoral meetings remarked in amazement on the vast numbers of Poles arriving armed to the teeth, arguing for
the length of the day, and soberly going home unbloodied.

Despite vicissitudes, the impetus continued. Poland was the first European country to open a public library, the first with a Ministry of Education, the first in Europe, too, to publish a Constitution, the famous
document of 1791 that startled statesmen around the world. The intention

was to build Utopia based on personal liberty and a strict respect for the law. The organization that for centuries enshrined this ideal was uniquely Polish too: the *szlachta*, a sort of patrician party, based neither on wealth nor property, nor religion or status, which had originally been a warrior class. Composed of clans provided with ancient, indecipherable coats-of-arms, it acted rather like a militant trades' union, and preserved its parliamentary franchise and rights (which included the right of veto) so jealously and rigidly that eventually, in the seventeenth century, the whole process of government had atrophied and ground to a halt for a time.

It was tempting to wonder how much had changed. The provision of public libraries had not. There's a small one right in the middle of Gdańsk, almost beneath the Town Hall. With its coffee bar in the corner, and a gallery beyond showing contemporary art, it's a good place for a rendez-vous, but in its pale green reading room, the atmosphere is studious. The rows of armchairs, where Rupert hunted sports results through the *Observer* and his neighbours were submerged in *Figaro* and *Die Welt*, were hedged by hatstands hung with all the main dailies of Europe (four or five days old) and a fair selection of journals. Outside, nearby, was a Solidarity name-plate and, not much further away, at the gates of the Lenin Shipyard, tall monuments of stainless steel to the workers who died in the 1970 disturbances.

There were other threads too, various authors and pundits averred, that ran through the Polish cloth. More than four centuries before, economists and visitors to Poland were already frowning on her policy of very cheap food as betraying a weak basic structure. It's still causing much of the trouble today; and then, it's claimed, there's the problem of temperament, attacks of idiosyncrasy at moments of national crisis. They instance the 60-year-old Hetman of earlier times, an army chief who interrupted a crucial assault to marry a girl of 16, and then more or less promptly died of exhaustion; eighteenth-century dissidents who kidnapped the King in Warsaw, lost their way through the streets, changed their minds, and put him back in his palace; and a modern farmer-Prime Minister who broke off delicate negotiations to go and get in his harvest. A general failure to get things together, they claim. Too high-spirited (why, even their most successful Prime Minister had been a concert pianist!), too idealistic for their own good, and unpredictable with it. We couldn't yet comment; but it was true that various people had already spoken of 'crisis', betraying a febrile feel in the air and a sense of not knowing what might come next, of not being able to see forward.

For the moment, neither could we. We had rounded the knuckle of Rozewie, the northernmost point of Poland, at nine the previous night, watching its three-second light flare out from a round, red tower nearly 300 feet high. But by dawn next morning, approaching Ustka, we were immersed in luminescent grey fog, the first in 3,000 miles. It's never a good experience.

'Foghorn, please, Rupert!'

Every two minutes on the brass horn he blew 'D', one long and two short; and every two minutes, longer and lower and louder, an ominous 'U' came back, two short and one long, visibly vibrating the wavering droplets of mist. Whatever it was, it was bigger than us and getting closer, and the relentless booming morse, being interpreted, warned, 'You are running into danger.' We could believe it. By now we were closing the coast obliquely, beating to and fro between the 20 and 10-metre lines, closely watching the echo-sounder, which here meant more than the Decca. Was it a ship that had us on radar, and was trying to warn us away? But no; it was only a phalanx of loudspeakers on the harbour mole which suddenly loomed over our bows – a 'U' for Ustka that hadn't yet found its way to the charts. We were glad that the fog was no thicker. The entrance, beyond the surrealistic mole-head clustered with two tiers of people, was nasty in the extreme: narrow and cluttered with piles and a half-submerged wreck to starboard. Further in, where it opened a little, and navy boats were ranged, we found a berth between a hydrofoil of the alarming Leningrad type, and an oddly-named lifeboat, the *Huragan*.

'I doubt,' said Susan, 'that I'd want a Hurricane to look for *Canna* during a storm!'

The third week in August was split between Ustka and Kołobrzeg, a similar port 50 miles on. The pair of them might have been twins: both had river-mouth entrances facing north-north-west, 'very dangerous in onshore winds'; both were popular beach resorts, with piers and hundreds of wicker shelters spreading east for miles on the sands; both had navy or military zones on the opposite bank to the west; both laid on high-speed sea-trips for tourists; both were fishing ports, too. The likenesses were uncanny, so much so that now it takes a bit of detective work to discover which was which.

'The one that smelt of stale vinegar?' (smells being the most acute of signposts). 'That was Ustka. The fish-processing plant, remember?'

Ustka was the smaller and more compact of the two, a big village of sinuous streets and tightly-packed fisherman's houses, some bricked or half-timbered, some plastered. The waft of over-strong fish-oil and brine mingled with the crustiness of baking bread and the fruity ripeness of *bigos*, a traditional dish of nameless mixed meats, with cabbage more sweet than sour.

Kołobrzeg was more rangy. Our berth in a municipal basin (the only place that charged for mooring, and the only place where *Canna* touched bottom) lay under an old brick fortress. The lane to serve it was almost rural, and smelt of grass and sweet-peas. The town, a mile distant, was wider and much more formal, with unkempt parks spreading for acres through its centre, the not entirely unpleasing result of earlier wholesale destruction; at least the place had huge green lungs that filled out its rather gaunt frame.

With Alan gone, we'd felt slightly depleted, but had responded with a change of pace. In Ustka the log read 3,000 miles; by now, the bulk of our Baltic circuit was done, and two-thirds, perhaps, of our voyage. Despite the vagaries of weather, with a little persistence and a lot of luck we'd kept to our programme and honoured engagements. There were no more crested envelopes from the Mayor of Dublin to present, and here where yachts ranged widely more often, less pressure for publicity. The four of us left on board had more time to spare for the people we met.

The Ustka lifeboat, with its red cross in a red circle on white on her bows, and her skipper, Andrej, soon became staunch friends. Andrej, like his boat, was built of steel. He took two-week turns of duty, heading a generous permanent crew. At the moment they had nothing to do, except to tend their substantial vessel and a tiny garden on the quay.

'Is not the time for accidents now . . .' he said, eyes always levelled at the horizon. Winter was the time when their work began, when the Baltic froze over and freighters and fishermen still tried to ply their trade. He knew the weather that brought the problems; he could almost feel the ice thickening, he winced, and in certain winds it would buckle and slide, and rear in pillars 40 feet high. If it got too heavy, it could cut through a trawler's hull.

News that *Das Boot*, the submarine novel, had been published in Polish, provoked a mild rush by the lifeboat's crew to a bookshop. On their way they helped us with shopping; picking out the best bread at the ochre-planked bakers, easing problems with cheese and meat, for which coupons are normally needed, pointing out which vegetable shops were private, and which were run by the State.

'Much better variety there, do you see?' – but it wasn't always obvious. If we ran out of zlotys, they lent us some, and Andrej presented strings of his favourite sausages, juicy and rotund affairs for boiling.

While strolling later, he pointed out Goering's house in the suburbs. (We were now already in the zone that had been German between the wars and where German is still widely understood. Previously, this Pomeranian coast was Prussian.) The gabled, russet-red holiday home of Hitler's lieutenant, tall among trees, with stables alongside it in the yard that must have rung to the click of heels and the clunk of limousine doors, had lapsed into quiet as a modest trades' union resort house.

But, despite his pocket radio, Andrej could never stay long. We drifted. We toured the art gallery on the quay, boldly converted from a warehouse.

We idly watched the crowds on the beaches. They came from all over Poland, and East Germany and Russia too. The summer had not turned out well; although sunny in Kołobrzeg, it was grey in Ustka, and the sea unsportingly stuck below its normal 64°F. Not that it had much effect. There were hectares of rippling and paunchy flesh; trunks staying up by the grace of God, clinging desperately to overhanging bellies like rock-climbers using pitons; bikini-straps stretched to a singing tone, or some-times discreetly unhitched, a small girl dressed only with bows in her hair, young bloods with footballs, and slim young things squelching sun-tan oil. Their pram-hood shelters, seating two and painted with big white numbers, faced downwind one and all, like an infinite series of sculptures.

NAPOJE. HOT-DOGI. BIGOS! clamoured the signs on toblerone cabins dotting a half-mile of promenade. Those that weren't beached, ate, and how! Canine-sausage was obvious, but the *zapiekankie!* To Poland they're what pasties are to Cornwall. Recipe – split one long roll, use half, layer with marinated anchovies, gherkins and cheese, decorate with a snake-like squidge of tomato, serve hot enough to skin the customer's tongue. You start at one end – scrumptious! – idling toward the pier as you go, follow up with a bilberry waffle piled to toppling with fruit and cream, nibble a few seeds from a sunflower head, wash down with *napoje*, sweet lemonade. After that, if still on your feet, you take a spin on the hydrofoil and, while along the dock railing, stare down to your heart's content at the only yacht in the harbour, and wonder where she has come from. If a small boy, you can go and ask for a print of their rubber-stamp, which any self-respecting yacht carries (we didn't).

It made a change all round, and even had its minor rewards, if one didn't mind people peering through portholes, and making a minute scrutiny of all our domestic arrangements.

Once, overcome by curiosity as Susan prepared a stew in the cockpit, a woman from among the crowd queried the ingredients.

'Fish,' she said.

'Fish, fisch, *feesh, feesh feesh*,' rippled down the line until it struck someone who understood; then, 'ryba, ryba, *ah, tak*, RYBA!' the muttering came rippling back, and all the faces swung towards her again and nodded.

Strangely, they didn't all seem happy.

'If I were you,' Susan heard from a vacationing priest one day, who had recognized our ensign, 'I should take down that little red flag behind (on our man-overboard buoy). Most people think you are Russian.'

The unpredictable had struck again. With some discomfort we did as bid, and for good measure posted a sign, IRLANDSKI. Was it imagination that the line of onlookers brightened? Or was it just that the queue had started to move? We kept an open mind as long as we could, but finally had to accept a sort of north-south Baltic symmetry: Russia's immediate neighbours treat her as a preoccupation, but whereas Finland had been avowedly non-Russian, Poland, in parts, was plain anti.

'How did you do in the Soviet Union?' some asked. 'Did you enjoy your time there?' – and shook their heads sadly when we said yes. Some of it might have been politics. 'You'll hardly find a communist here in the country,' more than one casual acquaintance told us. This was neither news nor heresy. Stalin himself had claimed that, 'establishing communism in Poland was like fitting a saddle to a cow', and a friend in Russia, counting off the true communist countries in Europe had hovered over the matter. 'Albania, Rumania, and Hungary, Poland . . .' the speaker's finger was bent down thoughtfully and then allowed to spring back, '. . . no, not Poland. They still have freehold business and property – they've never really accepted communism at heart.' It was a simple statement of fact, and from the look of the myriad smallholdings out in the country, it was easy to see what he meant; but most of the problems were monetary. The use of resources was criticized: the establishment of huge steel mills without raw materials to hand, and inter-country barters, such as Polish apples for petrol. 'One litre of petrol for one kilo of apples!' a fisherman snorted derisively, 'and we're told that that's a good deal! It ought to be more like a gallon.'

The tart joke went round that, for the sail-training ships built in Gdańsk for Russia, Poland might get a bus or two in return. The Soviet habit of procuring specialist goods from its neighbours, which had seemed natural and downright amusing in Riga ('Our trams are Hungarian, the rails are Polish, the cobbles between are from Sweden.' 'So what is Russian?' 'Maybe the tarmac!' they laughed), here didn't seem funny at all. In Russia, we realized, we'd heard very little about their immediate neighbours. Now, in Poland, we sometimes heard little else: another parallel with Finland, holding its corner across the water.

'Yes,' said a yachtsman, later, 'there are similarities. Finns say they regret not speaking Russian. But I learnt it, don't speak it and don't regret it at all.'

It was almost too embarrassing to pursue.

'But we did get a lot of help and warmth there . . .' we said.

'It's fine, the individuals can be good and friendly. But unfortunately government policies distort it, and make us dislike one another.'

'Why does an elephant have grooves in the soles of its feet?'

'To give the ants a fifty-fifty chance.' A nonsense jingle began to play in my head and and I had to stave off the possibly nonsense notion that, however quietly the elephant put his feet down, he wasn't aware of how strongly the ants might feel. The ants, after all, had been there first.

The other big grouse was exchange, but that was more an internal affair. 'We're not paid in dollars,' the complaint ran, 'but still we have to get them. We even have to give dollars for visas to socialist countries.'

If in the Soviet Union the black market wasn't perceptible (perhaps because we weren't obviously tourists), in Poland it was pervasive. Waiters, taxi-men and touts watched their chance to rip off their patrons with the very greatest of charm. No wonder we'd felt the difference. There was more than a whiff of corruption. The authorities were fighting an uphill battle. Rupert, walking alone one night, had been stopped by the *milicja*, who asked him to show what money he had and wondered if he'd stolen his passport.

Uniforms, in general, were fewer than in Russia, but more active. Photography was a particular phobia. Signs of red bars across cameras were posted not just on docks and railway crossings, but even on fishermen's compounds and tiny village town halls. Shay was queried in Gdynia harbour while filming, for the first and only time on the voyage. On that occasion I had accompanied him to the harbour office, but the matter was soon sorted out and, in fairness, in spite of darker hints from others, the officialdom itself was correct.

The customs officer in Ustka, an older man with heavily wired grey teeth, was especially conscientious. As crew's eyebrows, then tempers, began to rise, he checked items of our correspondence that his two young helpers in khaki passed him, delved into every locker, and poked in person behind the sail-bags.

'To see there are no extra body!' he quipped.

There was: a man for whom Shay had just video'd his disco in a marquee nearby piled in just then with a parting gift of waffles several storeys high. It helped to lighten the moment.

Kołobrzeg boasted Orbis hotels (like Intourist ones, but minus the door-men). Once an ancient bishopric, it also had a cavernous church, with columns crooked at the knees; a good museum (of military uniforms and weights and measures) and, unlike Ustka, a yacht club. Other yachtsmen were few, but varied. There was the young and solid Krzysztof Dubois, restoring the *Ark*, a black and white gaff-rigged sailing trawler, with all the fervour of Noah himself, and maybe more for lack of a Flood. It had taken five years, and his young volunteers were bending on sails as new and white and solid as cardboard. Her gunwales gleamed through their varnish. The boat was his own. Where the cash had come from he was too coy to say; but he'd negotiated a deal to train the sailing-club youngsters, and in a week or two more they would sail.

Then there was the Ancient Mariner, a Professor of Theoretical Physics, with very gentlemanly manners. Could he possibly call to talk? He wasn't, unfortunately, given the chance. I was press-ganged just then by a gang of pirates who arrived in a grubby, nameless sloop, surrounded by a cloud of smoke.

'A trip round harbour, you must!' yelped her skipper, with scarified hair and a pipe. His crew was a dwarf with an old man's face, who laughed like a flock of geese, and a serious, bespectacled, long-nosed type with a penchant for philosophy, dismembering salami with a wicked clasp knife and generously embowelling vodka. There was a dangerous crossfire of conversation, and all of them harangued at once. Manipulating a tiller like a shooting-stick, the skipper yelled down to the engineer, who was quite normal except for crossed eyes.

'Forward! *Nie, nie – Odwrotny! Odwrotny, Głupiec!* Fool!'

A diversion into the fishing harbour, for a dubious deal of tobacco for plaice – the yellow boats were privately owned, all other colours signified 'State', the reverse of what we'd supposed – then away down-river, past small coasters and navy boats to the harbour office at the root of the mole.

Intent on arranging a half-day outing tomorrow, it took them almost half a day to do it. Quite apart from surveillance, Poland has an elaborate system of yacht-crew qualifications and, without the necessary certified crew, no yacht can put to sea.

'Our skipper is not a "captain", so it won't be easy,' they said.

Clutching papers, he disappeared. Ages passed with no action, except fishing boats momentarily touching the pier (they too had to clock in and out), and as evening shadows climbed the mast, the crew dossed on the dock and horseplayed, whistled at passers-by and drank. Personally, I wouldn't have cleared them to sea in a fit.

'Is the lighthouse here from German times?' I enquired to kill a few minutes, unwisely.

'Not German! Is Polish,' the engineer scowled, already half-mad with impatience. 'Is *Polski!*'

His knife, by now, looked even more lethal, but just as I began to wonder if we might all spend the night 'in restraint', something suddenly snapped. Fuming and gesticulating like thoroughbred Latins, the whole crew converged on the offending building. For a minute, like the frames of a short cartoon, it vibrated and shuddered with argument, and the violent slamming of doors; then the victorious horde returned in spate through the dusk.

It was another instance of 'problems . . . but'. The small man had won another round.

Then there was the 'communal fridge'; even more wildly idiosyncratic as a way of getting by. For several days we'd been puzzled by a seemingly random selection of people suddenly kneeling in a busy road near a river bridge, and prising open a small, steel manhole – old women, children, and once a soldier, lying full length while his girlfriend held his jacket and cap. They all seemed to be fetching and carrying parcels. It turned out that the chamber beneath was part of the city water-main, and a handy place to keep food cool.

Getting by, it seemed, was the way of life. Many transactions were furtive or, at the very least, unofficial. Too bad – it had to be done. It was done with a pained and pristine sense of the fact that it shouldn't be necessary. If there was unpredictability and temperament, no doubt it had good cause.

'We're adaptable,' Poles had told us in Sweden. 'If you have difficulties, we'll straighten them out.'

They did do. By hook or by crook, and often both, charts or free diesel would be wangled on board, or a cherished photograph of a priest. Food and wine would be found for a spread, and, we belatedly realized, precious petrol coupons for outings. Whatever else might have to suffer, it wasn't hospitality; the historians of old had remarked on that too. Through it our various strings of contacts proliferated in wild progressions, and we followed on westward where they led.

CHAPTER 16

West Poland

Ustka fell astern on 19 August, and Kołobrzeg in the dusk of the 22nd, as we made towards Świnoujście, the port furthest west on the Polish coast. Once again there had been a brief debate about whether actually to call there. A direct route to leave the Baltic would take us nearer to the Danish island of Bornholm, a place of good repute with sailors, which Shay was keen to call in to; but the skipper, as was not unusual, turned obstinate. Fascinated by now with Poland's apparent contradictions, it seemed wilful folly not to take all our chances.

Polish towns, so far, with the exception of the centre of Gdańsk, had seemed tawdry: down at heel or not complete, and littered with badly finished buildings. People seemed to flee them for private worlds, for a fishing-stool or an allotment. Bordering the lane to the Kołobrzeg club had been a curious miniature world of Alice-in-Wonderland gardens, each of them spread with a neatly embroidered table-cloth of flowers and veg-etables, from which low-format fruit-trees sprouted like green Tiffany table-lamps. Each had a miniature timber cabin, with curtains and cuckoo-clock woodwork. It was a place where cats and grandmothers pottered, or dozed off under the sunflowers, or took tea in a suitably miniature café; and, in the evenings, young families visiting from the nearby flats that buttressed the town disappeared through their arches of dahlias. It looked suspiciously like a batch of tiny personal Utopias, laid out in default of a general one.

As Susan and I watched the coast pass, we reflected on what lay further inland. Roads hump and straighten through green and gold; beyond again, they wind slowly up among woodland and patchy pasture. There, the scale is more real. The private worlds are village houses, and fenced-off plots carved out from fields, strewn with ducks and pigs, and with poultry and plastic greenhouses: self-help, and partial subsistence.

Further on again, our reveries focus even more sharply: in Czaplinek, a small and almost anonymous town, farmworkers eat and drink and argue from breakfast-time onwards in the bar of a plain hotel, averting their gaze from the sign warning against excess alcohol ('Drunks are a danger to their families'), and abandonedly slamming down cards on the tables. The woman guarding its guest-rooms knits, and under its bare bathroom windows stands a horse-cart filled with pig-slops. The sunbaked main square is sleepy. Women sit out in the shade; the only monument of note, a tottering brick church, lies against heavy timber props as if resting its head on its elbow.

There's more air and space outside the village. Along unpaved tracks dark oak trees stand awaiting a breeze. Huge fields of corn swell out to the sky, and harvesters, competing with horses, very slowly strip their edges as if baring a cosmic bosom. A cluster of houses darken a hill, a girl dressed all in white walks by. At one of the farms, where we ask for water, we're given plum wine instead, and the very best of the seats in the parlour. The crop, they say is only average. Later, by tree-hung lakes in a rose-tinted evening, where along the path a drift of goose-down has been spilled, punts lie to unrippled shores and a single yacht paddles silently home.

As against the towns, the countryside felt generous, natural, fresh, extensive, and not a little beautiful. It seemed to be anyone's oyster – but not without its specks of grit. Along some of its undulating roads were endless army convoys in grey; off-duty soldiers rode the public buses, or made sudden storms if drivers turned them away when full; and once, walking in the middle of nowhere, we'd been asked for passports by a *milicja* on a motorbike. He'd come from behind, we hadn't seen him; but his aplomb had soon taken a painful setback. Straining to hear, he had cut the engine on his vintage machine by shorting two bare wires on its fuel tank. The shock he dealt to his undercarriage neatly matched what he'd done to our day.

Now, here at sea, it was much the same – quietness and unspoiled beauty mingled with threads of tension and minor farce. Those nights along the Polish coast were gorgeous – heady and dream-like, the very best we'd been blessed with. The scented breeze, that still blew steadily off the land, gave us six knots through water doubling a golden moon, and *Canna*, heeling gently, was soundless. Watches were changed in a whispering hush, and very few lights sparked out from the shore.

It was pure delight, but one in which we had little choice. To the west of Ustka and Kołobrzeg lay extensive military firing ranges – the range at Ustka stretched out 20 miles and more – unmarked on Admiralty charts. They could only be passed through by night, for which we'd conducted our own persuasions in the harbour offices.

'Keep two to three miles off the coast,' Polish skippers had told us. 'Not too far out, and not too close [for radar checks, was the implication]. It's best to keep to a parallel course.'

This wasn't difficult, apart from the occasional fisherman's dan buoy that clipped us far too close in the dark. Half a mile offshore, the average depth is at least ten metres, and currents here are often slight; but as we pressed on further, for a while the tension came to the fore. A light came close that we couldn't make out – a searchlight right on the water. It belonged to a miniature coastguard speedboat, even lower than our own low decks, that looked like a motorized saucer; then, 'Roger, quick, listen to this,' said Shay.

'Vessels are requested to watch for a yacht which left Gdynia for Świnoujście, and was due on the 23rd!' warned the radio, repeating the message in Polish and English.

But how could such a boat go missing? It could hardly have met with an accident, and nor, we quickly presumed, was it us, even though we too were aiming for that same last town on the Polish coast, squeezed into a chin-strap of land between the East German border and the mouth of the Odra river.

This was where our Polish friends had warned us to take good care; the East Germans had claimed a 12-mile territorial zone to seaward, which overlapped the only approach channel from the north; Poland, not surprisingly, was displeased and their navies were at a stand-off.

'Keep well east of the channel,' Adam Długosz had said. 'A friend of mine was in his right place and ended between Polish and German gunboats.'

True to prediction, at dawn a Polish navy squadron at anchor materialized on our bows, breaking the low mauve line of the shore.

The river entrance was a bigger version of Ustka's, and the customs berth, as warned, was poor; subject to the wash of huge freighters passing and turning, and to leeward of a commercial dock. Soon our decks and lungs were coated with a crystalline dust blowing down in clouds from a bulk carrier being unloaded.

To complicate matters further, Shay had run out of visas. By an unlucky chance we'd noticed only in Gdynia, he had permission for three entries, not four. The immigration guards changed duty at 8 am and, by arriving just before, we hoped, it might go through on the nod. Not a bit of it. I was summoned to the office, then Shay. The guard, at first, was impassive. 'No visa, no entry!' – and it began to look like a passage to Denmark. Eventually, tiring of my tortured Polish, he conceded, disappearing by car with some dollars to visit the main customs post. I apologized later for spoiling his breakfast.

'You *sorry?*' he snapped back, tapping his watch. 'What's this *sorry?* I no sleep here thirteen hours already.'

It was a relief to cast off and make up-river, winding through strings of docks and traffic, but still we weren't quite in the clear. It was not Świnoujście we actually wanted, but Trzebież, a village 15 miles inland, on the Zalew Szczeciński (Szczecin lake). In the Soviet Union, nearly everything was cut and dried; in Poland, there was mild confusion. The Consulate and the yachting fraternity affirmed and swore that all the ports in the Odra counted as one single 'entry'; but the immigration had demurred, and I'd made the mistake of stating 'Świnoujście'. For the first time, as we swung round the bends, passing more Polish navy, and then substantial Russian warships, moored and manned at the banks, we began to feel distinctly prickly. With the outflowing current of more than a knot against us, we couldn't make much speed; especially where the 'Old Swina' river swung in from port, and flat large ferries slewed across, carrying traffic from East Germany. It wasn't until a police launch, gaining on us from astern, had finally overtaken along the last four-mile stretch to the lake, that we began to feel a sense of relief. At last, we burst out to the Zalew, spreading for miles on all sides in the sun.

The Odra, or Oder, has always been an important waterway, serving a vast hinterland. The only heavily trafficked river in Poland, it runs down for 200 miles or so through the south-west of the country; shares its banks with East Germany for another hundred more, collects branches that serve Berlin, only 50 miles away, then veers east again a little through Szczecin. This major port, whose German name, Stettin, had provoked my near-disastrous error in London, had inevitably been fought for by Russians and Swedes, had exported ship-building oak to Britain, and been made the Prussians' main port for the Baltic. It had become Polish after the War. A few miles further downstream the river debouches into its lake, which spreads about 30 miles by 15.

'Flare-up' buoys mark the East German border, which cuts off part of its western arm. Denoted by bright red flames on the chart, they had put in a distant appearance, then vanished. Now there were only a few men in punts hauling fish, and yachts criss-crossing ahead of us, going our way and beating south. The lake is everywhere very shallow– barely a metre around the edges, and not much more than six in the centre. We elected to follow the shipping channel that cuts an arrow-straight line across it, for all the world like a farm track through fields, between the *Brama Torowa*, pairs of huge towers, four miles apart, marking the 'open gates'. *Canna* veered around a shrieking dredger-ship, dangling characteristic cones and balls to show on which side it was obstructed and hauling itself forward on a cable; and, as we made for the halfway harbour we sought, 100-yard trains of coal-barges groaned by in the opposite direction, driven by diminutive 'pushers'. This is a continuous traffic – the East Germans use the lake to link their inland waterways. Another multiple train soon passed, trailing an East German yacht, de-masted, a woman waving from the tiller; but by now the side-channel was so narrow that *Canna* was sandwiched tightly between them and children paddling close to starboard. Leading beacons defined the line. Straight ahead was a notch in the trees, identical to the alluring vignette in the Pilot, that opened to a sheltered pool.

We'd chosen Trzebież as a rendezvous with Polish sailors, and for a rest. We weren't to be disappointed – Trzebież would have been an excellent first stop had we been circling the other way. Artificial and squarish, the basin at the fringe of the village is entirely surrounded by trees. It harbours the marina and the modest schoolhouse of the principal Polish sail-training centre.

For the next few days we did little. We watched the comings and goings around us. The barges glided to a halt, for customs, under the island opposite. College staff, almost bridal in white and braid, and trainees of all ages, in blue, parade each morning to get their instructions, as bells are rung and flags are hoisted. They borrowed one of ours to hoist too. In due course, we chatted to the Director about his elaborate training courses, just barely prevented their engineer from servicing our engine, and collected diesel from the balcony of somebody's bedroom; and later, among varied boats around us, from half-deckers up to powerful steel cruisers, we noticed familiar prows and stems.

There was *Henryk Rutkowski*, for one, from Gdynia, a heavy old sail-training ship crewed by drug-addicts under rehabilitation.

'We had a bit of an incident with a freight-ship on the lake,' her skipper confided during a party. 'Her captain complained of me. I have to explain myself in Szczecin.'

Szczecin, we found, is now an oddly lopsided old city, coarsely split by a new river bridge slanting down from the Chrobry Embankment between the university and museum quarters. The university occupies the mediaeval castle of the Pomeranian Dukes and, from its terrace, while sipping liqueurs, one can look down across the docks, and the wooded outline of lakes beyond; or else towards the city, and its old Town Hall, with a mead vault in its basement, surviving in a condition of unsurprising drunkenness on a ragged patch of waste ground.

Not that the Poles do nothing but drink. Frustrated in Leningrad that the Kirov Ballet and Philharmonic were closed for the summer, Susan had patronized cinemas instead. In Poland, the halls were always packed for a very traditional night out: no advertisements, a strongly patriotic newsreel to start and then a western film with subtitles in Polish . . . but in Szczecin she and Rupert misjudged it. The audience all winked at her afterwards, everyone last one of them male to a man. A case of blue for boys, and the girls go pink.

'*Tsan-na. Tsa-na – ah, Italiano!*' young voices sang out alongside us. They were schoolboys, trailing along the dockside, spelling out *Canna* in Polish phonetics and gazing in wonder at our ensign.

'No!' we said, summoning a little energy. '*Nie. Jestesmy Irlandski.*'

It reminded us it was time to go home. At the back of our minds the North Sea was waiting, and threatening its autumn storms.

Reluctantly, we made preparations. At the village shop, we waited while a sailing-school skipper loaded a wheelbarrow with provisions for an extended voyage.

'How it costs! . . . nearly one-third more than last year. I must ask for 4,000 zlotys more from each crew . . .' And the queue behind us scoffed good-naturedly at the assistant who asked us for coupons. '. . . from foreigners? The very idea!'

We got all the salami and sausage we needed. Bread and milk, still cheap, was unlimited and very good. Tinned fish was ubiquitous. We were soon ready; but when the sailing manager warned of gales at Arkona, East Germany's northern cape, we promptly postponed for a day.

'*Słaby prognoza*,' we explained with defective idiom to the schoolmasterish customs official who advised a further extension to Shay's already temporary visa. 'Sick forecast.'

'Oh, yes?' he said ironically, shrugging up at the favourable wind and blue sky. 'But — what is the *real* reason? Shall we just put down "engine trouble"?'

In fact, had there been more urgency, we might have taken a chance and gone, but the real reason for staying, deep down, was that we were happy to be where we were, to cast one more lingering look around the gentle landscape of Trzebież: its whispering river-banks where people soaked up the soft, late sun under enormously heavy willows; its belts of sombre, spiky forest stretching away toward Germany, and pastures with ancient timber wagons. The village itself, with its clusters of classically-pillared farmsteads, its yards and orchards with stacks of firewood, its back lanes white with clatters of geese. Cartloads of hay being horsed through the streets, the odd motorbike plaintively whizzing by in the dust of a sunny afternoon, the strange gadget like a dustbin-trolley with gas-tanks, its twin nozzles haunted by wasps, dispensing syrupy drinks near the school.

There, in the narrow lanes and evenings, as hay stacks and roofs and the crowns of trees softened to a single purple outline, women called *dobre pies* to a sheepdog, or something sharper to bring children home; and there too, between laden trees and their plum-coloured shadows, an old man leaned from his garden window, talking on until dark of his time in England, decades before, of his friends and countrymen still there, and of how, for him, it was now too late and too difficult to travel to see them again.

We left Poland on 27 August. A few early fishing punts were dark against the sparkle of sun and the distant banks of woodland, as we unrolled the genoa for the last time and picked up speed across the lake. Wind and current hurried us on out through the straits and winding channels, and on again out to the sea at Świnoujście.

As we looked over our shoulders, until the coastline faded astern between a scatter of anchored ships, I had to admit that the subterfuge about 'engine trouble' still rankled. Why had it been necessary?

'Poland is ten times more different from the Soviet Union than the UK is from the United States,' a Polish diplomat had told us. Exaggeration? Even allowing for this Polish tendency, now we were not quite so sure. The ever-flexible Polish reaction, often invoked with the best of intent, was quite different from Russian exactitude. Coming from Ireland, it was all too familiar, and fitted like an old overcoat. Come to think of it, a lot of things did; the general scruffiness and lack of funds, the chaotic charm and spark of anarchy were very much more Irish than Russian.

But hadn't we forgotten something (a common feeling at a final departure), or perhaps just missed an opportunity? When we made contact with the local Polish radio station, to transmit our position to the Marine Rescue Centre in Shannon, we discovered it was both: 'What is this *yot, yot Canna?*' the operator asked in beautifully modulated English. 'Does your boat have two names? Nobody understands this "yot, yotty". – In Polish,' she corrected firmly, 'it is *jacht*, I spell . . .'

But she was much more distressed to hear we were leaving, not arriving. '*Canna*, have you paper and pencil? Here is my telephone number . . .'

We didn't really believe our ears: radio dating with half the world's ships listening in is not a common occurrence. 'And you can come to my place at any time,' sang the unlikely ambrosian voice. Shay has never forgiven me. We would have very few such chances left . . .

CHAPTER 17

The North Sea and English Channel

'Stay close!' said Susan, in bellicose mood. 'Don't encourage them, don't give an inch!'

For a day, we skirted the east German coast, indistinct and low, with a few tall buildings here and there jutting like single teeth. We had marked a dotted line on the chart, representing the 12-mile zone, and were keeping *Canna* just outside it. A single patrol boat ran up and down like a mildly demented dog, but the sound of what might have been gunfire was probably only the boom of frequent high-speed military aircraft; and by dawn next day, beyond the island of Rügen and its bold north-eastern headland, Arkona, we noticed that shipping was clipping the exclusion zone by a mile or two, and judged it safe to do likewise. As their coastline wavered and faded in turn, we felt sad for our friends from Stralsund.

In a momentary calm, Susan swam, reporting the water yellowish and bitty; but by then it was neither German nor Danish. Our first thought was of pollution. In the Baltic it's heavy generally, and in places acute, particularly the south and west. In Gdynia and elsewhere swimming was strongly discouraged, on account of industrial waste from Polish and East German rivers, and around the Danish islands, enormous algae blooms have occurred attributed to fertilizer run-off from wealthier western countries. Of dolphins and porpoises, once plentiful, we had seen not one, and no one could remember them either. But we had probably jumped to conclusions: yachtsmen of 100 years ago had reported the phenomenon hereabouts of a mass of weedy fragments, although their name for it, 'Fishes Wittles', betrayed they had no idea what caused it.

Those few minutes of stillness and silence, the only time we were stationary at sea, seem in retrospect a pivot, an end of a stage and a beginning, and the start of another hard race.

The return voyage wasn't easy and was to take us almost a month.

It was only partly a matter of distance. We had sailed 3,200 miles through eight countries, but were still a full 14° east of Greenwich; it was already nearly September and we had 1,200 miles more to go.

Also, by now, it was time to take stock of the crew. This, we'd discovered, was something our nineteenth-century colleagues studiously tried to avoid. They ran a strictly two-tier system of officers and men, of 'us' and 'them', to a degree now unbelievable. E. F. Knight, one of the foremost Victorian yachtsmen, in advising on 'Fitting out a fifty-tonner to go foreign', opines that: 'there is no man I would rather have at sea with me than the honest British yachting tar of the right sort; but it is difficult to get him to ship for a long voyage on a small [!] craft, and as a rule one has to put up with an inferior article.' How terrible that must have been!, especially when one recalls that it wasn't fitting to be seen sailing as if an equal even with one's own naval architect and, of course, there was always the example of the much-quoted Lord Cardigan to aspire to, who, on being asked, 'if he might wish to *take* the tiller', riposted that, 'he made it a habit to take nothing at all between meals.' Small wonder, perhaps, that the accounts and logs of those times manage to cover voyages of several months without once dropping the name of a single 'inferior article', or even of their professional skippers; and it was a mild relief to discover another who'd carried through to the logical extreme of not mentioning his own name either, nor indeed that of anyone on board at all.

On *Canna* it was otherwise. The crew simply sank or swam as one, and just now it seemed to be sinking. With our different programmes and different perceptions, what had been an efficient machine was beginning to drift asunder. Shay was in particularly bad shape: miserable, exhausted, laid low with fever, and now scarcely able to summon the interest even to open his camera bag. He had toppled over some kind of climax. An earlier incident gave the clue: when leaving Leningrad, I had started a new journal with the label RETURN, merely stating a fact of longitude, but Shay had been downright incredulous.

'That's surely not how you really think of the countries we have still to visit?' This pent-up impetus had carried him on without respite through the hectic weeks in the Baltic Republics and Poland, stoically humping the hefty clutter of movie equipment with little assistance and no complaint. Minus family connections on board, the continual making and breaking of friendships in port had caused added strain. 'Why must we leave now?' he would plead. 'Could we not just stay a day or two more?' Already gloomy, as we gingerly edged into a pastorale through the narrow Grønsund Channel between the islands of Falster and Møn, he finally hit rock bottom when we reached the marina at Stubbekøbing. Mouthing minor mutinies on the subject of pressing on, he was hurriedly despatched, with tall orders, to his friends in Copenhagen.

'Come back in two days – and fit,' we said, keeping all our fingers crossed.

For Susan and Rupert, soon to leave us for home and school, Denmark was a beautiful culmination, a tidy conclusion to a Baltic circuit. With nothing further to think about, they luxuriated in the neat red brick-and-tile towns, the biscuit-tin wonders of Aeroskøping and Marstal, pedalled airily through the manicured green and gold farmlands and stood fascinated by the clustered wind-generators on pillars spinning against their towering skies. Even getting themselves marooned on the island of Farø after the last ferry, and having to walk back 20 miles via a gangway on a mile-long motorway bridge (forbidden to pedestrians) at risk of being hurled into the sea by the blast of passing traffic, failed to dampen their spirits.

Between them, I was simply in limbo, and couldn't properly relax. For one thing, there was a sense of loss.

'How does it feel to be here?' Shay-the-journalist had enquired, in a final effort before his temporary departure, filming me topless in the marina ablutions. 'Distinctly odd,' was the answer. The contrast between Poland and Denmark was sharper than anything so far encountered, and almost everything but the showers felt cool. We were back in a world where self-conscious neighbours hosed and squeegeed their oversized cruisers on the stroke of eight bells each day, and handed down folding bikes from the bows to be unzipped from their plastic bags; where shops sported acres of bland plate glass, and bored girls bound for Copenhagen lay full-length on the train-seats with headphones clapped to their ears.

We had just consigned our last Soviet connection to a Danish recycling skip (Yuri's well-meant bottled smoked fruit from Riga tasted like soot congealed in syrup, the only ghastly food we'd encountered), and the warmth and comparative plainness of Poland still left intangible hankerings.

And then, no doubt, I was beginning to run a bit ragged.

'No gentlemen on board!' we had bragged to the mayor of Gdańsk, contrasting ourselves with the *Oriana*; but by now I almost wished we had. If a leisured owner, I could have written up my journals in peace, or spent more than a few brief hours in the Tivoli, reliving Martin and Corrigan's cavortings; if merely the skipper, I could have relished running the boat. Juggling both functions on twenty-four-hour alert for much of the last three months so far, even though I'd greatly enjoyed it, had undoubtedly taken its toll.

Worst, the weather was sending us signs. The light now slanted coldly along the interminable bollards and duckboards, and for only the second time on the voyage, as Shay rejoined us and we made to leave Stubbe-købing, a gale drove us back, whipping in from the west under the awesome arch of the Falster suspension bridge. It delayed us only a day, before we made on through golden sunsets via Vejrø and Langeland islands, and Aerø, but it served disquieting notice that the summer couldn't hang on much longer.

We reached West Germany on 3 September, groping into the enormous, anonymous Olympic Centre at Schilksee on the Kieler Förde in pea-soup fog at dawn, navigating at last by horns and sirens, and gliding under the bows of a square-rigged sailing ship; and it was there, before Rupert and

Susan abandoned *Canna*, that we had one last, strangely appropriate, rendezvous, with German sailors encountered in Sweden.

A curious network connected us back, in time and space: our older guests, sipping wine in the cockpit, had all been born in what is now Poland. Zabine's father, Horst, had been born in Kołobrzeg, Jochen and his wife came from Szczecin – and Jochen had just returned from a first visit to his homeland for 45 years.

'No trouble at all with visas,' he said. They had travelled through East Germany. Not for the first time, we were struck by the lack of rancour, the feeling of adjustment, of wounds knitting. A circle was being completed.

'Come and see Schleswig-Holstein!' they said, tempting us up toward Jutland. But it would have to wait. Temptations now could be dangerous.

On a beach near Derrynane Harbour, the ribs of an old timber sailing vessel have stuck up through the sand for as long as most can remember; her name, said Harry, the new crew who'd just joined us from Kerry, whose hotel overlooks it, was the *Elizabeth-Marstal*. Marstal was the name of our last port in Denmark! She'd been one of a famous fleet of traders; and we had now not only to follow her route, but also to avoid her fate.

At daybreak, the massive gate of the single lock at the eastern end of the Nord-Ostsee Canal (formerly the Kaiser-Wilhelm Kanal) finally closed us off from the Baltic: and from then on, climatic guillotines hovered ominously over our heads, just barely waiting for *Canna* to pass before slamming down behind her.

The weather held its breath, and we held ours, as we rushed the 60-odd mile cut in one day, grinding under a transporter bridge, with a railway spiralling up to its gantry, and a fragment of fluorescent roadway beneath alternately dangling from bank to bank; squeezing almost under trees to escape the slewing sterns of ships lining up for a bend.

At the further end, in Brunsbüttel, the atmosphere was even more fraught. Boiling brown clouds brewed a fearful heat and threw down flashes and torrents of thunder. An engine control cable broke. We welded it. It broke again next day as we entered the falling lock. Too bad: we pressed on and took our chance, out on the river we most of all dreaded.

'There is a tide in the affairs of men . . .' but the Elbe must be ridden out on the ebb: a mile or more wide, it runs at all of six knots. We rode it down at six more, making twelve knots over the ground.

The Elbe, the Weiser, the Jade! – a terrible trio of German river-mouths, spewing out their torrents north-westward through tongues of sandbanks viciously forked, and stretching far out to sea. If the wind should come in over them, they would froth in violent fury, and then there would simply be no way out.

Over the spreading estuary, the sky hung slack and greasy. Glinting yellow and black, or red, the channel buoys steamed towards us like ships, sluicing torrents down their sides. We hauled on the tiller to stay clear. Strings of traffic to port of them; to starboard ugly brown stains in the water where submarine banks pushed up, and here and there the dismal slanting masts of wrecks that hadn't quite made it.

The silhouette of Cuxhaven, our last conceivable mainland refuge, swung into view like a video run fast-forward. In minutes, we'd be carried past and unable to claw our way back – but sailors, I knew, had been stuck there for months, and a contrary wind was just now beginning. It was now or never to decide.

'It will come up soon,' the Met. Office said, 'and then it's going to be strong.'

We pressed on. Soon meant six to ten hours – time perhaps for a dash along the German coast toward Holland? – but banks of steadily-building cloud warned that the idea was far too risky. We made instead, like generations of seamen before us, toward the invisible Helgoland bolthole, the curious mile-square sandstone excrescence in the crux of the German Bight that someone put there for the purpose: a sort of Monopoly corner, 'Just Visiting', that had had far more sinister connotations as a base for Hitler's U-boats.

The gale barely held off until we crept in under the beam of its glaring lighthouse at midnight, and arrived before dawn with a bang, jostling the masts of a hundred yachts, wrenching their badly-moored trots into mangling collisions, freezing the legs of frightened crew scuttling on deck in pyjamas, and slamming behind us our exit door from West Germany, possibly for weeks to come.

The morning revealed a total confusion. Helgoland is a duty-free haven where Germans load drink and over-priced trinkets, and their yachts, like fat ants from a broken nest, were still milling around in frenzied haste. By degrees, being Sunday, they vanished in lulls to barely visible mainland burrows, leaving just those with long-distance pretensions – some Dutch, a Norwegian and one or two Poles.

The Poles alongside our berth were glum. They'd been dreaming until recently of the Canaries, but had guessed, as did we, that the equinoctial gales had set in, and that the best we could hope for now would be breaks.

So it proved. Stewed in impatience, we sat it out in the bleak square harbour as our foodstuffs finally dwindled to dregs.

'Spam?' I would quiz, without waiting for answers. It was either that or interminable tinned fish, or the dried mung beans we'd shipped in Kerry that now looked almost as tired as we did, but still lived on in the for'd lockers. In our low saloon, disloyal thoughts began again concerning those Victorian yachts: mirages of their gracious parlours with proper ceilings and panelled walls, soda siphons set out (what bliss!) by stewards, leopard skins a-sprawl on their floors, and, yes, aspidistras in their fireplaces, and heavily draped four-poster beds. Of course, they had minor disadvantages: with all their clutter and enormous draught, and what with the Kaiser's Canal not being fully complete, some had stuck in the River Eider instead, and been obliged to vomit 20-odd tons of ballast into lighters and send it on ahead. No matter! The crew would take care of that while the gentlemen presented their cards to likely country houses nearby, or took out their guns for a bit of sport – and at least they had space and plenty of weight (when reunited with it) to chance their bowsprits through such heavy weather with more impunity than we.

For four tense days, morale sank lower as the wind shrieked in from the west-north-west; perfect had we but turned the corner and been heading south along the Dutch coast, but impossible for us to beat against. On the third day a powerful English sloop stuck out her nose and was beaten back.

'Far rougher than you'd think,' they'd confided.

On the fifth, as the wind eased fractionally more north, we took a chance and set *Canna* to try it. No other yacht stirred. Our Polish neighbours, crossing themselves and looking soulful, sat tight – and out beyond the moles to the west, where the wind and sea burst in through our teeth, we were immediately on our own. It was another fairly desperate gamble. From the start, there was never a chance of laying Holland on starboard tack and, as the treacherous German coast slanted inexorably toward us, occasionally visible over the crests, all the bad dreams of the west coast of Ireland returned to spread their poisonous shades.

'What do you think?' Shay had asked. 'Will we make it?'

Once again, ironically, due to unlucky no-shows and defections, we were under strength when we needed it most; although stuffed to the gunwales in the Swedish canals, we were now down again to a skeleton crew and even weaker than at the start. Harry, although well-built and willing, had sailed with me only once before. Not just inexperienced, but hot-foot from his hotel kitchen, he could hardly have been less well attuned; he was expecting an easy cruise. Shay's new-found skills were offset by fatigue, and I had failed to find a fourth man in Kiel. Should I have commandeered Rupert to stay? The need for success weighed down on me darkly – could I bring the crew safely ashore?

For two days we slogged at the Frisian coast, straining in long un-balanced dog-legs to stand off from its string of islands and shun the riddle of their sands. They run for 150 miles, and for 16 watches in succession we beat and heeled and slammed and plunged, plugging tides, then running with them, shying away from shipping lanes, praying for the weather to hold while watching the slug-like silhouettes – Spiekeroog, Langeoog, Nordeney, Juist – drag laboriously astern over glittering trails of foam. The wind fluked us past the shelter of Borkum.

'So where are we going to put in now?'

It became a recurrent and plaintive query; Shay's wide face under his stocking cap was looking more and more grim and strained. It posed an acutely doubtful balance between weakening crew and strengthening weather. We could not now expect to reach Scheveningen, the port for the Hague far down the Dutch coast – a new storm was already brewing from there – but if instead we backtracked to shelter, we'd not even defeat the crucial knuckle, the bulge at the extreme north-west of Holland, and we'd have it all to do again later. If we could last out a few hours more, we might just scrape as far as Den Helder.

Ameland island crept by, then Terschelling, sixteen miles long: under a slashed and bleeding sunset we closed it to within a mile, cutting it as close as we dared, edging around the interminable curve. The wind bent too, with exquisite malice, to stay exactly ahead and block us. Its gusts became more menacing. Worse, the tide turned against us too, sluicing round the bend like a river, and by nightfall it had stopped us dead. Now we were like climbers caught out on a ledge, with neither room nor time to return: when the tide ebbed again, there'd be no way back, and ahead were only a few short hours to find shelter before the storm found us.

Well after midnight, the current at last relented and freed us. It was worth holding on for: the effect of the south-bound ebb was startling, as if *Canna* was being yanked by stretched elastic. Texel suddenly flew by to port, as we tore on southwards into the dark. Lights, stationary barely minutes before, now swelled and passed with amazing speed – ships to starboard, ships to port, red and green buoys to find through the spray, a web of revolving lighthouse beams meshing above us like radial wheels. Tangled in rigging, the moon raced with us, veiling and unveiling herself, and beckoned towards Den Helder's channels.

2 am. 3 am. Nearly 4. 'All crew on deck: and get into your harness!'

Suddenly the moon is down. Blackness swells on the starboard bow: a blanket suffocates the stars. It rears and hovers over the mast, now heeling further and further to port, whipping and shuddering under the strain.

Far too much canvas, but no time to de-power her. No time, either, to choose our course – too late already for the main 'sea-gate' from south-ward, too far to windward under the gale. Our only chance is the Molengat, the northern gap a few hundred yards wide, somewhere in the murk ahead. But how to find it – with no mistake?

The buoys, now, fast! I make a hurried check on the chart, one eye closed to preserve night vision.

'A quick flashing and a morse "A" to starboard; isophase red eight seconds . . . damn!' (as I'm thrown backwards across the cooker, and the lurching deck-head gouges scalp).

'A starboard cone, and a can, unlit . . . We should see most of them to port.' I chant them on the way back up as a wave drops down the companionway.

'Well, where are we then?' yells Harry.

'We need 180°, to allow for leeway. Keep your eye glued to the compass, and *call*. Shay – well done – stand by the main-sheet, and watch ahead.'

There's nothing there but wind and spray. Our eyes sting as the invisible shores rush closer, showing no inkling of the chink between. Where in God's name are those entrance buoys? We ought to be almost on top of them. Still nothing! Long minutes and aeons of shoaling water, of imaginations and phosphorescence, and phantoms on the retina. Pangs of doubt and germs of dread, as the wind howls louder through the shrouds. Were we in fact too far to the east?

'There! They're there!' We see them together, dit-dah and a quick one, slightly to starboard as they should be. But the channel markers beyond are alarming – a wicked tangle of reds and greens winking like Aladdin's cave, they're sliding slowly to the right as the gale shoves *Canna* bodily sideways. The current in the gap is unknown . . . Five minutes, ten – and we're still losing ground, being driven closer towards the lee shore. A desperate last jousting begins with the tiller – *to windward, you cow, just a fraction more!* Will she weather that first red buoy? She does! She tears by it with a few feet to spare – its iron bulk lunging viciously, its red eye gleaming along our rails. The second's no better, the third's to come. We simply have to stay on line: somewhere unseen in the dark to starboard sprawls the notorious Noorderhaaks bank with wrecks just five feet under the water. Its halitosis of sand and weed edges towards us closer and closer, and the blasts roaring across it turn suddenly foul.

'Shay! *Free the main!*' . . . but he's done it already. The sails seem almost flat to the surface, and gathering widening pools of spray. The decks tilt downward, further, further. The side decks are sliding under the water – it churns across the doghouse windows, and flies to port in a solid sheet. Still further over she goes, her three-ton keel a mere paperweight, and she's coming close to being knocked down.

'*More, Shay, more!* Spill more wind!'

But we're already standing on the cockpit coamings with the North Sea swilling around our boots. Harry loses his balance and falls as Buoy Four, gone missing under the sail, flashes out past the end of the boom.

'190°!' calls Harry, as she comes back up; and then at last, beyond Buoy Five, a pair of white leading lights, our landmark!

'That,' I affirm, once *Canna*'s secured in Den Helder's navy marina, 'was just *great* . . .' (the voice isn't mine; but sheer relief demands that something be said). 'Quite the best sail in the whole of the cruise!'

'Yes, we noticed,' Shay rejoined softly. 'So was that why you kept it all to yourself?'

He meant the way I had hogged the tiller, for which I had simply no excuse. I'd been far too scared to do otherwise.

We had made it with an hour to spare. Through our exhausted and fitful sleep, the storm built up to fever pitch. We waited and watched for five more days. Beyond the enormous, grass-clad dykes, the North Sea threshed itself to spume, and wraiths of it snaked over land and water like sand between Saharan dunes. Above us, a thicket of mast-head wind vanes screamed pointed accusations south-westwards, the direction, once more, of our destination.

'Cheers!' chinked Harry ebulliently. 'Many happy returns, indeed!' Just the one was all we needed. Incongruously, in a flock-papered Chinese restaurant, we celebrated the skipper's birthday while dust and miscellaneous signboards flew past at head-height outside the windows.

It seemed, now, an occulting storm – the breaks were shorter than the flashes. Some neighbouring yachts also bound for the Channel abandoned the direct sea-passage entirely and made off through the canals instead, intending to exit later at Flushing. We hung on from day to day with one ear tuned to the radio.

A sudden lull on 13 September, and another hurried dawn departure, just as Shay got back from the town. Another two or three days to face, another leg of 300 miles down through the sink of the southern North Sea. Once again we were on our own. Out through the churning gap to the south, a half-calm disfigured the swell, and sudden spits and banks of rain.

Under diesel, at first, as far as Noord Hinder, the central light-ship for North Sea shipping, near the spot, we reflected morosely, where Rudolf Diesel himself had committed suicide in 1913 by leaping from an overnight ferry; somewhere here, too, when sailing home from Riga, Adlard Coles had been caught in a storm, and been driven north toward Lowestoft.

Was another fight in store for us too? For a while it seemed so; once more the wind rose and the genoa was reefed down to storm-jib size; once more we had two heavy rolls in the mainsail and the mast-step shifted and shrieked in its socket. Down below, the wind-noise was drowned by a tedious roar as breakers turned the port-holes green and thundered on the cabin-top, and by sharp cracks as crockery took off like clay pigeons fired from their galley cubicles. Salt water began to seep everywhere.

The tides were now at full autumn springs, and our charted route looked like a concertina, alternately stretched to the limit and closed, until finally, near the Falls Head buoy in the dusk of the second day, the ebb came to our rescue once more, sweeping us on past the hungry crescent of the Goodwin Sands and their lightships, almost within touching distance in a single relentless scything curve through the dark of a moonless night.

This time, it was the mouth of the Thames, North Foreland and Ramsgate that fell astern like knackered horses; but our final fence was not a gale but the Straits of Dover, the most trafficked passage in the world. It boasted a route planning chart specially devised for avoiding collisions, which we hauled out on to the sodden table. There was no other chart of shipping quite like it – not a chart, in fact, but a diagram, layered with colour like a pattern of stresses. Blue hatchings showed the inshore zone (the only permissible portion for us), even shadings the main through routes, and along them wove threads of black and blue, the appointed tracks of deep-draught tankers, coming almost nose to nose a mile or two east of where we were. As if that weren't enough complication, the whole streaky pattern was laced like a bodice with wide blue ribbons labelled 'Ferries', stretched between French and English breastworks.

'Fast ferries leave Dover by both entrances – passing vessels should keep at least one mile off,' warned the instructions littering the margins.

'Indeed – they have been known to run down sailing boats that mistakenly got in their way.'

Harry's eyes widened as my comment slipped out; and the chart showed a pair of dotted lines, arching across the Straits at each end, marking a zone of radar surveillance. Big Brother watched everything that moved, and errant yachts had been arrested.

But no answer came back from Shay when I called up to ask what he could see. Now, where we needed perfect alertness, tiredness had become endemic. Were it not for the stalwarts at each end of the boat – the self-steering and the reefing genoa – it's doubtful if we'd have stood the pace. For the last two days, meals had been scratched up mechanically. Pots had to be forcibly held on the stove. We changed our watches like silent zombies, barely grunting positions and course, and keeping *Canna* north of the main through channels. Dover, in a blaze of sodium light, was coming up now on the starboard beam. We could do no more. Through the graveyard watch, from midnight to four, I kept an eye open for crew falling asleep; then it closed and I dozed off myself. A Channel ferry passed in the meantime and, once, a freighter last seen ahead reappeared in a lucid moment astern.

As the danger diminished, the crew slumped further, until all that persisted was the notion of progress. The Baltic by then was simply wiped out, another life already, submerged in the urge to keep heading west. Beyond Hastings, even recrossing the zero meridian was less marked by relief than new fears of delay: the engine, while charging the batteries, suddenly threw a violent fit and shook the boat from end to end. It turned out to be plastic wrapped round the propeller and, under the off-white cliffs of Beachy Head, I dived underneath to drag it clear.

'Right. That's it. I've had enough!' Harry left us in Brighton, unable to take any more, having finally succumbed, perhaps, to the ominous sight of my wet-suit. He'd done well to last as long as he did. Shay gritted his teeth and hung on, and my admiration for him rose even higher. Damian, our 19-year-old elder son, joined from Ireland; fit and strong and well used to the sea, he made another threesome for the final leg.

We stayed only long enough in Brighton to get the fraying genoa restitched.

'Get west, get west!' something kept urging – 'There's still a lot more bad weather to come!' The threat was almost tangible, like someone behind us cracking a whip.

Calms off the Isle of Wight, thick fog in Falmouth. One last envious comparison with our erstwhile nineteenth-century companions. With mixed winds, and temperatures up to 103°F, *Oriana* had long since passed through the Channel and left us trailing far behind. She had dallied between Newhaven, Portsea and Cherbourg, picking up friends here, heading for a ball there, shooting dolphins or fishing for sharks, and by now was home and dry in Dun Laoghaire; and even the *Ierne*, starting much later, had returned to the Mersey by her northern route.

A final hesitation in Scillies, while a deep depression makes up its mind. When it backs off, we chase it too soon and reap the turbulent consequences on the two days and 200 miles to Ireland – a wind turning once again contrary and the sea a succession of pyramids across the long Labadie Bank, the scourge of the ill-fated Fastnet Race.

Crash! Slam! *Canna* is bouncing from crest to crest and falling heavily into the holes.

'Let her. Nearly home. She can take it!' I mumble drowsily into my bunk; but Damian, berthing forward that night, feels a particularly heavy crack and, unknown to us, half our gunwale, 20 feet of solid teak, is carried clean away like matchwood. Had we hit flotsam? A log or a tree trunk, some floating cargo? If so, we'd been extremely lucky, and in case we'd not quite grasped the point, in the dying blasts of the wind at day-break, as we caught our first glimpse of the Irish coast, the mainsail, last restitched in Scotland, suddenly came apart at the seams. It could so easily have failed at Den Helder . . .

Mizen Head and Dursey Sound: at 13.00 on 25 September we edge under the cable-car bridging the narrow strait at the extreme west end of County Cork, back into the waters of Kerry. Familiar mountains at last reappear – it feels strange to approach from the opposite side – and the wind is still northerly, as when we left, but kinder.

'Don't arrive before 4 pm,' Susan had warned on the radio. Now we see why: boats have come out miles to greet us; there's a blazing bonfire up on the cliff, balloons and milling crowds on the pier. A banner yells out

'WELCOME HOME', and we are hauled ashore by a hundred hands. The circle is finally complete on 25 September.

The first yacht from Britain and Ireland to sail to Leningrad since the Russian Revolution. One hundred and eleven days. Thirteen countries; 50 harbours and ports; 4,400 miles; 80° of longitude; almost one-fifth of the way round the world.

But just then statistics were less important than the damage to boat and to crew. We had done unseamanlike violence to both. Should we have taken longer and pushed our return less hard? Probably not – our premonitions came all too true. Within a week, *Canna* was out of the water and propped; a week more, and the most violent hurricane within memory rampaged along the Channel and laid waste its shores, demolishing marinas and piers, setting ships and rigs adrift, crushing, maiming, killing and sinking. Who's to say that had we tarried and sat out gales, ours too might not have been one of the droves of beached and broken yachts that lined the shores of Normandy, Sussex and Kent, or were bodily hurled inland? We were glad in the end to have done as we did.

Postscript

'Lithuania,' a professor from its capital, Vilnius, told me, 'is astonishingly similar to Ireland. It has three and a half million people who are mainly Catholic, drink a great deal of beer, live largely by harvesting sugar-beet and whose national flag is mainly green. The climate is wet, and there are lots of bogs . . . and,' he said very firmly, 'you *don't* need a separate visa. You could have gone in from Latvia.'

He had been an altar-boy at 13, a Komsomol guide a year later, and the troupe of dancers he was chaperoning were scared half to death by the uncontrolled youth on the streets of Dublin, so obviously there were cultural differences.

For us, they would have to await another voyage. So would the odd-man-out, East Germany, along with Sweden and the Federal Republic, through both of which we'd skimmed with indecent haste.

Omissions aside, what had been the outcome of our efforts?

Initially, a heightened sense of history. It has been a surprise, in describing the voyage, to find how often reference has been necessary to historical wars, and the last War in particular. No doubt it should not have been, since the history of the Baltic has been one of more or less continuous struggle; but if it was a shock to discover on the spot how brutally heavy had been the toll they took of all the Baltic lands – very difficult for visitors from less-trampled countries to imagine – it was equally impressive to sense to what extent the trauma had been assimilated and discounted in favour of fresher perspectives.

Rounding out a Baltic history in the 1960s, Oliver Warner could just begin to sense this possibility. 'The enchanting Danes, who once ruled Norway, the serious Swedes, the resilient Finns, the all-enduring Russians, the unpredictable Poles, the obedient Germans, look out upon the Baltic from their various windows and points of vantage. If few heads lie easy, there are signs, as yet they are no more – that the future may be less devastating than the past.'

What we had done, which would not have been possible then, and perhaps not even one year sooner, was to take a quick and presumptuous peep in at nearly all of those windows in the Baltic courtyard, and present ourselves on the front doorstep of the country that, for better or worse, now plays the leading role in its affairs.

The specific results were very modest: suggestions of twinning with suitable towns, invitations to eastern bloc regattas, a return visit by a Polish yacht; but bit by bit wider realizations dawned. Instead of viewing the Soviet Union's 'avalanche of hopes' from a distance, it became apparent that *Canna*'s journey had been a tiny fraction of it, a mere pebble on the fringes of a vast flood of change which has spilled across the media headlines and alters the perceptions of half the world almost from day to day. The avalanche will be hard to keep ahead of, because almost no one is prepared for it. We're still labouring under a mountainous rucksack that should now be unpacked and scrutinized piece by piece: stuffed with ideas that no longer equate with the facts, and many that never did.

It has been that way for centuries, in spite of long and extraordinary connections – perhaps, it's amusing to conjecture, ever since Ivan the Terrible had unsuccessfully sought a wife at the court of Elizabeth I.

'You'll be caught by the Rooshians and knouted to death,' the blood-thirsty sounding Revd R. E. Hughes was told when embarking his yacht for the 1854–5 campaign, even though the English had been received with kindness and even deference in St Petersburg for decades before, and were again to be afterwards.

As for the Baltic itself, that too has always had a bad press, and in that the Victorian yachtsmen were serious culprits. The Revd Hughes' own accounts were scathing, speaking of the natives almost as if of a separate species, and of the shores as 'dreary, uninteresting and uninhabited' (an unsurprising condition, considering how enthusiastically he participated in their bombardment) and that, 'but for the excitement of war, few yachts I fancy would be tempted to make a second cruise in the Baltic.'

The reports quickly seem to have become self-perpetuating. Why else should the widely-read E. F. Knight, for instance, comment that, 'A few English sailing yachts visit the Baltic every year – but that wind-swept sea can scarcely be termed one of the favourite grounds of our fleet'; and go on to refer to 'violent northwesters and howling wintry afternoons', when the logs of the few vessels to penetrate the Gulf of Finland since Hughes, for instance, told more often of 'heat and stillness so fearful that crew suffered from recurrences of malarial fevers, contracted elsewhere, or had to repeatedly dive in to cool off'?

No wonder that more than a century later we were sometimes asked, 'and how did you cope with the ice . . . ?' and that the headline to a newspaper feature (the only part of it we didn't pen) informed tens of thousands of readers that we had 'braved the chill waters of the Baltic', with a bland disregard for the fact that a bad summer there is at least as warm as a good one in the Irish Sea.

Much of the problem, of course, is instinct. What is north is cold. The people too, presumably. Let's just leave it at that – there are warmer places to go to (in the 1900s the sailing men were already extolling Marmora, for instance: 'easy of access, with Constantinople only two days and six hours by train from London') – and the notion has been hammered, impacted, embedded, compounded by generations of unconscious reinforcement from all kinds of sources.

'An excellent read!' another Lithuanian academic had commented, waving a bestselling east-west spy-thriller, 'but it really does us no good at all, and how does one fight against it?'

Perhaps partly by simply wandering through each other's countries and sorting things out on the spot.

'How peaceful it is here in Ventspils!' I'd commented to the Inflot secretaries, referring to the pace of life.

'Well, what did you expect – something aggressive?' one of the girls had promptly retorted, putting the wrong foot forward. It's no wonder that wider politics are so fraught.

Now, it seems odd that the idea which took shape in such an accidental way should have produced results as rewarding as they have since become.

It was indeed a great delight to have been the first yacht to have sailed our route, after an overlong interruption, and to savour in memory the thrill of anonymous moments in the cities or countryside; but the most enduring pleasure is that of new contacts. From now on we shall watch and worry as our eastern friends struggle to adjust their lives, or survive an earthquake in Armenia. The bond is made, and reciprocated. Letters wing in like homing pigeons; Polish sailors send postcards from Singapore. Riho, we hear, did get to his longed-for college. The Volgograd crew head off again for another regatta in Vladivostok.

There are invitations to revisit and, when we do, we shall still have funds in Russia. A few months after our return, an Inflot Disbursement Account arrives, listing the exact breakdown of *Canna*'s costs in Leningrad:

> *Pilotage in and out*: as per Bills Nos:
> *Telephone and Telex*: 16 roubles
> *Car expenses*: as per vouchers attached:

right down to a small subvention I'd asked for:

> *Cash paid to Master*: 10 roubles 50

The upshot of the lengthy form? We hold credit in the city of Peter the Great in the sum of $1.61. There are deletable options to decide its fate. We score them all through except the last, and the 'Master' gladly returns the message: 'Please keep balance on hand for our next ship.'

APPENDIX

Practical Observations for Cruising the Baltic Coasts of USSR and Poland

Visa Requirements

Generally, for yachts visiting the Baltic from British, Irish, and other European waters, visas are required only for the Soviet Union, Poland and East Germany.

For the Soviet Union, the procedure for obtaining visas has been streamlined since *Canna*'s visit. An authorization from the Moscow authorities is not now necessary. Yachtsmen should make direct contact with the Inflot shipping agencies in the ports they wish to visit, stating dates proposed and giving details of boat and crew. (See below on Ports of Entry.) Contact is best made by telex. If the yacht's crew do not need onshore accommodation (such as a hotel) Inflot will take complete charge of the arrangements. Inflot's confirmations of berth reservations should then be presented to the appropriate local Russian Embassy for issue of visas. These will be 'ordinary visas' for which a small processing charge is made. The visas will be valid for the dates booked with Inflot.

For Poland, visas are granted on the basis of formal or informal invitations from yachtsmen, or direct from a Polish Embassy. Visas are issued which are valid for specific ports. The charge may be as much as £15 per crew member per port visited. It is possible to apply for a 'multi-entry' visa, listing all the ports you may wish to visit, and from which you will select when in Polish waters. A total of three or four ports is normally permitted within a stated period, but without indicating specific dates, itineraries, or berthing arrangements.

Visa charges may be reduced or waived on the basis of an invitation from a yachtclub. Formal invitations are made through the Polish Yachting Association:

Polski Związek Żeglarski
00–791 Warszawa
ul. Chocimska 14
Poland

It is normally required, after a visit by formal invitation, that the visiting skipper advises the appointed 'host' member of the Polish Yachting Association of the actual itinerary and any official personae contacted.

After an initial visit, subsequent visits may be arranged by direct informal invitations from one of the many sailing clubs. Initial contact should be made through the Polish Embassy, or the Polish Yachting Association.

For East Germany, visas are not as yet generally available to yachtsmen.

Ports of Entry, Port Facilities and Charges

USSR

Ports of entry in the Baltic at which Inflot offices exist, and for which permission may be sought, listed clockwise from the Finnish border:

RUSSIAN SOVIET FEDERATIVE
SOCIALIST REPUBLIC

Vyborg Mainly a commercial port, approached through complex channels. Town of approx. 70,000

Inflot: POB 40, Vyborg 188900. Telex 121521

Leningrad The jewel in the Russian crown, but berthing facilities may be limited. Pilotage normally required for entrance channel.

Inflot: 10 Gapsalskaya Street, Leningrad 198035. Telex 121505/121506

ESTONIA

Tallinn The very attractive and historic capital of the Republic. Excellent facilities at Pirita Marina, three miles away. Easy of access and pilotage not normally required.

Inflot: 54a Tuukri Street, Tallinn 200102. Telex 173273

LATVIA

Riga Gracious and lively Latvian capital, well worth a visit. Basic but convenient yachtclub near centre. Straightforward access via river channel, but pilotage normally provided.

Inflot: 6 Vilis Lacis Street, Riga 226180. Telex 161118

Ventspils An oil-exporting and commercial port, not geared to the needs of yachts. It is a useful port of refuge with easy access. The small town is at some distance from the docks.

Inflot: 18 Dzintaru Street, Ventspils 229100. Telex 161822

LITHUANIA

Klaipėda A medium-sized commercial port on the narrow strait at the outflow of the Kurskiy Zaliv. The entrance is direct, but exposed to westerly winds. The historic part of the town lies to the north of the Dange River.

Inflot: 8 Geguzhes Street, Klaipėda 235801. Telex 278113

Descriptions of the ports are given in a booklet published by the Ministry of the Merchant Marine of the USSR, *Briefings on USSR Sea Commercial Ports*. Certain of the information is relevant to yachts, in particular details of pilotage arrangements, and radio channels for contact with port authorities. Normal VHF channels are used and a VHF should be considered essential, even though it is sometimes difficult to contact port control offices. If the yacht is berthed under Inflot (Shipping Agency) auspices, berthing charges are heavy (typically £40 –£50 per day), but include an estimate of costs for full ship's services, e.g. pilotage, transport on shore, city visits, chandlery,

laundry, bunkering, telephone services, etc. If full use is made of these, reasonable value can be obtained. In ports where pilotage is not required, charges may be less.

A yacht crew with limited time available, if selecting one USSR port, would do well to visit Tallinn, which has the easiest approach and by far the best facilities. Elsewhere, amenities are generally basic.

Crew changes could conceivably be made *en route*, for instance at Leningrad or Tallinn, but all details of transport, hotel accommodation, etc, would have to be advised and booked well in advance, which would involve Intourist, the tourist agency.

POLAND

Ports accessible to yachts, listed from east to west include:

Gorki Wschodnie A small fishing port east of Gdańsk, with one yacht club, few facilities and an exposed and sometimes difficult entrance.

Gdańsk There is a yachtclub upriver opposite the docks area. Visiting yachts normally prefer to berth at Gdynia, where facilities are more extensive. The towns are connected by frequent electric trains (approx. 35 minutes' journey), and by excursion boats. A superb city and the best centre from which to explore the country.

Gdynia The premier Polish sailing port, easy of access, well sheltered and convenient to sailing clubs and the town.

Władysławowo A small fishing port suitable for shelter only.

Łeba/Ustka/Darłowo Small coastal towns, resorts and fishing ports at river mouths, of which Ustka and Łeba are particularly attractive. Entrances from seaward face north or north-west, and are difficult or dangerous in strong onshore winds.

Kołobrzeg Medium-sized coastal town, resort and fishing port, and small commercial port. The harbour entrance can also be difficult. Basic yachtclub in a pleasant municipal basin.

Świnoujście A spa and holiday resort on the west side of the mouth of the Odra.

Beyond the east bank lies the attractive Wolin National Park. The river entrance is easy, but the customs berth is uncomfortable, and the river itself heavily trafficked.

Trzebież A very attractive small village in unspoilt countryside, adjoining a secluded harbour 15 miles upriver from Świnoujście.

Szczecin A major city 30 miles inland from Świnoujście. Yachts can lie to the main quays on the pier, but there are also a number of yachtclubs in the approaching and surrounding lakes.

Permissible ports of first entry are shown on Polish maps as Gdynia, Kołobrzeg, and Świnoujście. Coming from eastward, Gdynia is recommended as having the best range of clubs and facilities for yachtsmen. From west Świnoujście/Trzebież/Szczecin would be a good alternative. Pilotage is not required at any port. There are normally no berthing charges when hosted by clubs. At a municipal pier (as at Kołobrzeg), one can be asked for 1,500 zlotys (£2) per night.

Crew changes can be effected at Gdynia via Warsaw airport (although internal travel is slow and crowded). Poland Ocean Lines also run a London–Gdynia service. Świnoujście is conveniently connected by ferry to Copenhagen and Ystad in South Sweden. It has internal connections by road, rail and hydrofoil to Szczecin. Trzebież is connected by bus and train to Szczecin.

Customs

SCANDINAVIA
In Sweden, particularly, there are extremely strict rules concerning wines and spirits, which may prohibit the carrying of liquor on board in excess of duty-free allowances. This should be carefully checked before laying in stocks for the voyage.

USSR
Customs are independent in each Republic. In practice, this means a customs check in and out of each port. Advance notice of duty-free amounts could not be obtained, but reasonable quantities of liquor and tobacco for personal use appear to cause no difficulty. All personal valuables, cameras, etc, are required to be declared, and it is useful to have a list prepared beforehand.

POLAND
Generally as for USSR. Customs checks also operate in and out of each port.

Currency and Exchange

USSR
1 rouble = £1 sterling (1989, approx. official rate of exchange). There is no compulsory daily exchange, i.e. no requirement for visitors to exchange a set amount of currency daily.

Major credit cards, Eurocheques and Traveller's Cheques are acceptable in western currency 'Beriozka' shops. Official bodies, such as Inflot, may accept Eurocheques at their discretion.

It is desirable to carry a full range of types of currency including dollars or sterling in small denominations. All currencies are required to be declared on entering and leaving each Republic, together with any exchange made into roubles. Roubles cannot be obtained abroad or carried out of the country.

POLAND
800 zlotys = £1 sterling (1989, approx. official rate of exchange, but subject to considerable inflation). For tourists travelling independently a compulsory daily exchange of dollars is normal. The visa charge substitutes for this. Cash in dollars or sterling is more acceptable for exchange than other forms of currency. All currencies and exchanges must be declared in and out of each port. Zlotys may not be taken out of the country.

Stores and Supplies

FOODSTUFFS AND GENERAL SUPPLIES

In Norway, Sweden and Finland, all victuals are extremely expensive by comparison to the UK. A yacht ought to be self-sufficient there except for essential fresh supplies. Mosquito netting for deck hatches is very desirable.

In the USSR, if recourse is possible to Inflot chandlers, a good supply of all types of food, including fresh vegetables and fruit, will be found at prices generally rather less than in the UK. In the general shops, basic foodstuffs of excellent quality, particularly bread, dairy produce, tinned fish, bottled vegetables, etc, are very economical. Fruit and fresh vegetables are more readily available in markets than in shops. Certain items, such as concentrated fruit juices, and spirits (vodka is one US dollar a bottle), vacuum-packed coffee, and salami, are obtainable at foreign-currency shops, 'Beriozkas'.

In Poland, ship's chandlers stores are not available. 'Pewex', foreign currency stores, are the equivalent of the Russian 'Beriozka' and are found in most tourist hotels, and elsewhere in bigger cities. Otherwise, as for USSR.

A yacht should carry a full stock of any essential delicacies, and keep good supplies of items such as kitchen and toilet paper, plastic bags and sacks and toiletries, which are not always available.

GAS

Canna carried three Camping Gaz cylinders,
each 2.72 kg (6 lbs) – butane
one Calor Kosangas cylinder,
11.34 kg (25 lbs) – butane
An extra Calor Kosangas cylinder, 5.0 kg (11 lbs) was purchased *en route* and found to be unnecessary.

Camping Gaz supplies are generally sparse in Scandinavia. They are available at a few outlets in Norway, fewer in Sweden, and could not be found at all in Finland. Camping Gaz is not distributed in Poland or the USSR, but is freely available in W.

Germany and Denmark. Lists of agents and charts of suppliers are available from Camping Gaz, 9 Albert Street, Slough SL1 2BH.

The Calor Kosangas cylinders supplied in Ireland are also in general use in Finland and the USSR. Refills are available at marinas and merchants in Finland, and at depots in the Soviet Union. Note that this is *not* the same cylinder as standard British Calor Gas – if relying on this, very adequate supplies would be necessary.

In Poland, an entirely different type of cylinder is used, incompatible with Camping Gaz or Calor Kosangas. We had sufficient supplies in hand not to need refills (although Polish sailors assured us this could probably have been achieved by improvisation if necessary).

WATER

Canna carried 60 gallons in fixed tanks, and 15 gallons in containers. The quality everywhere in the USSR and Poland was satisfactory.

FUEL

Canna carried 15 gallons in a fixed tank and 8 gallons in containers.

In the USSR diesel was available through Inflot.

In Poland, supply through clubs is informal and *ad hoc*. Tanks should be kept topped up.

Repairs

In the USSR and Poland, boats are often encountered with engines in a semi-permanent condition of breakdown. Spares for most Western engines would be hard to come by. Full spares, tools, and manuals should be carried. Similarly, major items of rigging and chandlery are in short supply. In Poland, chandler's stores exist at some clubs and ports, with a limited stock of smaller items. Minor sail repairs could probably be arranged at some of the Polish clubs. Batteries for on-board equipment are non-existent in both countries and an adequate stock must be carried.

Charts and Pilotage Information

Admiralty charts are issued for all of the Baltic. Their degree of detail and coverage are, however, more suited to commercial traffic than yachts, and are in any case largely based on local national charts. Local charts are very desirable, and in many cases essential, as for:

SCANDINAVIA

For Sweden, including Göta Canal

For Åland Islands, and Finnish mainland: standard charts and special Batsportkort chartlet books give full details of navigation routes, and military restricted areas.

Main sources of supply

Via main Admiralty chart suppliers, or from suppliers *en route*, e.g.:

Kiel-Holtenau (Germany), Nautischer-Dienst
Copenhagen Iver C. Weilbach & Co. A/S
Göteborg Esselte Bokhandel
Gumperts
AB Nautic
Stavfeldts Nautiska AB
Malmö Lundgrens Bokhandel

Göteborg Stavfeldts Nautiska AB
AB Nautic
Stockholm Esselte Kartcentrum
Helsinki OY Maritim AB

USSR

Admiralty charts give adequate detail for approaching main ports by main channels. Local charts and pilots necessary for diversion, e.g. to Leningrad sailing club.

Russian charts are not available to foreigners.

POLAND

For details of restricted zones on coast, and approaches to smaller ports Polish charts are essential. Sailing clubs can often oblige with a loan.

No yachtsman's pilot in English exists for the east and south Baltic. The Admiralty Pilots, in three parts, contain a great deal of relevant information, are almost the only source of information on local weather, currents and water levels and, despite their bulk, are worth carrying.

Foreign pilots which cover the USSR and/or Poland include:

Hans Gades: 'Harbour Pilots'

Chart shops in Gdynia and Szczecin – Government chart correction office available in Gdynia.

50 Norrevoidgade, Copenhagen

Hafen-Handbuch (loose-leaf file), German,
3 vols.
1. North Sea
2. Skagerrak, Kattegat
3. West Baltic, including E. Sweden,
   Åland, SW Finland, Poland,
   E. Germany.

Hamnboken, Ostra Delen. Swedish version   Esselte Kartor AB
of above in book form

Pilot books in Polish of west Baltic ports
are also available in Poland. Pilots that may
be useful on the Baltic approaches include:

Cruising Association Handbook   Cruising Association
Norwegian Cruising Guide by Mark   Stanford Maritime Ltd
Brackenbury (includes part SW Swedish
coast)
Frisian Pilot by Mark Brackenbury   Stanford Maritime Ltd
(Den Helder-Kiel)
Baltic SW Pilot by Mark Brackenbury   Stanford Maritime Ltd

Lights, Radio Communications, Forecasts, etc.

The standard UK Almanacs (Reed and Mac-millan) do not extend into the Baltic. For the USSR and Poland, the Admiralty 'List of Lights', Volume 'C' should be carried, as full details of lighthouses are not shown on all charts. Similarly, the Admiralty 'Lists of Radio Signals', particularly Volumes 1, 2, 3 and 6 should be carried, or excerpts from relevant sections, for details of Coast Radio Stations, Radiobeacons, Weather Services and Port Radio Operations respectively.

Sweden has an excellent sea area forecasting system, which covers all of the western Baltic and western approaches in English twice daily, and in Swedish five times daily. With a little practice, and the official sea-area key card, the Swedish can be readily understood.

Navigational Aids

Decca: Decca coverage of the Baltic is excellent, except in the eastern extremities of the Gulf of Finland, and in the southern Gulf of Riga, where the two Finnish stations are out of range, and to a lesser extent along the west Polish coast. It is undoubtedly the best navigational aid for most of the area.

RDF: Radiobeacons exist on all coasts, including Russian and Polish, although good signals were hard to obtain from these, and they would not be accurate enough for close-quarters navigation.

Radar: Radar is likely to be of limited benefit, especially in the southern areas with very low, receding sandy shores.

Selected General Bibliography

CRUISING ACCOUNTS

Coles, K. Adlard, *Close-hauled* (London, 1926)

Graves, S. R., *A Yachting Cruise in the Baltic* (London, 1863). An account of a voyage from Liverpool to Leningrad and back in 1862

Hughes, Revd R. E., *The Log of the Pet, 1854–55* (London, 1856). An extraordinarily vivid and bloodthirsty account of the British campaigns in the Gulf of Finland

Ransome, Arthur, *Racundra's First Cruise* (London, 1923; paperback, London, 1984)

Sullivan, Sir Edward, Brassey, Lord and Others, *The Badminton Library of Sport and Pastimes*, 'Yachting' (London, 1904)

HISTORY

Agar, Capt. Augustus, VC, *Baltic Episode* (London, 1963). The inside story of the Baltic Raids

Anderson, R. C., *Naval Wars in the Baltic, 1522–1850* (London, 1969)

Ascherson, Neal, *The Struggles for Poland* (London, 1987)

Bater, James H., *Studies in Urban History: St Petersburg – Industrialization and Change* (London, 1976)

Bishop, Marian and Dobrzcki, Jerzy, *Copernicus, Scholar and Citizen* (Warsaw, 1972)

Greenhill, B. and Giffard, A., *The British Assault on Finland, 1854–55* (London, 1963). A superbly researched and detailed new history

Ireland, John de Courcy, *Ireland and the Irish in Maritime History* (Dun Laoghaire, 1986)

Mitchell, Mairin, *The Red Fleet and the Royal Navy* (London, 1942)

Pitcher, Harvey, *When Miss Emmie Was in Russia* (London, 1977). An account of English governesses and society in Russia before and during the Revolution

Ustinov, Peter, *My Russia* (London, 1983)

Warner, Oliver, *The Sea and the Sword – The Baltic 1630–1945* (New York, 1965). An excellent, comprehensive account of historical power struggles

Zamoyski, Adam, *The Polish Way* (London, 1987). A superbly illustrated and comprehensive general history

TRAVEL AND SOCIAL COMMENT

Heine, Marc, *Poland* (London, 1980)

Post, L. van der, *Journey into Russia* (London, 1964)

Smith, Hedrick, *The Russians* (London, 1976)

Thubron, Colin, *Among the Russians* (London, 1983)

Walker, Martin, *The Waking Giant* (London, 1986)

Index

Roger Foxall is an English architect who has practised in Ireland for the last twenty years. At Derrynane Harbour in South Kerry he and his wife and two sons farm a traditional coastal small-holding. He is also an experienced yachtsman who has twice won the Hamble Cup (previously awarded to Clare Francis and John Ridgway) for voyages of particular enterprise, and – based on his cruising yacht *Canna* – he runs a charter business and navigational school.

Sailing to Leningrad is Roger Foxall's first book, though he frequently writes – and lectures – on navigation and cruising for the yachting press.